Korean Buddhist Nuns and Laywomen

Korean Buddhist Nuns and Laywomen

Hidden Histories, Enduring Vitality

Edited by
EUN-SU CHO

SUNY
PRESS

The cover photograph was taken in 1996 by JOO Myungduck at Unmun-sa Monastery in Cheongdo, South Korea. The novice nuns (who are studying at the Unmun-sa seminary) are washing vegetables at the stream. The image is used with the permission of the photographer.

Published by
State University of New York Press, Albany

Printed in the United States of America

For information, contact
State University of New York Press, Albany, NY
www.sunypress.edu

Production, Laurie Searl
Marketing, Anne M. Valentine

Library of Congress Cataloging-in-Publication Data

Korean Buddhist nuns and laywomen : hidden histories, enduring vitality / edited by Eun-su Cho.
p. cm.
Includes bibliographical references and index.
ISBN 978-1-4384-3511-4 (hardcover : alk. paper)
ISBN 978-1-4384-3510-7 (pbk. : alk. paper)
1. Monastic and religious life (Buddhism)—Korea. 2. Monastic and religious life of women. 3. Buddhist nuns—Korea. I. Cho, Eun-su, 1958–

BQ6160.K6K67 2011
294.3'65708209519—dc22 2010023371

10 9 8 7 6 5 4 3 2 1

To my late mother, who lived in a world

where few of these wonderful opportunities

were available to women.

Contents

Foreword

Despite having a 1,600-year history within the Korean Buddhist tradition, ordained and lay women have been neglected in both traditional and contemporary accounts of the religion. Korean Buddhist monastic records offer little information on the religious activities of women. There are some brief references to nuns during the Paekche and Unified Silla periods, a bit more material about women during the Koryŏ-dynasty golden age of Buddhism, but next to nothing during the Chosŏn period, when women suffered under an oppressive social system and Buddhists endured a centuries-long persecution at the hands of Confucian ideologues. This paucity of records has long discouraged scholars from attempting any kind of comprehensive narrative of the place of women in Korean Buddhism. Although scholars have acknowledged the presence of nuns within the order since virtually the inception of the religion, the specific contributions that ordained and lay women have made to Korean Buddhism have yet to be examined systematically.

Anyone who encounters Korean Buddhism in its modern setting, however, soon recognizes that nuns and laywomen demonstrate a tenacity of purpose and religious commitment that is incommensurate with the modest recognition, respect,. and support they have traditionally received. Thankfully, conditions for women are changing, and changing rapidly. Perhaps most fundamentally, the difficulties nuns have been compelled to overcome in the modern age have clearly made them particularly dedicated practitioners. Even though there are about as many ordained nuns as monks within the tradition, nuns have far fewer monastic institutions available to them. For those crowded institutions to function, ordained women have had to be especially cognizant of the role that precepts play in the Buddhist way of life and the importance of nonattachment. Perhaps precisely because of the hardships nuns have learned to endure every day, many of these women display remarkable self-reliance, tolerance, and humility in their religious practice, exhibiting a palpable sense of the joy of renunciation.

As the status of women in Korean society has more broadly improved over the last few decades, so too has the status of ordained Buddhist women. It is now common to find nuns studying and teaching in Buddhist seminaries and universities, training in meditation halls, and holding important ecclesiastical office. Nuns are at the vanguard in eleemosynary activities, religious propagation, social engagement, and environmental activism. Indeed, there are now nuns who are as eminent and as widely known as monks in virtually all aspects of the contemporary Buddhist tradition: as meditators and Sŏn masters, scholars and academics administrators, painters and calligraphers, even vegetarian chefs and tea masters.

This engagement with society at large has led in turn to nuns having increasing influence with communities of laywomen. As Korean society has undergone a dramatic shift from intimate village life to a crowded, but often isolated, urban environment, nuns have become sounding boards for laywomen who no longer can draw on the extended family as their support system. Nuns have thus become especially adept at negotiating the divide that has typically separated the lives of monastic and laypersons in Buddhism.

For all these reasons, the influence of nuns in the Korean Buddhist tradition has arguably never been greater than it is at the present moment. Thanks to the efforts of editor Eun-su Cho and her collaborators, this volume takes important strides in documenting the crucial contributions that women have made to Korean Buddhism and restoring Korean Buddhist nuns to their rightful place in any comprehensive accounting of that tradition. Their coverage will help to transform the women who have all too often been silent partners into eloquent exponents of the best that Korean Buddhism has had to offer throughout history.

Robert E. Buswell, Jr.
Los Angeles, California

Preface

This volume was conceived with the intention of breaking new ground in a neglected area of Korean history and culture—the tradition of female Buddhist practice—for those in the broader academic community already focused on the topic of women and religion. It addresses the roles and accomplishments of women in Korean Buddhist history, including the role and status of nuns in the Three Kingdoms, Koryŏ, Chosŏn, and modern periods, and also examines the systemic and organizational aspects of nuns' lives. The contributors to the volume detail the sorts of education and training the nuns received in their lecture halls and meditation rooms, as well as the relations between that system and the modern order of nuns.

All the chapters except chapters 4 and 6 originated as papers presented at the May 2004 international conference entitled "More Than Women: Korean Nuns within the Context of East Asian Buddhist Traditions," held at and sponsored by the HanMaum Seonweon (One Mind Zen Center) in Anyang, Korea. As the first international conference on Buddhist nuns and female practice in Korea and East Asia, this gathering drew attention from both academic and religious communities inside Korea, which consequently led to a surge of interest on this topic of the lives and practice of Buddhist nuns. Considerably more papers were delivered at the conference, yet not all were included in this current volume. Our focus in narrowing the selection targeted only those papers devoted to Korean tradition. Thus, papers on Chinese and Japanese Buddhism that had been presented with the intention of providing comparative and contextual material were not included. A few papers pertaining to cultural studies, art history, and literature in the Korean tradition were not included as well, as we decided to limit our focus to historical overviews specifically addressing the development of female Buddhist practice in Korea.

Some chapters have been previously published elsewhere. An earlier version of chapter 2 was originally published in the *Seoul Journal of Korean Studies* 22, no. 1 (June 2009), as "Reinventing Female Identity: A Brief History of Korean Buddhist Nuns." An earlier version of chapter 3 was originally published in Korean in the journal *Ihwa sahak yŏn'gu* (Study of History at Ehwa Womans' University) 30 (2003), as "Koryŏ Chin'gak kuksa Hyesim ŭi yŏsŏng sŏngbullon" (Koryŏ Master Chin'gak Hyesim's Theory of Women's Attaining Enlightenment). An earlier version of chapter 5 was originally published in Korean in the journal *Chŏngsin munhwa yŏn'gu* (Study of Intellectual Culture) 27, no. 4 (2004 Winter), as "Chosŏn ŭi Chŏngyu wa Koryŏ ŭi Chinhye." An earlier version of chapter 7 was originally published in *The Review of Korean Studies,* 11, no. 4 (December 2008). I thank these publishers for their generous permission to use them.

As the first collection of its kind in the English-language press, this volume was compiled through a group effort to identify and appreciate the unique tradition of women in the Buddhist monastic communities of Korea. The contributors sincerely hope that this book will shine light on heretofore undiscovered aspects of the lives and practices of Korean Buddhist women. We also hope that it will illuminate Korean culture, religion, and thought through the experiences of Buddhist nuns and laywomen, both modern and premodern. Women remain seriously underrepresented in Korean culture and history, especially in books on Korean religion and thought, even while interest in Korea has been growing steadily in the West, so we hope this volume will contribute to filling in the gap.

Several people led me to this new area of interest, which contrasts with my earlier research on Buddhist doctrinal thought. Through his own writings on the topic and personal encouragement, Samu Sŭnim, a Korean monk who moved to America a few decades ago, inspired me to study the remarkable tradition of female practice in Korea. He is indeed a pioneer in this area of research, and, to the best of my knowledge, his articles on three Korean Buddhist nuns in the 1986 issues of *Spring Wind,* a Buddhist magazine that he headed, should be recognized as the first English-language publications highlighting Korean nuns' lives. I was also influenced by the nun Sukdham Sŭnim who helped me more directly understand Buddhist nuns' practice and ways of life. She showed me her own personal essays about leaving home to become a nun when she was young and this impressed upon me the importance of the determination of these brave female practitioners. Another friend, Shi Zhiru, also a Buddhist nun and an academic in Buddhist studies, has given me advice at various stages in the publishing of this volume.

Many people and friends have contributed to this venture: Matty Wegehaupt, my former student at the University of Michigan, extended his unlimited helping hands without considering his own busy schedule, from the initial stage of organizing the conference to correcting transliterations and grammar mistakes of nonnative writers. Victoria Scott, a freelancer copy editor, also improved the manuscript considerably by copy editing most of the chapters. I would also like to thank Nancy Ellegate of State University of New York Press, to whom I am deeply indebted for her encouragement throughout this long process and especially for her crucial advice in sharpening the focus of the volume at the time of its initial submission. I must also thank my students Sangyop Lee, Ahrim Won, and Inga Kim Diederich for their assistance in providing proofreading to the text as well as their help in the laborious process of indexing this multi-faceted project. Many thanks are due to Joo Myungduck for sharing his fine photograph, which captures the spirit of the community of Buddhist nuns in Korea, for the cover of the volume.

Last but not least, without the sponsorship and support of HanMaum Seonweon, led by Reverend Daehaeng, my aspiration to reveal the significance of this religious tradition of practice would never have materialized. Many other people—including the Venerable Hyewon Sŭnim of Dongguk University and another Hyewon Sŭnim, the abbot of HanMaum Seonweon—also provided the initial connections that enabled me to organize the 2004 conference. The present volume is dedicated to the Reverend Daehaeng and her community.

Eun-su Cho
Seoul, Korea

1

Introduction

Eun-su Cho

While the modern study of Buddhism has witnessed impressive development over the years, the shape of this progress has not always been balanced. Perhaps most notable in this skewed progress has been the lack of focus on women and their role in the religion. With Korean Buddhism, this has certainly been the case, but the time has come for this situation to change. The life and culture of Korean Buddhist nuns and laywomen deserve serious attention from scholars not only in the Western world, but in Korea as well. This is not merely a pursuit for a superficial balance, but a remedy to correct a flawed vision of the complex history of Buddhism. Through an examination of historical records and biographical excerpts from Buddhist nuns, we can see, albeit fragmentarily, that Korean nuns have maintained a tradition of religious practice and commitment to the Buddhist teaching from the very inception of Buddhism in Korea, despite the common perception that such a history is merely the history of monks. To the contrary, the research supports the notion that when the monks' order was formed upon the transmission of Buddhism to Korea, a nuns' order was established at almost the same time. This leaves Korean nuns with a long history of some 1,600 years, a rare and remarkable feat that stands out in the history of world religion. This achievement runs contrary to the dominant narrative of a long moribund female Buddhist tradition, and calls for a much-needed focus to be brought on the unique place Korean Buddhism holds in Buddhist culture.

Evidence of the existence of female monastics is found in Buddhist scriptures from the beginning of the history of Buddhism. The Buddhist bhikṣuṇī saṅgha was formed during the time of its founder. The Buddha pronounced that the Buddhist community should consist of male monks, female monks, laymen, and laywomen. Though the reality of a persistent power discrepancy between male and female monastics must never be ignored, it should be emphasized that Buddhism is one of the few major religions in which female clergy exist alongside their male counterparts with independent organizational structures and religious functions, and have done so from the beginning of the religion. That said, egalitarian ideas could not surpass the social prejudices and historical turmoil of the societies in which Buddhism developed, and the closest descendents of the earliest bhikṣuṇī saṅgha of South and Southeast Asia died out around the eleventh century. From then on, the tradition has remained defunct for many centuries, due to the bitterly ironic situation that there were no bhikṣuṇī to perform bhikṣuṇī ordination, as required by the scriptures. Only at the end of the twentieth century did brave women from these countries without bhikṣuṇī forge a path to China, Taiwan, or Korea to receive bhikṣuṇī ordination from sister communities that had persisted. This daring effort to reinstate bhikṣuṇī orders in Sri Lanka and Thailand, while met with some skeptical resistance in their home countries, has received strong support from the international Buddhist community. In a recent meeting of the International Congress on Buddhist Women's Role in the Saṅgha, organized for monastics and scholars in Hamburg, July 2007, a resolution was passed stating that the establishment of the bhikṣuṇī saṅgha where it does not currently exist is a significant event and should be applauded. Yet even as we recognize that this tradition founded in great turmoil continues to struggle to maintain its birthright, it is imperative that such conflict does not paint an overly bleak picture of the tradition as a whole. Whatever difficulties may have accompanied the long history of the bhikṣuṇī saṅgha, its accomplishments are what should more properly define it.

While the bhikṣuṇī saṅgha faced major difficulties in South and Southeast Asia, its fortunes were much brighter in the East Asian countries, where the Mahayana tradition had been established some centuries after the founding of Buddhism in India. The scriptures and the way of practice reflecting the Mahayana Buddhist development of Northwest India, the so-called northern tradition of Buddhism, were transmitted to Central Asia first, and then to the countries of East Asia—China, Korea, and Japan. As a part of this process, the Vinaya texts were also introduced to China on a few separate occasions and one prominent set among them became the basis for bhikṣuṇī ordination. In ancient Korea, the historical evidence indicates that Buddhist nuns were ordained by these precepts and it is these same precepts that remain today as the foundation of the contemporary bhikṣuṇī order.

At this point, the most striking question one might pose is why the fates of these two bhikṣuṇī communities were so disparate; why did the Theravada bhikṣuṇī literally die out and the East Asian tradition survive? This area is in desperate need of further explanation. As we hope that further historical and textual study will bring answers, I would like to add my own candid opinion by comparing their means of sustaining themselves, that is, their economic basis. Theravada Buddhists are known for their strict adherence to the Vinaya precepts, even now following the early teaching of the Buddha not to engage in any kind of economic activity to support themselves other than getting food by alms rounds. There is a famous story that when a Brahman criticized the Buddha, "How come you don't work or grow anything but depend on others giving," the Buddha answered that he and his followers do work, but work on the field of their mind. A phrase found in the Pāli scriptures states that donations to bhikṣus—not bhikṣuṇīs—bestows upon the donor great merit, conspicuously omitting mention of bhikṣuṇīs; this might be the reason why when societal resources during war and famine grew thin, female monastics were neglected, lacking enough external support to sustain themselves.

On the other hand, early in the sixth century the Chinese Buddhist community began to establish new sets of precepts called "pure precepts," which were also introduced to Korea in which labor and work for self-support and sustenance were encouraged. There is a famous saying in the monasteries that if you don't work one day, there is no food for one meal. For example, in Koryŏ, women received equal estate inheritance from their parents as well as from deceased spouses; some widowed women entering the monastic life would bring their resources with them. This might provide the monasteries with land and attached labor in the form of serfs so that they would not have to solely depend on almsgiving for their daily food. This kind of materialistic foundation may be the reason why Korean Buddhist nuns were able to survive even when society passed over them. This unique and characteristic Mahayana interpretation of the Vinaya precepts, which can be viewed as leniency, may have been a factor in East Asian bhikṣuṇī economic equality and independence.

In Korea, the health of the bhikṣuṇī saṅgha followed that of the religion in general. Buddhism flourished during the first millennium of its history in Korea, through the ancient period of the Three Kingdoms of Koguryŏ, Paekche, and Silla, and United Silla (opening date ?–935). The subsequent Koryŏ dynasty (918–1392) saw Buddhism enjoy prosperity and respect as the national religion. Such benefit led to a backlash as it struggled to survive during the Chosŏn dynasty

(1392–1910), which had adopted a neo-Confucian ideology to organize society and enforce an explicitly anti-Buddhist policy. Buddhism was suppressed and Buddhist monks and nuns were disrespected in public, suffering self-doubt and treated as outcasts. Buddhist nuns suffered double oppression as both Buddhists and as women. The neo-Confucian Chosŏn society treated women as the property of their fathers, husbands, and sons. Given these adverse circumstances, Buddhist nuns were encouraged to hide themselves and lead quiet, uneventful lives away from the outside world. Most of them lived and died anonymously without leaving much information about their lives.

However, the environment for female clergy in Korea has changed rapidly in the past thirty years. The remarkably increasing presence of Buddhist nuns in the public religious sphere of modern Korea has forced us to question the invisibility of Buddhist women in modern research, not only in the Western world but also in Korea. Scholarly research in English on Buddhist nuns and laywomen, gender in religious history, and female spirituality in general are available in the West as there has been a considerable amount of new research on the subject in recent years.[1] Serious studies of the history of Chinese, Taiwanese, and Japanese Buddhist nuns have already been undertaken. The biographies of eminent Buddhist women past and present have been researched and disseminated to the world outside of these individuals' respective traditions.[2] International organizations like Sakyadhita have held international conferences on Buddhist women over the past two decades, publishing edited volumes of their research and serving as an important venue to distribute information on Buddhist women around the world.[3] Such works should provide comparative context through which the Korean tradition can be understood as well as insight into the diversity of Buddhist women's practice. More thorough treatment of the significance of the similarities among the East Asian Buddhist traditions, which would bring a shared sense of the implications of social prejudices and historical circumstances that shape perceptions on religious women in East Asia, is needed in the future. However, specialist research on Korean nuns has been alien not only to the non-Korean academic world but to the Korean academic world as well. The number of writings on Korean nuns can be counted on one hand, and it is no exaggeration to say that the fruits of this academic research had been almost nonexistent until a few years ago.[4]

Although there are a number of reasons for this, the most important is the scarcity of textual materials and historical evidence. The activities of women in general had been neglected and left out of official histories. The accounts that do exist are found mostly through indirect mentions of spouses and daughters of remarkable men. As renunciants without close ties, Buddhist nuns left no records about themselves, nor were their life stories recorded by their relatives. Instead, we must look to tangential descriptions that appear in more general works. The major historiographies telling about women of the Three Kingdoms period are *Samguk sagi* and *Samguk yusa,* but the former only comments on the transmission of Buddhism and lacks records of individual activities. The latter introduces many stories relating to pious women and Buddhist teaching, but since they are mostly tales of the miracles and magical events of bhikṣuṇīs and laywomen, it is hard to use such literature as an historical record, even though it may give us solid proof for the general notion that women did indeed play an important role in the religious landscape of Buddhist practice at that time. As for the Chosŏn period, given its massive volume and quantity of records, the Chosŏn dynasty annals (*sillok*) stand as the most important account of Buddhist females, but these are almost entirely of a fiercely negative tone. In fact, on almost every occasion when Buddhist nuns were featured in the Chosŏn *sillok,* it was for criminal cases or appeals to the throne when the women were prosecuted due to supposed sexual misconduct or prohibited religious activities. Sadly, this lack of historical materials is notable not only in classical texts, but persists into our recent history. What few records that do exist of the deeds of important nuns of the recent past have been scattered and even now are not being properly preserved.

The most formidable obstacle to our research of the near past is that Buddhist women and monastics' own writings about their lives and religious practice are almost nonexistent. This marks a sharp difference compared to records from China or Japan. This absence is largely due to a widespread reaction of Korean nuns in their personal attitudes in which they developed common outlooks on practice that had a significant impact on their presence in the historical record. Specifically, one of their key coping mechanisms was to seclude themselves entirely from the outside world. Many Korean nuns lived and died anonymously, leaving little if any information about their lives. Because Korean nuns in the past five hundred years experienced both the oppression of Buddhism and the ideology of male primacy, later nuns seem to have accepted the fact that seclusion was their traditional, normative lifestyle. Determined to preserve such a tradition and to avoid revealing their personal abilities, nuns have virtually quarantined themselves in their meditation rooms and lecture halls in the mountains of Korea, even up to the present day. Hence, it is an urgent task for researchers to document nuns' achievements in modern Korean Buddhist history and record oral interviews with elderly nuns before they die. These women are the last generation of witnesses to the Buddhist practice of the colonial period. They alone might offer us insight into whatever changes and challenges were brought to the way female monastics had lived and practiced toward the end of the Chosŏn dynasty. In terms of understanding nuns' roles in Korean Buddhism, the urgency of this task, and the loss that will be incurred should it fail, cannot be overstated.

The passive, eremitic atmosphere of their community contributes to other difficulties in research beyond simply the dearth of primary text source material. Reliance on personal testimony brings its own methodological conundrums. The prevailing views of informants can restrict our information about the past, present, and future and, within such limits, there is a propensity to create new forms of misunderstanding. That is, within the limits of the testimony of surviving people, one is often forced to reproduce the achievements of the past according to the stipulations of the current ideology and the contemporary lineage environment. Therefore, one may unwillingly duplicate the biases of one's living informants. Moreover, while many nuns complain about the external prejudices toward them, they themselves harbor varied prejudices as well. In particular, the lineage adherence that exists among them can be fatal to reliable research. As secondary and tertiary prejudices come into play, later research about nuns will likely be forced to grope among the differing biases, potentially giving rise to even more distortions and unnecessary disputes.

Our research faces the additional difficulty that it cannot be carried out without considering the relations of nuns with the order of monks in general and also with monk teachers individually. For example, it would be contradictory to posit the ideological and practical independence of nuns whose lives were voluntarily dependent on the position and influence of the monk teachers under whom they studied and practiced. The viewpoints of nuns' male patriarchal teachers must also be given our attention and their impact analyzed accordingly. Recent research on the status of female clergy inside religious orders seems to show that women's religious orders that operate independently of men in terms of their education, faith, and proselytization make more progress than those whose operations are dependent on male institutions. A full accounting of such relationships must be brought to bear on any appraisal of the achievements, or lack thereof, of the bhikṣuṇī saṅgha.

The case of Myori Pŏphŭi, whom I deal with at length in chapter 2, is instructive here. She was one of the greatest female masters of modern Korea and was a remarkable guide to the first generation that established the modern order of nuns. Yet when giving her membership in the lineage of the dharma, her teacher, the monk Man'gong, said to her, "Go before the congregation, since you have been venerated of late, but do not preach."[5] Pŏphŭi followed her teacher's words to the letter. Although she had a renowned career as a Sŏn master, received many contemporary male masters for dharma exchanges, and nurtured many disciples, she never once ascended the dharma podium to preach. Her case thus shows the ambivalent position a female disciple could fall into with her male guide in the religious order: these relationships were often of simultaneous guidance and restraint that men offered women in the Buddhist monastic orders.

Another area of concern when considering the obstacles our research must contend with is that most research on nuns has been hampered by the overarching concern that "nuns are women." There are cases premised on the vague expectation that "nuns must essentially be feminists," or must have aims or starting points similar to those of feminists. However, some care needs to be taken in this approach. Many contemporary Korean Buddhist nuns certainly expressed, through their writings or personal meetings with me, that their desire to become nuns was to overcome their present "bondage" as women. Yet they also mentioned that the way to do this was through spiritual practice and its final goal of attaining enlightenment, and that this spiritual quest was the ultimate reason they wished to become nuns. That is, people who choose ordination do so in anticipation of the highest religious ideal; questions of gender differences or their oppressive environment are secondary.

The practice journey of Reverend Daehaeng is an instructive case. She was the founder of the HanMaum Seonweon (One Mind Zen Center), and her rise as a woman in the Korean saṅgha was a stormy one. However, Reverend Daehaeng's explicit desire was always to open up the possibility of a "new humanity," regardless of gender. While she challenged the existing male-centric system of practice, her achievements were always aimed toward an enlightenment that totally transcended such issues, receiving recognition of the universal position existing beyond lay or cleric, male or female. Her practice and teaching have discarded the particular form of "a nun," since for her and her disciples, the idea of femaleness or maleness is itself a useless delusion. Her disciples see Reverend Daehaeng as a universal human and as a teacher.[6]

Given all the social and intellectual obstacles against researching Buddhist nuns and women, the seven papers collected in this volume aim to present a freshly coherent and collective picture of the life and history of Korean Buddhist nuns and laywomen, from the fourth century to the twentieth century, as we seek to resurrect the history of Buddhist nuns and laywomen in Korea. It is our hope that this work will serve as a major step forward in researching the female practice of Buddhist Korea.

Chapters 1 and 2 set the foundation for the text and the remaining chapters deal with more specific women and periods of Korean history. Chapter 1 serves to contextualize the chapters within the general discussions on gender and religion in East Asia, providing both a summary of the main ideas and insights of each chapter in the volume and detailing the linkages binding the pieces chronologically and thematically. Chapter 2, "Female Buddhist Practice in Korea—A Historical Account," serves as a prolegomena offering a survey of the entire history of Korea in a more descriptive way. It was written with the intention of presenting a larger picture of the religious milieu within which the individual chapters fit, so that the historical incidences and religious events in those chapters will be presented to the readers with more coherence and meaning. At the same time, I also reiterate the implications of the accounts of religious women in the larger historical and social context of traditional Korea, providing a more integrated view of female Buddhist practice in Korea.

Chapter 3, "Male Sŏn Masters' Views on Female Disciples in Later Koryŏ" focuses on the religious practice of the notable bhikṣuṇīs and laywomen practitioners of the later Koryŏ period, namely, Sŏn-practicing elite women. The information on these women was drawn from the related records of their male teachers, including one of most notable Sŏn monks in the period, Chin'gak Hyesim (1178–1234). He was the successor of Pojo Chinul and continued the flourishing expansion of the Sŏn community at Songgwang-sa after its initial establishment by his teacher. Most of all, he played a key role in popularizing the *hwadu*[7] meditation method. This chapter analyzes Hyesim's inscriptions and collection of writings and shows how he received and trained his female disciples. The inscription of his epitaph states that female disciples participated in summer retreats under his guidance and also contains names of women disciples, a fact well worth noticing as the first of such records in the epitaphs of eminent monks found in Korean history. The fact that these Buddhist nuns were gaining visibility must relate to and reflect the changed attitudes of Sŏn masters in late Koryŏ society.

The value of Hyesim's collected records is especially great in his written communications with his disciples. It is here, particularly in the letters from disciples inquiring abut *hwadu* meditation practice, that the religious zeal and aspirations of his female disciples are displayed most vividly. The fact that these women were most seriously engaged in meditation and awakening to the buddhahood is also clearly established. The most notable finding may be his strident insistence that he was teaching explicitly that enlightenment can be achieved in this life and in this body, even for women. Such a stand is quite advanced, given the traditional position on women's enlightenment presented in the *Lotus Sūtra,* which states that women have to first become men in order to reach enlightenment. With his acceptance of female disciples and the inclusion of female disciples' names in his epitaph, Hyesim presents the most progressive male view about women's Buddhist practice in Korean history.

Chapter 4, another chapter on Koryŏ women, titled "Koryŏ Ladies and the Encouragement of Buddhism in Yuan China," discusses a different group of Koryŏ women—expatriates in thirteenth-century Yuan China. The conclusion of hostilities with the Mongols in 1259 and the foundation of the Yuan dynasty brought many changes to the Koryŏ political and societal landscape for the next one hundred years. The conditions of peace were harsh. Among other concessions, Koryŏ had to pay tribute to the Yuan court in the form of young women. These court ladies often became wives and concubines of high Yuan court officials and Mongol princes. Outside of these women, however, tens of thousands of other Koryŏ people migrated to China for many other reasons. This chapter details the various activities of these expatriates so as to understand the meaning of these women's role in the promotion of Buddhism and the kind of faith they professed. These records are accessible due to the fact that the Koryŏ communities that sprung up in Yuan China were often centered around Buddhist temples. Many of these temples had been founded by well-to-do Koryŏ ladies, who, thanks to their backing, could often afford the means to fund Buddhist temples and promote initiatives in favor of the Buddhist saṅgha, both in China and in Koryŏ. Wives of Koryŏ officials in service at the Yuan court also distinguished themselves as active promoters of the Buddhist religion. The most exemplary case is that of Lady Ki, who became the last empress of the Yuan and was prominent in sustaining Buddhist establishments. The chapter concludes with a tentative evaluation of the meaning of their activities both in terms of Buddhist history in general as well as the specific Korean history relating to the period of Mongol control.

Chapter 5, "Two Female Masters of Two Eras: Differences and Commonalities in Roles," offers a comparative analysis of two bhikṣuṇīs, Chŏngyu (1717–1782) of Chosŏn and Chinhye (1255–1324) of Koryŏ, both of whom were from aristocratic families and became Buddhist nuns after their husbands died. Though they lived almost five hundred years apart, this comparison yields an interesting observation about the shared values and practices that guided them. The author chose to introduce Chŏngyu first, arguing that she is the most unique and notable of the two, having been referred to as "woman-master," a rare title for a woman in the harsh Confucian society of mid-Chosŏn. After then detailing Chinhye's development, the author illustrates how even though both were already from illustrative family backgrounds, they rose to prominent levels of spiritual authority on their own accord as Buddhist practitioners, noting how each individual's personal history flourished within the Buddhist cultural sphere.

Moving on chronologically, we find that the Chosŏn period is an extremely problematic one for studying either Buddhism or women. Not only the paucity of historical records and textual reference materials, but also the harsh and negative depiction of Buddhist women makes it nearly impossible to draw an objective and accurate account of women during the period. Nevertheless, despite the consistently negative tone, the abundance of records about women found in the dynasty annals, when given a close reading, are indeed useful in helping to conjure an image of the Buddhist women of this age. Chapters 6 and 7 successfully provide such readings.

Chapter 6, "Marginalized and Silenced: Buddhist Nuns of the Chosŏn Period," concentrates on the dynasty annals. It presents appeals made to the throne by Confucian officials to have the Buddhist order restricted or dissolved, in order to prevent elite women from visiting monasteries, or to prohibit women of elite families becoming nuns. The state wanted men for military and agricultural service and women for bearing children. For elite women to become nuns would set a bad example, and there was a desire to maintain class and gender boundaries. In addition to accounts of women in the Seoul-based monasteries found in the dynasty annals, the author uncovers records of women in the country through the careful excavation of various temple gazetteers. This is a new methodology and such records have never before been utilized as research material on Buddhist women. These records detail the many temple donations made by women and offer information about women who led monastic lives. Such material is invaluable in providing solid proof of the existence of bhikṣuṇīs' lineage.

Nevertheless, the optimism offered by the new discovery is somewhat tarnished with the conclusion that Buddhist nuns were triply marginalized: first, as Buddhist clergy in an increasingly fundamentalist Confucian society; second, as women within a patriarchal Confucian and misogynist Buddhist hierarchy in which males were always superior spiritually; and, third, as a consequence of the general lack of education in classical Chinese in which all "serious" writing was done. What is revealed is that one of the major reasons records about Buddhist nuns are so sparse is because the nuns did not write classical Chinese, and literate males, especially monks, could not write about nuns, for to do so might invite accusations of violating the rules of gender separation and hierarchy. Possibly the only serious public attempt to cater to the religious education of nuns was the composition of *han'gŭl* Buddhist texts, mainly by monks of one lineage in a restricted time frame. This mixed bag of hope and disappointment helps ground our vision for the future of our studies of Korean Buddhist women and makes clear that our progress will only come in fits and starts.

In contrast to the previous chapter's historical perspective, chapter 7, "Buddhist Nuns and Alternate Space in Confucian Chosŏn Society," takes a feminist approach in its analysis. Where the previous chapter focused on the social and institutional history, chapter 7 pays attention to the inner and psychological world of the women, the motivations as to why and how they wanted to become Buddhist nuns, and how they invented their own paths of life to overcome the obstacles of the harsh neo-Confucian milieu. With nuanced and daring comparisons and aggressive and positive interpretations, the author argues that the women chose alternative lives outside the boundaries prescribed by the Confucian patriarchal ideology, and their creative engagement as women in the religious sphere allowed them to simultaneously conform to, reject, or appropriate the existing gender system. While the women submitted themselves to the dominant gender ideology through various strategies and tactics, they still found ingenious and subversive ways to exercise their power and resist the status quo. For these women, Buddhism was a means to provide for the creation of an alternative space outside Confucian social norms and a life, at least somewhat, separated from them.

The last chapter, chapter 8, "The Establishment of Buddhist Nunneries in Contemporary Korea," examines the period of Korea after forty-five years of Japanese colonization. These monasteries began to appear after the Purification Movement during the 1950s and represent the emergence of the independent operation of nuns in Korea who established their own lecture halls (*kangwŏn*) and meditation halls (*sŏnwŏn*). This chapter gives a detailed analysis of the status of

Korean nuns at the major nunneries and the pioneering women who built them, namely, Suok, Inhong, and Pŏbil Sŭnim. These founding nuns built the compounds from scratch, with little assistance from the administration of the saṅgha, and through their efforts accomplished the great task of providing an environment for generations of nuns to come. The author concludes that despite Korean nuns being ignored in the central politics of the saṅgha, they accomplished a great deal through their self-sufficiency. Their alienation from the central administration even helped them, ironically, by sheltering them from the hegemonic battles that often characterized the saṅgha.

With the eight chapters presented in this volume, we sought to achieve through a collective effort the rewriting of the history of religious Korean women. Even though the primary source materials, and even modern secondary scholarship, are almost nonexistent—most of the records utilized here are being brought to scholarly attention for the very first time—we have taken on the task of being trailblazers in this quest. As such, I must emphasize our acknowledgment that we are understandably restricted by the sources available. In short, at this point in the development of the scholarship, we are still left reaching and are fated to a somewhat partial success. That said, this volume will undoubtedly bring to light new evidence that though the many female practitioners of old were anonymous, their very existence made them bearers of a remarkably long-sustained tradition of female spirituality in Korea. It is our sincere hope that this will bring a new awareness to this field of study and raise critical questions that not only make this work relevant and important, but will serve to encourage future growth. The very purpose of this volume is thus not to offer any defining conclusions, but to stimulate questions and provide the impetus for much more research on each of the periods examined.

NOTES

1. Rita Gross's *Buddhism After Patriarchy: A Feminist History, Analysis* (Albany: State University of New York Press, 1993) should be mentioned as a pioneering work in discussing women and Buddhism from a feminist perspective and it still serves as the classic of this field.

2. There are numerous books and articles on Chinese Buddhist women, not all of which can be mentioned here. Chün-fang Yü, Beata Grant, Miriam Levering, and Ding-hwa E. Hsieh are leading scholars in the field. Recent works have appeared in Western academic circles that trace the remarkable growth of the nuns' saṅgha in Taiwan, such as Heng-Ching Shih, "Buddhist Spirituality

in Modern Taiwan," in Yoshinori Takeuchi, ed., *Buddhist Spirituality—Later China, Korea, Japan, and the Modern World* (New York: Crossroad Publishing Company, 1999), 427–431; Chien-Yu Julia Huang and Robert P. Weller, "Merit and Mothering: Women and Social Welfare in Taiwanese Buddhism," *Journal of Asian Studies* 57, no. 2 (May 1998): 379–396; Charles Jones, *Buddhism in Taiwan—Religion and the State 1660–1990* (Honolulu: University of Hawai'i Press, 1999); Elise Anne DeVido, " 'The Infinite Worlds' of Taiwan's Buddhist Nuns," in Karma Lekshe Tsomo, ed., *Buddhist Women and Social Justice: Ideals, Challenges, and Achievements* (Albany: State University of New York Press, 2004); and Wei-Yi Cheng, *Buddhist Nuns in Taiwan and Sri Lanka: A Critique of the Feminist Perspective,* Routledge Critical Studies in Buddhism (Abingdon, NY: Routledge, 2007). For Japanese Buddhist women, representative books are Paula Kane Robinson Arai, *Women Living Zen: Japanese Soto Buddhist Nuns* (New York: Oxford University Press, 1999), and Barbara Ruch, *Engendering Faith: Women and Buddhism in Premodern Japan,* Michigan Monograph Series in Japanese Studies, no. 43 (Ann Arbor: Center for Japanese Studies, University of Michigan, 2002).

3. Karma Lekshe Tsomo edited *Buddhist Women Across Cultures: Realizations* (Albany: State University of New York Press, 1999); *Innovative Buddhist Women Swimming Against the Stream* (Richmond: Curzon, 2000); *Buddhist Women and Social Justice: Ideals, Challenges, and Achievements* (Albany: State University of New York Press, 2004); and *Bridging Worlds: Buddhist Women's Voices across Generations* (Taipei: Yuan Chuan Press, 2004).

4. Beginning in 2002, a group of young scholars from a wide range of disciplines, including religious studies, Buddhist studies, literature, and others, began to discuss collaborative approaches to this important area of study. After scattered talks and meetings, they gathered face-to-face and confirmed each other's enthusiasm at a one-day planning workshop entitled "New Directions and Strategies for Research on the History of Korean Buddhist Nuns," held in New York on February 15, 2003. This event—organized by Barbara Ruch, a pioneer in the study of Japanese nuns, and hosted by the Center for Medieval Japanese Studies at Columbia University—brought vital momentum to the initial effort, propelling it in a more organized direction. Among those who attended the workshop and became major researchers in the project were Samu Sŭnim, Bongak Sŭnim, Haewon Sŭnim, Sukdam Sŭnim, Hyangsoon Yi, and myself. Samu Sŭnim in particular had already been a pioneer in this area by publishing accounts of notable twentieth-century Korean Buddhist nuns, such as Eunyeong Sŭnim and Manseong Sŭnim, in his articles "Eunyeong Sŭnim and the Founding of Pomun-Jong, the First Independent Bhikshuni Order," and "Manseong Sŭnim, a Woman Zen Master of Modern Korea," in *Spring Wind, A Buddhist Cultural Forum: Women and Buddhism* 6 (1986): 129–162 and 188–193, respectively. Martine Batchelor, who was not present at the workshop, published a nonacademic but very important anthology of stories about the lives of contemporary Buddhist nuns, *Women's Buddhism, Buddhism's Women: Tradition, Revision, Renewal* (Boston: Wisdom Publications, 2000). Her *Women in Korean Zen—Lives and Practices* (Syracuse: Syracuse University Press, 2006) is

an impressive work that provides vivid in-depth interviews and the personal history of Sŏn'gyŏng Sŭnim, a nun who lived through the end of the Chosŏn dynasty, Japanese colonization, and into the era of modern Korea.

5. Ha Chunsaeng, *Kkaedarŭm ŭi kkot* (Flowers of Enlightenment; Seoul: Yŏrae, 1998), 121.

6. Many of her writings have been translated into English and other foreign languages, including her most recent work, *No River To Cross: Trusting the Enlightenment That's Always Right Here* (Somerville, MA: Wisdom Publications, 2007).

7. In *hwadu* (C. *huatou*; J. *wato*; literally, "word-head") practice, meditators focus on the point, or key line, of a *kongan* (C. *kungan gongan*; J. *kōan*; "public case").

2

Female Buddhist Practice in Korea—A Historical Account

Eun-su Cho

How can there be [gender distinctions between] monks and nuns
in the Buddhadharma?
How can there be the worldly and the nonworldly?
How can there be north and south?
How can there be you and me?

Pon'gong Sŭnim (1907–1965)

One of the fundamental tenets of Sŏn (C. Chan; J. Zen), which forms the basis of modern Korean Buddhism, is that in the Buddhadharma there is no distinction between male and female, worldly and nonworldly phenomena. There is, however, a considerable gap between this nondualistic ideal and what is actually practiced. Pon'gong's verse quoted here[1] seems to question this gap, as the author is conscious of her dual status as a woman and as a Sŏn teacher who defies that womanhood.[2] Poems and other overlooked sources offer us glimpses of the enduring vitality displayed by Korean nuns, who have maintained a history of thorough practice that has been almost completely ignored: the history of Korean Buddhism has so far always been restricted to the history of monks alone.

The nuns' saṅgha began when the historical Buddha, Śākyamuni, ordained his maternal aunt and foster mother, Mahāprajāpati, and five hundred other women. When the Buddha permitted the ordination of nuns, he demanded that they observe eight chief rules of respect to monks. For anyone concerned about the status of women in Buddhism, this is a problem that causes considerable anguish. Scholarly research to date on this subject is largely divided into two camps. The first maintains that these regulations did not reflect the thinking of the Buddha himself but were created in later times by his conservative disciples. The second holds that although the Buddha may have said this himself and his own disciples may have created these regulations, this was merely an expedient means, an empty statement to placate Indian society of the day. This second view emphasizes the fact that Buddhism is one of the few major religions in which female clergy exist alongside their male counterparts, with equally independent organizational structures and religious functions. Regardless of which interpretation is adopted, at the time of Śākyamuni it was codified that the Buddhist order is made up of the four assemblies—female and male clergy, and female and male lay believers—a fact that in itself indicates the longevity of the egalitarian and democratic nature of the social and political ideas of Buddhism.

However, unlike the Buddha, who advocated and practiced the idea of gender equality within the limitations of his time, the later institutions of Buddhism were corroded by the patriarchal societies and cultures in which they formed. Korea was no exception to this, and its nuns suffered constant ordeals solely and specifically because they were women.

KOREAN BUDDHIST NUNS FROM THE FOURTH CENTURY TO THE PRESENT

Despite the paucity of historical materials, it is generally agreed that a Korean nuns' order was established at almost the same time as the order of monks, namely, on the transmission of Buddhism to Korea. The two seminal historic sources for ancient Korea, the *Samguk yusa* (Memorabilia of the Three Kingdoms; written by the monk Iryŏn [1206–1289] toward the end of the thirteenth century) and *Samguk sagi* (History of the Three Kingdoms; an official history compiled in 1145 by Kim Pu-sik and others), both contain records of Buddhist nuns and female lay practitioners, proving the existence of Korean nuns from the very beginning of Buddhism in Korea some 1,600 years ago.

Buddhism came to the Korean peninsula in the latter half of the fourth century through China, during the Three Kingdoms period. Koguryŏ (37 B.C.E.–618 C.E.) in the north was the most powerful of the three kingdoms, and received the new religion first. There is a record stating that the introduction of Buddhism to Koguryŏ took place in 372 C.E., when King Fu Jian (r. 357–384) of the former Qin dynasty (351–394) sent the monk-envoy Shundao (K. Sundo) to the Koguryŏ court with scriptures and images. Around the same time, the Paekche kingdom (18 B.C.E.–660 C.E.), occupying the southwestern part of the peninsula, was introduced to Buddhism in 384 through another monk-envoy who had come from Eastern Jin. The kingdom of Silla (57 B.C.E.–935 C.E.), in the southeastern part of the peninsula, was officially introduced to Buddhism about two centuries later than the other two, in 527. However, even though these dates are regarded as the official introductions of Buddhism, it is believed that actual contact happened much earlier, probably by the third century.[3]

The Three Kingdoms Period and Unified Silla (676–935)

The earliest record of Buddhist women in Korea comes from the *Samguk yusa*, which records a woman known only by her surname, Sa, a younger sister of Morye, a local leader in the Ilsŏn area of Silla. Both of them are said to have helped Ado, a monk from Koguryŏ, perform his missionary work of spreading Buddhism some one hundred years before it was officially accepted by the Silla court. Lady Sa became a nun, thus marking the first recorded appearance of a Buddhist nun in Korean history. The queen of King Pŏphŭng (r. 514–540), along with her husband, converted to Buddhism at the time of its official acceptance in 527. When the king became a monk after renouncing the throne in 540, the queen also became a nun, "out of respect for Lady Sa's path." However, Lady Sa and the queen could not have received official ordination. Women were only allowed to become Buddhist nuns after a decree was issued to that effect in 544, the fifth year of the reign of King Chinhŭng (r. 540–576),[4] the successor of King Pŏphŭng.

It is well known that nuns from Paekche went to Japan and played a definitive role in the establishment of a nuns' order there. The first record of Paekche nuns comes from a Japanese history, *Nihon shoki*, which states that Paekche sent Buddhist missionaries, including a nun, to Japan in 577. It is known that Paekche began to regularly dispatch Buddhist doctrinal specialists, psalmodists, iconographers, and architects to Japan over its well-developed sea lanes, thus transmitting the rudiments of Sinified Buddhist culture and laying the foundation for the rich Buddhist culture of the Asuka (552–645), Hakuhō (645–710), and Nara (710–794) periods.[5] It is also mentioned that a Paekche nun named Pŏmmyŏng went to Tsushima Island in 655 and cured a Japanese high official of an ailment by reciting the *Vimalakirt-nirdeśa Sūtra*.[6]

This exchange also went in the opposite direction. There is a record that three Japanese nuns, whose names are recorded as Zenshin-ni, Zenzo-ni, and Kenzen-ni, came to Paekche in 584 and received novice precepts as well as full ordination in 588.[7] An envoy from Paekche explained their ordination ceremony to the Japanese court as follows:

> The way to receive their bhikṣuṇī ordination is thus: they receive their *pratimokṣa* precepts from ten bhikṣuṇī preceptors and then they go to a bhikṣu temple and request ten bhikṣu preceptors, such that they receive precepts from twenty monks and nuns. However, in this country [i.e., Japan] there are only bhikṣuṇīs. There is no bhikṣu preceptor or bhikṣuṇī preceptor, thus if these bhikṣuṇīs want to receive the bhikṣuṇī ordination properly, they should establish a bhikṣu order. Also, they have to invite bhikṣuṇī preceptors from Paekche.[8]

This description of the process and requirements for bhikṣuṇī ordination shows that the first ordained Buddhist priests in Japan were women and that they became ordained without meeting the standard requirement of receiving precepts from ten bhikṣus and ten bhikṣuṇīs, a fact that may have caused some controversy. At any rate, this passage tells us that a formally recognized female order existed in Paekche in a much-advanced form at that time.[9]

Once Silla adopted Buddhism and ordained Buddhist nuns, the religion flourished throughout their society, which had previously been without any organized form of religion, and thus regarded this new tradition as providing an advanced worldview and a loftier principle of morality. It was during this time in Silla and the subsequent Unified Silla period (676–935) that the doctrinal study of Buddhism made its greatest advancements in Korean history. At the same time, the society of Buddhist nuns also seems to have flourished. The existence of a position called Toyunarang,[10] apparently denoting the head of bhikṣuṇī affairs, also indicates that there was a bhikṣuṇī order with a substantial number of members.

After Silla's unification of the three kingdoms in 676, the Unified Silla period brought great prosperity in Buddhist activities and the deepening of doctrinal understanding. The two most important historiographies dealing with the Three Kingdoms period, the *Samguk yusa* and the *Samguk sagi,* were both written during the subsequent Koryŏ dynasty, and contain many stories related to Buddhist women.[11]

The *Samguk sagi* details historical events of the three kingdoms from the rulers' perspectives, arranged in chronological order under the kings' names. It records women from royal and aristocratic families such as the wife of King Chinhŭng who became a nun, and the wife of Kim Yusin, the general who assisted King Muyŏl's war for unification (she herself was the third daughter of the king), who entered priesthood after her husband's death. To the contrary, the *Samguk yusa*, compiled at the end of the Koryŏ dynasty by Buddhist monk Iryŏn (1206–1289), features many stories of miraculous deeds of religiously pious women from different walks of life: from ladies of royal and aristocratic families and bhikṣuṇīs, to the wife of a poor man and a slave girl. Their accounts are found in the form of tales, life histories, and historical Buddhist events.

Chihye, from the period of King Chinpyŏng (r. 579–632), performed many meritorious deeds. While staying in Anhŭng-sa, she devoted herself to the restoration of a Buddha's hall, but was short of resources. In answer to her prayers, a celestial woman appeared in her dream and offered help.[12] Another tale, this one with a nun, involved the famous scholar-monk Kyŏnghŭng, who lived during the reign of King Sinmun (r. 681–692), after he became seriously ill. After a few months of suffering, he received a visit from a nun who looked at him and said that his disease was caused by worries and fatigue, and thus joyfulness and laughter would serve as his cure. She then made an eleven-faced comedic mask that she wore while performing a dance, providing a ridiculously funny sight. It was so silly everyone laughed uproariously. Without him even noticing, the monk's illness disappeared. The nun vanished into a Buddha hall, with only her walking stick left behind in front of the eleven-faced [Bodhisattva] statue in the hall.[13] Tales like this involving mysterious women and bhikṣuṇīs are abundant in the *Samguk yusa*. It must have been a local legend passed down to Iryŏn's time and it would be too much of a stretch to use this tale to provide any general statement on the status of bhikṣuṇīs and how they were perceived by society. Yet, this is an unusual story in that a nun is credited with curing one of the most renowned Yogacāra monks, someone who had been appointed as "Kungno" (National Elder) by King Sinmun. Thus, the rendering of this history and the unusual laughter therapy (the *Samguk yusa* indicates she must have been an incarnation of Bodhisattva Kwanŭm) tells us that bhikṣuṇīs were indeed worthy of entering the mystical pantheon of the Three Kingdoms period.

The story of Ungmyŏn, a slave girl who entered the Western Paradise by chanting Amitābha Buddha's name, may perhaps be the most moving narrative about women's religious practice found in the *Samguk yusa*. One day she followed her master's attendance at a ten-thousand-day chanting ceremony and made a resolution that she herself would do the practice as well. Upon returning home, she didn't stop chanting and her master became jealous, so much so that he burdened her with the weighty task of milling ten bushels of grain every night. However, she would finish the work by early evening and return immediately to the temple for prayer where she stood outside in the courtyard, continuing her chanting. One evening, the assembled worshippers heard a voice from the sky inviting her to enter the main Buddha hall. Suddenly the sound of heavenly music was heard from the west, and a swift whirlwind swept into the palace of the Buddha. Ungmyŏn was lifted into the sky through a gaping hole in the ceiling and roof, rising higher and higher as she flew toward the western side of the temple.[14]

Beyond these tales of magic and mysticism are the records of more quotidian acts of donation. Such records detail not only aristocratic women who gave money as donations for the building of bells, stupas, and stone lanterns, but also poor women who donated their labor to the Buddhist community as meritorious acts. Many such stories are found in the *Samguk yusa*.

The works of such women were not limited to the Korean peninsula. There are also records of nuns active in missionary work in the expatriate community outside of Silla. Ennin's diary records the presence of Korean nuns outside of Korea as early as 839–840 in a monastery called Fahua-yuan (Lotus Cloister) in the Shandong area of China, originally built by Chang Pogo, a Korean general.[15]

The Koryŏ Dynasty (918–1392)

After the Unified Silla period, the Koryŏ dynasty made Buddhism a state religion and the Buddhist order became more organized and secularized. There was a centralized administrative body that dealt with clerical affairs and the monks' examination system. Many notable monks were appointed to various positions and given various titles throughout the dynasty, whereas nuns were apparently excluded from both examinations and official positions and titles. Bhikṣuṇī ordination ceremonies were performed, but contain no records of female masters whose names are singled out for notable Buddhist practice or deeds. The only exception is Bhikṣuṇī Chinhye (1255–1324), who was granted the posthumous title of *yŏdaesa* (literally, "female master"), as illustrated in chapter 5, "Two Female Masters of Two Eras: Differences and Commonalities in Roles."

Because Buddhism was the Koryŏ national religion, royal family members played key roles in promoting it. The women of the royal families of the Koryŏ dynasty were especially avid practitioners of Buddhism and fervent supporters of the religion and the saṅgha as well. Some of them went so far as to become nuns themselves later in their lives, such as the wives of the founding King T'aejo, Queen Sinhye (family name Ryu) and Lady Sosŏwŏn (Kim), and the wives of King Kongmin, Queen Hye (Lee) and Queen Shin (Yŏm).

Queen Mother Inye, the wife of King Munjong (1019–1083), left conspicuous footsteps in the history of Korean Buddhism and the religious life of Buddhist women in Koryŏ as sponsor of the Ch'ŏnt'ae sect founded by her son, the famous Taegak National Preceptor, Ŭich'ŏn. Inye was a daughter of Yi Chayŏn of the Inju Yi family, the mightiest aristocratic clan at that time, and, along with her two younger sisters, married King Munjong as part of a political scheme to further establish family influence and produced eleven sons and two daughters. Among her sons, three became monks, including Ŭich'ŏn. She herself commissioned the publication of the *Hua-yen sūtra*, copied important Yogācāra Buddhist treatises in silver calligraphy, built a thirteen-story golden pagoda, sponsored dharma gatherings for confessional purposes in the Ch'ŏnt'ae style, and established Kukch'ŏng-sa Monastery as her own home temple. Most significantly, she helped Koryŏ Buddhism turn toward a new direction by sponsoring her own son, Ŭich'ŏn, with generous funding to embark on a number of endeavors in Sung China and later provided the material foundation for his new Ch'ŏnt'ae sect via the establishment of Kukch'ŏng-sa Monastery. These elite women exerted a great influence on Koryŏ Buddhism and served as critical patrons of many Buddhist works.[16]

On the other hand, the bulk of nuns and laywomen of this period remain generally anonymous. In the few cases when nuns' names do appear, it is in the lists of disciples on the stelae inscriptions for great male masters. In such cases, the women are all from distinguished family backgrounds. The bhikṣuṇīs found in the stela inscription for Hyesim (1178–1234), who was the successor of the famous Pojo Chinul (1158–1210) and was posthumously invested as National Master (*kuksa*), can be cited as examples. As chapter 3, "Male Sŏn Masters' Views on Female Disciples in Later Koryŏ," indicates, altogether only three inscriptions have been found so far that record the names of male masters' female disciples, and these masters were all Sŏn monks, rather than monks belonging to the doctrinal schools.[17] For example, a letter from a female practitioner inquiring about her progress in *hwadu* meditation and her teacher Hyesim's response shows how serious they were as practitioners of Sŏn. Unfortunately, those communications were kept in the anthologies of male masters, and they usually presented only the male masters' responses and perspectives on Buddhist women's practice, not those of the women themselves.

However, given the social milieu of Koryŏ as a Buddhist state and with the direct governmental support of the religion, it is assumed that numerous aristocratic women became Buddhist nuns after their husbands' death, and that Buddhist practice by women believers was flourishing. It has also been argued that there is a relative abundance of historical information on the financial and spiritual support of Buddhism by Koryŏ women in Yuan China, where a good portion of the ladies attending the court, as well as some women married to high officials, were of Korean origin. Such is the story examined in chapter 4, "Koryŏ Ladies and the Encouragement of Buddhism in Yuan China."

The Chosŏn Dynasty (1392–1910)

Chosŏn society has been understood as that of a monolithically Confucian culture, so ideologically dominated that Confucianism controlled both the public and private spaces of peoples' lives while Buddhism was suppressed and forced underground. However, a closer look reveals that this cannot be true. Confucianism and Buddhism surfaced and submerged alternatively, fluctuating with political fortunes. The existence and nature of the bhikṣuṇīs and Buddhist women during the dynasty might serve as crucial keys to shed new light on a more nuanced understanding of the state.

From the beginning of the Chosŏn dynasty, the government promulgated an anti-Buddhist policy, challenging a Buddhist establishment that had long enjoyed the privilege and support of both the public and the government as a state religion. With the advent of Chosŏn, which adopted neo-Confucianism as the prevailing ideology for the country, the Buddhist community faced social suppression and discrimination and suffered a subsequent decline. The government's restrictions included a law that monasteries could not be built near cities and towns but had to be constructed in the mountains. Monks and nuns could not enter the capital and had to wear large hats to cover their faces when they went out.

Buddhist women suffered a form of double oppression, in that (1) their religious lives were curtailed as a result of anti-Buddhist policies, and (2) their social lives were restricted by the legal and cultural oppression of women authorized by neo-Confucian ideology. Monastic and laywomen practitioners became subjects of moral scrutiny. Whenever Buddhist laywomen or bhikṣuṇīs were recorded in Chosŏn-dynasty annals, they appeared due to their accused involvement with Buddhist monks and under charges of violating Confucian moral codes, especially chastity. The worst examples were accusations of adultery between bhikṣus and bhikṣuṇīs, and assumptive charges of adultery between monks and laywomen, based on the latter's frequent visits to monasteries. Some records even accuse certain women in Buddhist robes living outside the city as having been involved in prostitution.

One particularly momentous scandal involved a group of high-class women and bhikṣuṇīs attending a Buddhist ceremony in the earlier period of the dynasty, during King Sejong's reign in 1434. Hoeam-sa was an important Buddhist monastery of the Chosŏn dynasty. Located near the capital, it was famous for the notable monks who resided there, such as Muhak, who was the personal advisor of the founding king of the dynasty, and also as a dedicated temple for a deceased queen. However, the monastery had recently fallen into serious disrepair. The king suggested using government funds for renovations but was rebuffed due to his ministers' objections. Monks wrote letters "encouraging merit" and circulated them in person to powerful families. Donations came in, the reconstruction was planned, and a commemoration ceremony was announced. Many women of aristocratic families came to participate in the ceremonies and attend dharma talks. As three monks were performing a Buddhist dance, some women donated their robes and silk as gifts. When details of the gathering became known, an investigation commenced with the interrogation of the temple monks and the women involved in the incident. The investigation revealed that a few government officials and many women from royal or aristocratic families attended the ceremony and bhikṣuṇīs accompanied their visit to the monastery. The king's own mother-in-law had also attended. The women's participation in the religious activity, and specifically their occupying the dharma hall with male monks and staying overnight at the temple, were highly criticized as being in violations of the state code that decreed: "Women who go to Buddhist temples along with monks will be regarded as having lost their chastity." Such women violated not only the Confucian social norm of separation of men and women, but engaged in the activities of "heresy" and "religious deceit." More than twenty people, including the monks and the aristocratic women (most of them widowed), received beatings, and the higher aristocratic women paid fines in exemption. The royal family, on the other hand, was exempted.

Such were the strictures that limited women's Buddhist participation in the highly Confucian Chosŏn dynasty, when visits to Buddhist temples by women were controlled or sometimes prohibited outright, depending on the reign. The Buddhist women who were leaving home to become nuns were also denounced as disobeying patriarchal authority. Unmarried women who became nuns were argued to be damaging the harmonious force of the universe by not marrying. Widowed wives who sought to become nuns were thought to be trying to go beyond the patriarchal law's boundary. Where they once had a father, and then a husband who had died, they were expected to then remain in the care of their sons. Thus, women who tried to become nuns were seen as trying to escape from the Confucian moral realm, acts perceived as not only threats to the social order but even violations of the very fabric of the universe. Confucian officials and fervent Confucian students brought numerous petitions banning unmarried women from becoming nuns and requesting that bhikṣuṇīs be sent back to their home. In this way, the religion, especially in the institutional space, fell under the control of the state. As the number of ordained monks and nuns were controlled, the state had the power to disrobe monks or nuns and send them back to their homes. Nevertheless, the state was never fully able to control their personal choices and could not simply disrobe the monastics without reason.

The Buddhist women were seen in many ways as beings who were dangerous to the social order the Confucians were trying to build. Buddhist women were frequently depicted as tainted and potentially tainting because of their Buddhist faith and their status as women, so frequently the accusations naturally implied and linked them with sexual impropriety. The annals of King Sukjong (1661–1720), whose reign saw the harsh suppression of Buddhism, record a petition received in regards to a bhikṣuṇīs temple's flourishing religious activities, in which Buddhist nuns were summarily described with the following characteristics: "lewd and seductive," "shrewd," "destructive of public morals," "betraying of husbands and masters," "unchastised," and "cunning practitioners of adultery." These records obviously reflect a less than charitable view held by Confucian historians and statesmen toward women and Buddhism.

Throughout the dynasty, these types of accusations and petitions brought to the court and persecutors' offices were incessant. Yet, given official declarations of Confucian piety, the charges served as an ironic reflection that Buddhist practice was still quite alive. Despite an environment of fierce anti-Buddhist criticism and rampant accusations against them, Buddhist women were recorded as visiting temples and entering the priesthood. There were copious accounts of women who dared to leave home once their husbands had died, directly challenging the social mores that prohibited widows from any such behaviors. The story of an aristocratic woman who "ran away" on the funeral day of her husband to become a nun is just one example. She would later become a renowned nun and abbot of Chŏngŏpwŏn, a royal nunnery. Many women incorporated the Buddhist religion as a part of their lives and Buddhist monasteries were their spiritual refuges. They chose a countercultural religious path in their personal space and the state tried, but could not fully intervene within it.

The less than totalizing aspect of anti-Buddhist cultural policy is reflected not only in its application, but also among personalities at the highest levels of the government enforcing it, chief among them the aforementioned King Sejong, the fourth king of the dynasty. He was respected as the greatest and most literary among the Chosŏn kings for establishing an administration based on Confucian rule. Yet Sejong himself suggested that his ministers support the restoration project mentioned earlier as his own elder brother Prince Hyoryŏng, a pious Buddhist, requested. However, the ministers adamantly objected that pitiful people's labor and the country's precious resources would be spent for that sort of purpose. Ultimately, the king relented. Regarding petitions aimed at curtailing Buddhist monasteries, the king replied that the Buddhist teaching had a long history and it would be difficult to reform the religion by diktat. He repeatedly beat back the tedious accusations and anti-Buddhist harangues lodged by Confucian officials' regarding all matters of temple affairs. The affairs of Hoeam-sa Monastery alone were brought up a total of forty-eight times in the annals during the thirty-two year reign of King Sejong, and he defended the temple in most of these. Even after the incident, when there were reports of local government harassment, he intervened on behalf of the monastic community. Toward the end of his life, he visited the temple and also granted gifts, including an exemption from taxation.

In fact, we find many Chosŏn kings who were scrutinized under suspicion of their Buddhist faith. For instance, King T'aejong, the third king of the dynasty, prohibited temple construction on behalf of late kings and queens and sought to control the number of monks via a quota system. However, after a brutal political career, he then converted to Buddhism in his old age and personally visited many monasteries. What these examples reveal is that at the core of these controversies, it was never simply a struggle between Confucian ideology and Buddhist religion, but also a struggle for power between the king and the ministers, embedded within the cultural matrix of the Confucian political system surrounding them. In other words, the anti-Buddhist criticism might have been a superficial cover for an underlying desire to check the king's power using the excuses of religion and culture. King Sŏnjo (1552–1608) in the mid-Chosŏn period suffered repeated accusations and petitions from the students of the Confucian academy attacking his and his cohorts' suspicious activities involving Buddhist worship inside of the court. Running on the basis of a check-and-balance system, the Chosŏn ruling system allowed ministers the power to correct the king if they had to, even as the king was considered a being bestowed by heavenly order.

The survival of Buddhism as an important religious and social practice of the Chosŏn people was particularly dependent on female members of the royal family and wives of state officials and Confucian literati. Not only in this case, but in many others, there were many kings and queens who also defended for the Buddhist community. When a government proposal was submitted calling for all bhikṣuṇī temples in the capital to be centralized into one single bhikṣuṇī temple for ease of oversight and control, it was the royal family who eventually stopped the proposal. Women in the court were also the major force in maintaining the Buddhist faith tradition, for there were royal nunneries within the palace grounds during both the Koryŏ and Chosŏn dynasties. These royal bhikṣuṇī convents (*piguni-wŏn*) were located attached or adjacent to the palace, and were institutions where women of the royal family and nobility took the tonsure and led religious lives. The fortune of these nunneries waxed and waned depending on the king in power, with the most severe period being that of the violent despot Prince Yŏnsan (r. 1476–1506), who evicted the nuns—erstwhile court ladies of his late father—and turned them into slaves. Except for this brief period, however, nunneries for the court ladies existed throughout the dynasty.

The Buddhist activities of Chosŏn women were not necessarily always in direct competition or conflict with the standards of society. In fact, their form of religious practice can sometimes be considered to have been a new form of faith that appeared in Chosŏn society precisely to avoid trouble between the two religions. For instance, these royal and aristocratic women also acted as major patrons of Buddhist art in early Chosŏn. Their activities suggest that, compared to men, women were less directly subject to the strictures of Confucian ideology and policy and thus were able to bypass the possible conflicts that would have arisen had their husbands taken part in such activities. These women chose to express their Buddhist faith by providing financial support for the construction of Buddhist temples and monasteries, the production of new paintings and statues, and the building and repairing of pagodas. Indeed, in the beginning of the dynasty, there was a marked increase in the number of Buddhist artworks commissioned by upper-class women, who became the most powerful patrons of Buddhist art, taking over the role of male patrons in the previous dynasty. They also promoted the publication of Buddhist scriptures, translated from Chinese into Korean.[18] From records of donations (such as paintings and statues of the Bodhisattva Kṣitigarbha and the Ten Kings of the Underworld) and of the dissemination of related scriptures and the like made by the wives and daughters of respectable families praying for the positive rebirth of their deceased parents and other family members, we can see the union of Buddhist faith and the Confucian moral concept of filial piety.[19] It might even be argued that these women developed their Buddhist faith as a religion of the private sphere and Confucianism as a religion of the public sphere.

Despite the ideological attacks and social denouncements from Confucian scholars, we nevertheless find in the annals of that age individual practitioners of Buddhism, even among literati. For example, Yulgok Yi I (1536–1584), one of the two most renowned Confucian scholars and statesmen during Chosŏn, committed himself to Buddhist practice upon the early death of his mother. He left home and became a monk in the famous Diamond Mountains for a short time, an act that marked him, even posthumously, when he was temporarily prevented from being properly enshrined in a Confucian shrine, despite having openly attacked Buddhism at the height of his career. Other members of the Confucian elite remained steadfastly Buddhist in their private lives, engaging in scholarly exchanges with monks or making pilgrimages to monasteries and worshipping there. Although Confucianism, as a social conception of the state, and Buddhism, as a faith in the private domain, thus would seem to have been mutually exclusive, there were overlapping elements.

Toward the later days of the Chosŏn dynasty, with orthodox Confucian rule well established in every nook of society, all forms of public Buddhist practice began to disappear. With a mid-dynasty policy banning monks and nuns from entrance to the city now firmly entrenched, temples disappeared from the capital and other cities; only those in the countryside survived. Whether or not such charges were true, accusations against the practice of Buddhism by women in the later half of the dynasty diminished, becoming mixed in some cases with shamanistic practices. An epic poem composed by the progressive Confucian scholar Tasan Chŏng Yag-yong (1762–1836) while he was on exile in To'gang (present-day Kangjin), "To'gang goga pusa" (A Story of a Woman Who Married a Blind Man of To'gang) introduces a young girl who was forced to marry an old blind man by his threatening father and the deceit of a matchmaker. She escapes from this brutally abusive husband to a temple and shaves her head to become a Buddhist nun. However, her destiny didn't stop there. She was dragged to the court as her husband reported her to the magistrate. This tale of women using the temple as a refugee from harsh life is telling not only as simple evidence of the enduring presence of female Buddhist institutions, but also of the role these institutions played in a society that was often cruelly repressive to women. The Buddhist temples persisted, as did bhikṣunīs, and the survival of their practice until the very end of this dynasty is itself a testament to its vitality.

The Colonial Period (1910–1945)

The Japanese colonial period provided a platform for experimentation within Korean Buddhism. At the beginning of this period, some Korean Buddhists reacted ambivalently to the favorable attitude of the Japanese toward Buddhism and the actions of Japanese missionary-monks who were supported by the colonial government. This ambivalence was rooted in the wariness of colonization in the guise of religious affinity—a concern borne out by the official annexation of the country by Japan in 1910.[20] Selected Korean Buddhist monks gained access to higher education and received support in Japanese monasteries, yet stood vulnerable to the charge of collaborating with an aggressive colonizer. In contrast to the "mountain Buddhism" of the late Chosŏn period, however—which had been characterized by private and individual modes of practice and hence almost devoid of any institutional vigor for participating in public affairs or opportunity for self-restructuring—the colonial period allowed modern Buddhist monks the social space in which to play an active public role. The Japanese incursion thus forced Korean Buddhists to face the social demands for modern initiatives. This sense of urgency, from both inside and outside, demanded a response.

Amid this rapid social and political change, Korean Buddhist women, who had long been silenced, emerged to form their own modern community. After centuries of social disdain both toward Buddhist practice and toward women taking part in religious life, what these women found were crumbling, humble monasteries that inspired in them a fervent desire to establish bhikṣuṇī shelters where they could live and practice. It is remarkable that in such a challenging time female clergy were able to commence the institutionalizing of their community.

Under the leadership and with the support of Man'gong Sŭnim (1871–1946), a renowned Sŏn master monk of the time, a bhikṣuṇī Sŏn meditation facility, or community (*sŏnwŏn*), was established at Kyŏnsŏng-am hermitage belonging to Sudŏk-sa Monastery, and accepted bhikṣuṇī meditators for the retreat season in January 1916. This is the first record of such a meditation facility for nuns in modern Korea. In many ways, Man'gong Sŭnim was the founding father of the bhikṣuṇī practice traditions that resumed in modern times. Many of the nuns whom he accepted as his disciples and encouraged to practice later became leaders of bhikṣuṇī society.[21] In 1918, Ongnyŏn-am of T'ongdo-sa was designated a seminary for doctrinal study (*kangdang*, or *kangwŏn*), and doctrinal education for bhikṣuṇīs was resumed after a long period during which the community of female monastics seemed to have lacked any strong organizational basis.

After the opening of Kyŏnsŏng-am in 1916, Seman Sŭnim opened the meditation facility Sorim *sŏnwŏn* of Naejang-sa in 1924; Sŏngmun Sŭnim opened Pudo-am of Tonghwa-sa in 1927, Sŏjŏn of Chikchi-sa in 1928, Yunp'il-am[22] of Taesŭng-sa in 1931, and Samsŏn-am of Haein-sa in 1945; Pon'gong Sŭnim opened Chijang-am of Wŏlchŏng-sa in 1937; and Taewŏn Sŭnim opened Kugil-am of Haein-sa in 1944. And after the 1918 opening of the seminary at Ongnyŏn-am of T'ongdo-sa, two other seminaries for doctrinal studies were opened at Pomun-sa and Namjang-sa, in 1936 and 1937, respectively. The *Pangham-nok* records (a register maintained at meditation facilities for their biannual, three-month-long summer and winter retreats) show that many Buddhist nuns were actively engaged in meditation practice during this period.[23]

Although the social perception of Buddhism had been changing—and Korean Buddhists' yearning for serious practice increasing—during the colonial period, the actual conditions of living and practice were utterly poor. The facilities for Sŏn meditation and doctrinal studies previously listed were opened in ancient hermitages attached to main monasteries in the countryside. This meant that bhikṣuṇīs had to rehabilitate and rebuild these long-neglected structures from scratch. They gathered wood for repairing the buildings and collected rice and other alms on foot. Sometimes their donation-collecting trips to other parts of the country took many months. They also walked many miles to find masters and listen to dharma talks and teachings. Stories of these brave women circulated in meditation halls and temples, encouraging many serious practitioners who became dedicated to the religious path.

Myori Pŏphŭi (1887–1974) stood out in this period. She spearheaded the movement to revive religious practice and Sŏn meditation among bhikṣuṇīs and is regarded as the builder of the modern Korean bhikṣuṇī saṅgha. Myori Pŏphŭi was born to a humble family in a village in South Ch'ungch'ŏng Province. Her father died when she was three years old. A year later, her Buddhist grandmother took the four-year-old girl to Mit'a-am, a hermitage of Tonghak-sa temple on Kyeryong-san Mountain, where she was cared for by Kwiwan Sŭnim, the abbess of the hermitage, who treated her like her own daughter. Her mother accompanied her and became a nun, taking the name Toch'ŏn. When Myori was eight years old, her mother suddenly died. From then on, separation and death became central questions in her life. At the age of fourteen, she took the ten *śramanera* precepts from Tong'ŭn Sŭnim and received the dharma name Pŏphŭi (dharma Joy).

Her life at Mit'a-am was spent as a novice nun, taking care of daily temple affairs, studying Buddhist scriptures and the teachings of various Sŏn masters, and practicing rituals and ceremonies. In 1910, when she was twenty-three years old, Pŏphŭi received full ordination as a bhikṣuṇī from Hae'gwang Sŭnim at Haein-sa temple. She then traveled to the Ch'ŏng'am-sa Temple in North Kyŏngsang Province and studied the *Lotus Sūtra* under the guidance of Kobong Sŭnim (1890–1961), a renowned doctrinal master. Kobong encouraged her to meditate and told her about his teacher Man'gong Sŭnim. As a dharma successor to Kyŏnghŏ Sŭnim (1849–1912), a renowned master who has been labeled a "superstar in modern Korean Buddhism" because of his revival of the Korean Sŏn Buddhist tradition after the stifling Chosŏn period, Man'gong was the first male master in modern Korea who received bhikṣuṇīs as his students, trained them in Sŏn practice, and certified them as Sŏn masters.[24]

Pŏphŭi resolved to study with Man'gong and left for Chŏnghye-sa Temple on Tŏksung Mountain, where he was teaching. Man'gong had a vision of her arriving and came down the mountain to greet her. "Who are you?" he asked. "My name is Pŏphŭi, but I do not know who I am or where I came from." Man'gong accepted Pŏphŭi as his student, and she stayed at the nearby nuns' hermitage, Kyŏnsŏng-am (Seeing into One's Nature Hermitage). Other nuns gathered, and together they rehabilitated Kyŏnsŏng-am to make it their meditation facility. Man'gong once wrote a poem recounting the pitiful sight of young nuns carrying soil and wood in their A-frame backpacks, and encouraging them to bear these burdens as if they were the Buddha's golden robes.[25]

Pŏphŭi later devoted herself fully to *hwadu* practice under Man'gong's guidance. She eventually experienced enlightenment and truly understood all the words of the Buddhas and the masters. In front of the general assembly, Man'gong recited a dharma poem and then issued the following challenge to the audience: "Tell me something about the flagpole!" The assembly remained silent. The silence was finally broken when Pŏphŭi rose quietly and said, "A fish is swimming around and the water gets clouded; a bird is flying in the sky and a feather is falling down." Later, Man'gong publicly acknowledged Pŏphŭi's enlightenment, granting her another dharma name, Myori (Mysterious Principle), and composing a poem endorsing her dharma transmission. Pŏphŭi was thirty years old at the time.

She later gained an impressive reputation and enormous respect as a Sŏn master, both among her own disciples and from other Sŏn masters. The most eminent male Sŏn masters—Ch'unsŏng, Kŭmo, Chŏn'gang, Kyŏngbong, Hyanggok, Kobong, and others—visited her for dharma exchanges. In 1966, she returned to Kyŏnsŏng-am, which she turned into a modern institutionalized Sŏn meditation facility for bhikṣuṇīs. For the next ten years, she served as the center's headmaster and devoted herself to training disciples. As a result of her efforts, monastic training centered on Sŏn practice became the basis of the Korean nuns' tradition.[26]

Another of the great nun masters of the twentieth century was Mansŏng, who was ten years younger than Myori Pŏphŭi and also famous for her practice of Sŏn. She was renowned in the Pusan area for her excellent preaching. Mansŏng's life is vividly described by Sŏn'gyŏng Sŭnim (1903–1994), a Sŏn nun who studied under her:[27]

> She was born in 1897 in a poor farmer's family. She was married at a young age but, to her great distress, lost her husband very soon afterward. One day she went to Sangwŏn-sa to hear a dharma talk from Master Hanam. His talk comforted her, and she asked him, "I have heard there is a method for invoking the spirit of the dead. I have no other wish but to meet my husband one more time." Master Hanam looked at her carefully and said, "You can only meet him if you become a nun. If you want to be free

> of suffering, take refuge in the Buddha!" Later she visited Master Man'gong and received instruction. She continued to investigate her *hwadu* for five years, still as a laywoman, until she received confirmation of her awakening from Man'gong. Unfortunately Man'gong's poem of transmission to her has been lost. Shortly afterward, in 1936 at the age of thirty-nine, she became a nun and Master Man'gong gave her the dharma name of Mansŏng (Manifold Nature).

Mansŏng later stayed at Taesŏng-am in Pusan and taught many female disciples. She also raised dharma topics with visitors, and there is a famous story of her bold words when she met Ch'unsŏng and put her leg on top of the male master, asking, "Is this leg mine or yours?" This exchange became legendary among the meditation practitioners (this anecdote was told by Samu Sŭnim).

These women practitioners practiced both together and separately. Even before the meditation halls and seminaries for bhikṣuṇīs were established, individual practitioners are known to have received teachings from notable teachers. For example, Myoŏm Sŭnim (who is the dean of the Pongnyŏng-sa Bhikṣuṇīs Seminary, one of the two most prestigious in Korea, the other being Unmun-sa Seminary) recalled that she practiced meditation along with male practitioners at Taesŭng-sa *sŏnwŏn* in 1944—men such as Ch'ŏngdam, Sŏngch'ŏl, Ubong, and Sŏam, who became patriarchs and leaders of Korean Buddhism after the 1960s.[28] There were also nuns who sought out individual scholar-monks to learn the sūtras.

Taken together, these women's individual stories give us an overview of how they began to revive the long-lost traditions of meditation and doctrinal studies for Buddhist nuns in Korea. Their diverse and scattered efforts, combined with more structured activities, were later transformed into an institutionalized effort to reestablish the bhikṣuṇī saṅgha in Korea.

Besides the nuns' efforts to restructure the Buddhist saṅgha and rejuvenate the traditional way of practice during the colonial period, there was also a resurgence of Buddhist practice among laywomen, after long years of suppression during the Chosŏn dynasty. However, just when the Korean Buddhist saṅgha was focusing on the discourses of modernization of Buddhist society, laywomen's practices were often undermined as "superstitious" and "irrational." For example, Manhae Han Young-un (1879–1944), a leading ideologue-monk for the modernization of Korean Buddhist society and an anti-Japanese activist, put the "old" ways of practice at the center of his criticism, believing them to be a major obstacle to Korean Buddhism's prospering and adapting to the changed era. He criticized the practice of "group chanting of Buddha's name" (*kosŏng yŏmbul*); Buddhist practice combined with folk religion, such as worshipping the seven stars of the Big Dipper, mountain gods, and others; and praying for good fortune—the very modes of practice that were most popular among Korean laywomen during the 1920s. His criticism was not explicitly directed toward women, but with the weighted influence of his call for modernization, a negative social perception labeling women's practice as superstitious had entered the mainstream by the 1930s.

Against this backdrop, a meditation facility called *puin sŏnu hoe* (literally, "an organization for women meditator friends") was established under the Sŏnhak-wŏn Institute in Seoul in 1931. Later, another facility was opened at P'yohun-sa Monastery, called the P'yohun-sa *puin sŏnwŏn* ("women's meditation facility at P'yohun-sa"), in the Kŭmgang-san Mountains area.[29] Many intellectual women were converted or entered monastic life, such as Kim Iryŏp (1896–1971), the famous writer and social commentator, who converted to Buddhism and began the life of a monastic at the age of thirty-eight, upon the instruction of Man'gong Sŭnim. Although the emergence of women as intellectuals, writers, and artists during the modern period in Asia is often assumed to have been prompted by the introduction of Christian beliefs and civilization, many such "New Women" in Korea found Buddhist religious practices and perspectives interesting to explore and of use in their professional worlds.[30]

The Postcolonial Period (1945–present)

After the Korean War of 1950–1953, the Korean bhikṣuṇī community made remarkable advancements in its social presence and internal strength. Nuns rebuilt monasteries that had either fallen into ruin because of the war or had been unoccupied for a long time. They also served as frontrunners in the 1954–1955 Purification Movement.[31] They saw this movement as providing the strategic momentum necessary to gain their rightful place in the saṅgha as a whole. After the Japanese colonial period, only a handful of celibate bhikṣus remained in Korea (most well-educated elite monks had either converted to Japanese Buddhism or joined the order of married monks), so at the peak of the movement, when married monks were purged through street demonstrations and legal suits, bhikṣuṇīs outnumbered bhikṣus.

At the beginning of the Purification Movement, some bhikṣus opposed the participation of bhikṣuṇīs, and the title of the first rally was

"National Bhikṣus Rally." But the third rally, in December 1954, was called the "Third National Rally of Bhikṣus and Bhikṣuṇīs" (*chŏn'guk pigu piguni taehoe*), and thereafter, whenever a proclamation was read, usually by a monk, it began, "We bhikṣus and bhikṣuṇīs. . . ." Thus, the monks clearly acknowledged that the saṅgha should actually denote a community of both bhikṣuṇīs and bhikṣus, with each group having the other as an indispensable and equal partner to make a whole. Indeed, at the rally of December 11, 1954, the number of bhikṣuṇīs who attended was 221, whereas the bhikṣus numbered 211. The final document, signed when the protracted struggle was drawing to a close, bore the signatures of those who had attended or had sent in their letter of vote/attorney: 571 bhikṣuṇīs and 430 bhikṣus, for a total of 1,001 votes. It is interesting that the numbers of both monks and nuns attending had doubled in the course of a year.[32]

In the middle of this long process of activities and discussions, the central administrative body for the saṅgha (*chonghoe*) and other committees were formed, and bhikṣuṇīs came to participate in those committees. Also, new agendas for the renewed saṅgha were discussed and written down.[33] A document submitted to the superintendent general's office in December 1954, as a response to the public negotiation initiated by the police after a series of public disturbances, called "Plan for the Purification of the Buddhist community," with 807 signatures (366 bhikṣus and 441 bhikṣuṇīs) is noteworthy in many ways. First, it defined roles, functions, and responsibilities in explicit form: monks and nuns (*sŭngnyŏ*) are those who are dedicated in five areas of Buddhist practice—keeping the precepts, meditation, chanting, studying sūtras, and reciting mantras. Second, it mentioned the criteria for becoming the head of a monastery, but does not specify gender: no matter what the size of a monastery or temple is, monastics must complete a certain number of meditation retreats and finish their studies at the seminaries to be considered. Therefore, it is no wonder that, after the successful conclusion of the Purification Movement, many bhikṣuṇīs were actually appointed as abbots of monasteries.[34] Even the abbot of Tonghwa-sa Monastery, one of the twenty-three head monasteries of the nation, was a bhikṣuṇī, Sŏngmun Sŭnim (1893–1974).[35]

After these years of turmoil and toil, the bhikṣuṇīs added to their power and institutional structures. Many meditation halls were established or reopened for formal training of nuns: Kugil-am of Haein-sa by Pon'gong Sŭnim in 1948, Hoeryong-sa by Tojun Sŭnim in 1954, Taesŏng-am by Mansŏng Sŭnim in 1956, Sŏnhae Illyun of Naewŏn-sa by Suok Sŭnim in 1957, Pudo-am of Tonghwa-sa by Sangmyŏng Sŭnim in 1957, Tongguk Cheil Sŏnwon of Taewŏn-sa by Pŏbil Sŭnim in 1957, Chŏngsu Sŏnwŏn of Sŏngnam-sa by Inhong Sŭnim in 1957, Yangjin-am of Tonghwa-sa by Sŏngnyŏn Sŭnim in 1958, and Naewŏn-am of Tonghwa-sa by Changil Sŭnim in 1959. In addition, bhikṣuṇī seminaries such as Unmun-sa and Tonghak-sa began to be rebuilt in 1955 and 1956, respectively, and Hwaun-sa Seminary was opened by Chimyŏng Sŭnim in 1957.[36] Monastic education and doctrinal study, which had been neglected throughout the Chosŏn and colonial periods, thus began to receive a lot of attention. Initially, the emphasis was on meditation practice, but with the modernization of Korean society, the importance of Buddhist education was agreed upon by masters and disciples alike. Along with the establishment of modern education facilities for Buddhist monks and nuns (such as Myŏngjin School in 1906, which later became a university of general education), support for the traditional education occurring at *kangwŏn* (monastic seminaries for doctrinal study) was also under way. No longer perceived as an outdated and obsolete way of educating young minds, the traditional *kangwŏn* education regained its status as a legitimate way of training monks and nuns. At first, male doctrinal masters and lecturers taught at the reestablished bhikṣuṇī *kangwŏns*, but later the lineage of scholarship was handed down by female masters to female disciples.

The Contemporary Situation

After the dramatic social changes of the 1960s and 1970s—economic growth, adoption of general education for the nation, and the subsequent elevation of women's social status—the community of Korean Buddhist nuns entered a totally new stage. Over the last thirty years, the Korean nuns' saṅgha has grown to such an extent that half the ordained clerics of the Chogye order are nuns.[37] Not only have their numbers grown but their status has risen significantly. Martine Batchelor, who lived in Korea as a Buddhist nun from 1975 to 1985 and traveled extensively in Asia, has observed that Korean Buddhist nuns have the second highest social status among Asian countries, next to that of Taiwanese nuns. She points out that Korean monks tend to offer the most respect to the nuns, coming closest to treating them as equals, and notes that all nunneries in Korea operate with a high degree of autonomy and are not supervised by monks.[38]

My own candid assessment of contemporary Korean Buddhist society identifies the following six factors as possible explanations for the remarkable development in the Korean nuns' saṅgha over the past thirty years. In the absence of any in-depth research of the factors behind the success of the Korean Buddhist nuns' order, these are some subjective reflections based on my observations and discussions with nuns and other believers:

1. *Collective cohesive power*. In a number of reforms in the saṅgha, the cohesion shown by the nuns served as a striking display of their capacities within the saṅgha. The nuns had formed a comparatively large collective inside a relatively narrow environment. Their lecture halls and meditation rooms were always overcrowded, and their living facilities were usually insufficient and inferior. Ironically, this challenging environment helped them come up with better survival strategies and a collaborative spirit with which to cope with unfavorable political and economical situations.

2. *Improvement in the economic environment*. From the 1970s on, in accord with developments in the Korean economy, the economic strength of the Korean saṅgha rapidly improved. Over time, even the nunneries were able to secure considerable economic power. In particular, the nuns efficiently applied their characteristically frugal and diligent attitude to establishing a secure livelihood for themselves, unlike their monk counterparts. This increased their inner self-confidence as female monastics. Due to the deepening of their practice and their activities in the greater society, and by extending the breadth of such activities, they also gradually enlarged the basis for the populace at large to trust them.

3. *Changes in ideals and the environment of their practice*. The modern Korean saṅgha has been governed by an ideology that put practice first—namely, Mahayana meditation as a direct path to enlightenment. As a result, there tended to be a strict division between the *ip'an* (meditators) and *sap'an* (support staff). The *sap'an* were viewed as mere supporters of the *ip'an*, performing the tasks necessary for the latter's subsistence. In this atmosphere, some *sap'an* came to feel shame at being monks who merely labored. Until the 1980s, the *ip'an* had absolute influence both inside and outside the saṅgha. For example, they had the authority to change the power structure of the entire order in a single morning at a monks' conference. Beginning in

the late 1980s, however, the *ip'an* recognized the importance of administering the order and began to actively participate in it. After that, the division between *ip'an* and *sap'an* gradually blurred, creating an environment in which the importance of the *sap'an* was sometimes greater than that of the *ip'an*. From then on, interest in various methods of practice besides *hwadu* meditation began to gain attention inside and outside the saṅgha. Practices that had been excluded as heretical—such as prayer and *yŏmbul* (chanting/mindfulness of the name of a buddha), as well as austerities and altruistic service to others—began to rise in prominence. Such changes led to a recognition of the proper attitude toward practice and toward the strict regulations themselves. Again, in direct contrast with the corruption and power struggles of the monk-led order, the practices of the nuns were highlighted during this period of renewed emphasis on proper practice.

4. *Changes in the* saṅgha *following changes in Korean society.* Problems such as the role of religious groups, their altruistic activities, and their place in the greater society had been largely ignored due to the primacy given to meditation practice in the modern Korean saṅgha. Traditional monasteries located in the mountains had focused on ensuring their own economic base and were the main support for the formation of the modern saṅgha that gave primacy to the cultivation of meditation. However, as Korean society grew and changed quite drastically, the saṅgha became a large-scale organization and its role in the greater society also began to increase. Extending beyond the scope of the traditional monastery, new, modern-style monasteries appeared. They began to question the importance of the internal issues of transmission of the dharma and conversion of laypeople, and the external issues of the role of religion in the greater society.

5. *The rapid rise in the status and role of women in modern Korean society as a whole.* The extent of social participation and the position of women in Korean society have improved rapidly. Of course, there has been great resistance to this, and a huge differential exists between the

calls for a gender-equal society and the reality of that society. However, the Buddhist world, seeing itself as a participant in the movement struggling to revise those outlooks, is actively seeking to progressively influence such trends. A few years ago, there was a news report that a nun was appointed chief of the Bureau of Culture in the general administration of the Chogye order, which was a clear sign that the order wants to at least appear conscious of this need for gender equality. This had been welcomed heartily by many people, not just inside the religion, and the enthusiastic welcome nationwide, in newspapers and other media, shows that Korean society was much more liberal, progressive, and flexible than the order had thought it to be.

6. *The change from a society of extended families to a society of nuclear families*. There has been a recent tendency in Korean society to replace the traditional concept of filial piety with an increased interest in child-rearing and education. In this tendency, there is more sympathy than before for the emotional and psychological conflicts between the family and the individual. Female clergy, who know from experience how to interpret the nuances of such problems, will naturally be able to understand and empathize with lay believers and disciples on such matters.

Within the contemporary religious landscape of Buddhism, nuns are equal and indispensable partners with monks, regardless of whether or not this fact is always acknowledged. In the past, monastic Buddhism was almost entirely a man's world, but, these days, radical changes have been taking place. Like monks, nuns receive full ordination (at present, only the Korean and Taiwanese institutions maintain the traditions of full ordination for nuns). Not only does the total number of nuns equal the number of monks, nuns are active participants in the tradition in various capacities: as avid mediators, compassionate caretakers for the needy, adept administrators of social welfare facilities, attentive and powerful leaders of city-based Buddhist centers, and ardent activists demanding democracy and opposing prejudice, within both the Chogye order and the broader society. Korean nuns have built a viable monastic community that has survived near obliteration and established its own power of regeneration, as reflected in its continual growth, its social activism, and its meditation programs, making the Korean nuns' saṅgha one of the most flourishing female monastic communities in the modern religious world.

Now that Korean nuns no longer have to focus exclusively on reestablishing their monasteries and places for practice and study, they have expanded the scope of their activities to include proselytization and social welfare work. These women also play a prominent role not only as practitioners but in the areas of education and the direct management of monasteries. They receive systematic training in lecture halls and meditation rooms, are aware of the history of their own tradition through lineage and teacher-disciple inheritance, and live a communal life in nunneries with other practitioners, in joint ownership of their own true character as a distinct movement within the larger Buddhist order. They assert this ownership by actively creating a constructive image of themselves through their engagement in everything from running children's summer schools and social welfare facilities to popularizing Buddhist songs for younger generations as both performers and disk jockeys. The culmination of these efforts lies in the formation of the bhikṣuṇī association. It started as a loose association of nuns called "Udambala hoe" (Udambara Association) in 1968, which became the formal National Bhikṣuṇī Association in 1985, with Hyech'un Sŭnim as its first president. As an umbrella organization of Buddhist nuns, based on membership, it has been successful in various educational, intellectual, and social activities. With the successful hosting of the 8th Sakyadhita International Conference on Buddhist Women in Korea in 2004, the organization also proclaimed the vitality of the Buddhist nuns' tradition to the international Buddhist community as a whole.

NOTES

An earlier version of this chapter was published in the *Seoul Journal of Korean Studies* 22, no. 1 (June 2009), as "Reinventing Female Identity: A Brief History of Korean Buddhist Nuns."

1. This poem was composed in 1935. It is featured in Pon'gong Sŭnim's biography in *Kkaedarŭm ŭi kkot* (Flowers of Enlightenment; Seoul: Yŏrae, 1998) by Ha Ch'unsaeng, a volume that has contributed to the recent upsurge in interest in the lives of Korean nuns.

2. The locus classicus of the metaphor of north and south in the poem is the famous dialogue between Hongren and Huineng; upon his arrival at Hongren's monastery, Huineng was asked where he is from and what he is

looking for. Hearing that he is from the south, Hongren challenged Huineng by saying: "If you're from Ling-nan then you're a barbarian. How can you become a Buddha?" Huineng replied: "Although people from the south and people from the north differ, there is no north and south in Buddha nature." Translation from Philip Yampolsky, *The Platform Sutra of the Sixth Patriarch* (New York: Columbia University Press, 1967), 127.

3. Robert E. Buswell, Jr., *Tracing Back the Radiance: Chinul's Korean Way of Zen* (Honolulu: Kuroda Institute, University of Hawai'i Press, 1991), 5.

4. *Samguk sagi*, fascicle 4, in the third month of the fifth year of King Chinhŭng.

5. Robert E. Buswell, Jr., "Buddhism in Korea," in Joseph Mitsuo Kitagawa and Mark D. Cummings, eds., *Buddhism and Asian History* (New York: Macmillan, 1989), 152.

6. Nukariya Kaiten, *Chōsen zenkyōsi* (Tokyo: Shunjūsha, 1930), 30.

7. The three Japanese women traveled to Korea to receive full ordination and that event marks the beginning of Japanese Buddhist nuns. See Akira Hirakawa, translated by Karma Lekshe Tsomo, "The History of Buddhist Nuns in Japan," *Buddhist-Christian Studies* 12 (1992): 49; Karma Lekshe Tsomo, ed., *Sakyadhītā: Daughters of the Buddha* (Ithaca, NY: Snow Lion Publications, 1988), 128 and 131.

8. Kim Yŏngt'ae, *Paekche Pulgyo sasang yŏn'gu* (Study on the Buddhist Thought of Paekche) (Seoul: Tongguk taehakkyo ch'ulp'anbu, 1986), 75.

9. From early on, Paekche developed a strong tradition in the study of Vinaya (the Buddhist precepts and moral rules), as indicated by the record of the monk Kyŏmik, who went to India in 526 to study Sanskrit and acquire Vinaya texts. He returned with an Indian monk specializing in the Vinaya in 531, after which he is known to have translated the *Vinaya pitaka* in 72 fascicles. Kyŏmik's disciples composed commentaries, and the entire project was then dedicated to King Sŏng, the ruler at that time. Based on these records, we can assume that the Paekche Buddhist order already had a well-established protocol for the ordination ceremony by 588. However, it has been argued that the record of Kyŏmik's travels is suspect because it only appears in Yi Nŭnghwa's 1918 *Chosŏn pulgyo t'ongsa* (General History of Korean Buddhism). See Best, "Tales of Three Paekche Monks Who Traveled Afar in Search of the Law," *Harvard Journal of Asiatic Studies* 51, no. 1 (1991): 139–197, esp. 152–178.

10. Samguk sagi, chikkwan-ji section.

11. For an in-depth analysis of the types of Buddhist women appearing in *Samguk yusa*, see Kim Young Mi, "Silla Pulgyo-sa e nat'a'nan yŏsŏng ŭi sinang saenghwal kwa sŭngnyŏ dŭl ŭi yŏsŏng-kwan" (The Religious Life of Women and Monks' Understanding of Women in the History of Buddhism in Silla), *Yŏsŏng sinhak nonjip* (Feminist Theology Review), vol. 1 (Ewha Womans University, Yŏsŏng Sinhak Yŏn'guso, 1995).

12. The *Samguk yusa*, chapter 7, "Tales of Devotion."

13. Ibid.

14. The author of the *Samguk Yusa*, Iryŏn, notes that several different sources for the story existed: one was a contemporary account based on a local history (*hyangjŏn*), while another was based on a monks' history (*sŭngjŏn*). As for the development of Pure Land tradition and the ten-thousand-day chanting community in the later period, see Eunsu Cho, "Re-thinking Late 19th Century Chosŏn Buddhist Society," *Acta Koreana* 6, no. 2 (July 2003): 87–109.

15. Edwin O. Reischauer, trans., *Ennin's Diary: The Record of a Pilgrimage to China in Search of the Law* (New York: Ronald Press, 1955), 131–161.

16. Ch'oe Pyŏng-hŏn, "Women of Royal Families and Buddhism in Koryo: Focusing on the Queen Mother Inye and the Establishment of the Ch'ont'ae Sect," presented at the HanMaum conference in 2004.

17. Cross-cultural comparative study might help us understand why women's names were better preserved in Zen (C. Chan; Kor. Sŏn) communities. On female teachers who appear in the history of the Chinese Chan school, see Miriam L. Levering, "Miao-tao and Her Teacher Ta-hui," in Gregory and Getz, eds., *Buddhism in the Sung* (Honolulu: University of Hawai'i Press, 1999); and idem, "Women Chan Masters: The Teacher Miao-tsung as Saint," in Arvind Sharma, ed., *Women Saints in World Religions* (Albany: State University of New York Press, 2000). Because so few primary source materials on Korean nuns have thus far been unearthed and introduced academically, these records about the elite nuns of Song dynasty China have significant bearing on our understanding of the faith and activities of Koryŏ Buddhism.

18. Heejong Kang, "Women as Patrons of Buddhist Art in the Early Chosŏn Dynasty," paper presented at the 2002 Association for Asian Studies annual meeting in Washington D.C.

19. See Zhiru Ng and Sunkyung Kim, "Women and Kṣitigarbha Worship: Examples from Tang China and Chosŏn Korea," in proceedings for an international conference titled, "Korean Nuns within the Context of East Asian Buddhist Traditions," held in HanMaum Zen Center in Anyang Korea in May 20 to May 22, 2004, sponsored by the same foundation.

20. A survey by the Japanese government's domestic affairs division records that in May 1910 there were 958 Buddhist temples in Korea, with 5,198 monks and 563 nuns, according to the reports by *Hwangsŏng Daily* (May 5, 1919) and *Taehan Maeil sinbo* (May 6, 1919). See *Han'guk kŭnhyŏndae Pulgyosa yŏnp'yo* (Chronicles of Buddhist Affairs in Modern and Contemporary Korea), (Taehan Pulgyo Chogye-jong kyoyuk-wŏn pulhak yŏn'guso [The Institute of Buddhism of Education Division of Korean Buddhist Chogye Order], 2000), 21; requoted from Chŏn Horyŏn (Haeju Sŭnim), "Han'guk kŭnhyŏndae piguni ŭi suhaeng e taehan koch'al" (Study on the Religious Practice of Korean Bhikṣuṇīs in the Modern and Contemporary Period), *Han'guk sasang kwa munhwa* 33 (2006): 307.

21. Without historical materials to attest to their existence, we cannot say that there were doctrinal lecture facilities or meditators' communities for nuns during the Chosŏn dynasty, yet because there were meditation facilities and seminaries for monks during this period, we cannot rule out the possibility

of such communities for nuns. The establishment of Kyŏnsŏng-am *sŏnwŏn* is well noted in various histories and the training and living there took an institutionalized form, so this facility can be considered the first modern *bhikṣuṇi sŏnwŏn*. How Buddhism was practiced during the Chosŏn dynasty needs further investigation.

22. Yunp'il-am meditation hall was the essential glue that held together many activities of *bhikṣuṇi* meditators in the 1930s. How this important meditation hall came to be established and who its leader was are not known. *Pangham-nok* records are available only from the year 1936, so we do not know who the resident meditators were before that. However, it is known that this facility was established in 1929 for monks, and was converted into a nuns' facility in 1931. We also know that Yongsŏng Sŭnim, another great Sŏn monk and revitalizer of Korean Buddhism in the modern period, resided there and supervised the meditators in the community in 1931, so we can make a circumstantial guess that he had played some role in drawing together the community of meditators, making the establishment of the facility possible.

23. Chŏn Horyŏn (Haeju Sŭnim), "Han'guk kŭnhyŏndae piguni ŭi suhaeng e taehan koch'al," 308.

24. Hwang Ingyu, "Kŭndae piguni ŭi tonghyang kwa Tŏksung ch'ongnim pigunidŭl" (Trends of Modern Korean Buddhist Nuns and the Tŏksung Forest Lineage), in *Kyŏnghŏ Man'gong ŭi sŏnp'ung kwa pŏmmaek* (Kyŏnghŏ, Man'gong and Their Sŏn Buddhist Practice and Lineage), edited by Taehan Pulgyo Chogye-jong kyoyuk-wŏn pulhak yŏn'guso (Chogye Order Publishings, 2009).

25. Wŏlchu Chimyŏng Sŭnim, *Talpit ŭn uju rŭl pich'une* (Moonlight Brightens the Cosmos), (Seoul: Pulch'ŏn, 1996), 144. This is a memoir of Pŏphŭi Sŭnim written by her disciple Wŏlchu Sŭnim.

26. See Eun-su Cho, "From Anonymity to Self-Reinvention: Korean Buddhist Nuns in the Twentieth Century," in Karma Lekshe Tsomo, ed., *Bridging Worlds: Buddhist Women's Voices across Generations* (Taipei: Yuan Chuan Press, 2004), 125–130.

27. From Martine Batchelor's interview of Sŏn'gyŏng Sŭnim, in her book *Women in Korean Zen: Lives and Practices* (Syracuse: Syracuse University Press, 2006), 98–99. This interview provides a rare personalized and vivid account of life as a nun in early twentieth-century Korea.

28. Chŏn Horyŏn (Haeju Sŭnim), "Han'guk kŭnhyŏndae piguni ŭi suhaeng e taehan koch'al," note 9.

29. The information here on laywomen practitioners in the colonial period is based on Seung-mi Cho, "Kŭndae Han'guk Pulgyo ŭi yŏsŏng suhaeng munhwa—Puin Sŏnuhoe wa Puin Sŏnwŏn ŭl chungsim ŭro" (On Women's Practice of Buddhism in Modern Korea—Focusing on the Women Sŏn Practitioners' Organization and the Women's Meditation Hall), *Han'guk sasang kwa munhwa* 34 (2006): 383–410.

30. Jin Y. Park's "Gendered Response to Modernity: Kim Iryeop and Buddhism" (*Korea Journal* 45, no. 1, 2005) approaches Kim Iryŏp from the perspective of modernity in colonial Korea.

31. For the role of the Buddhist runs on the purification movement by the Buddhist saṅgha, see Pori Park, "The Establishment of Buddhist Nunneries in Contemporary Korea."

32. Chŏn Horyŏn (Haeju Sŭnim), "Han'guk kŭnhyŏndae piguni ŭi suhaeng e taehan koch'al," 310.

33. During the colonial period, Japanese Buddhist cultural practices (such as ceremonies, robe style, and, most important, allowing married saṅgha) had been imposed; to renew the Korean saṅgha, these influences had to be removed and Korean practice traditions reestablished.

34. *The DongA* (Tonga) *Daily* reported on August 14, 1955, that bhikṣuṇīs had been appointed as abbots at 623 temples in the nation. Quoted from Chŏn Horyŏn (Haeju Sŭnim), "Han'guk kŭnhyŏndae piguni ŭi suhaeng e taehan koch'al," note 18.

35. Chŏn Horyŏn (Haeju Sŭnim), "Han'guk kŭnhyŏndae piguni ŭi suhaeng e taehan koch'al," 312; the document also set criteria for selection for the central administrative body (*chonghoe*), without mentioning gender. However, the number of bhikṣuṇīs to be selected for the seats was agreed to be limited to one-sixth the number of bhikṣus.

36. Ibid.

37. According to *Sŏnwŏn ch'ongnam* (Comprehensive Review of Sŏn Meditational Centers), published by the Chogye-jong headquarters in 2000, during the Buddhist year 2542 summer retreat, there were 32 *bhiksu sŏnwŏn*, with 567 monks participating, and 32 *bhiksuni sŏnwŏn*, with 716 nuns participating. As of 2008, the most recent survey record says there are a total of 5,413 monks and 5,331 nuns, according to the official statistics of the Chogye order.

38. Ibid., 21–22.

3

Male Sŏn Masters' Views on Female Disciples in Later Koryŏ

Young Mi Kim

The idea that women can become enlightened follows naturally from the core Buddhist belief that enlightenment can be achieved by all creatures. When we review the history of Buddhism in Korea, however, we find that, due to the patriarchal nature of society and religious establishments, the possibility of enlightenment for women was not always recognized.

There is historical evidence that after Buddhism was accepted in Paekche and Silla, bhikṣuṇīs (fully ordained Buddhist nuns) came to exist in both these kingdoms. There are records of the formation of associations of both bhikṣus (fully ordained Buddhist monks) and bhikṣuṇīs in Paekche and Silla,[1] while in Silla there was a nuns' government position called Toyunarang (scholars' opinions differ as to the meaning of this title). Nonetheless, when we look at available stelae inscriptions from Silla, there are no records of any nuns' activities. Because nuns were required to receive ordination from monks as well as from other nuns, their names ought to appear in the lists of students on the stelae of National Preceptors and Royal Preceptors. However, no name of any nun appears on a stela predating the Koryŏ period.

To date, the earliest known record of the name of a nun in an inscription is the one on the stela of National Preceptor Chin'gak Hyesim (1178–1234), which lists her as his disciple. On this stela, which was found at the Wŏllam-sa site, Chin'gak's disciples are divided into the categories of Taesŏnsa (Great Zen Master), Sŭngt'ong (Governing Monk), Sŏnsa (Zen Master), Sujwa (Head Seat), Yangga-sŭngnok (Monk Recorder of the Two Rows), Samjung (Three Repetitions), Taesŏn (Great

Choice), and nuns. This stela was composed by Yi Kyu-bo four years after Hyesim's death, between the twenty-fifth and twenty-seventh year of King Kojong's reign (between 1238 and 1241), and was erected and carved in the thirty-seventh year (1250).[2] The next stelae that record nuns' names are the stela of the Indian monk Chigong (1235–1361)[3] and the stelae of the Koryŏ monks Naong Hyegŭn (1320–1376)[4] and T'aego Pou (1301–1382).[5] Nuns are also listed as having been student assistants in the bottom part of the *Recorded Sayings of Paegun Kyŏnghan* (1298–1374) and in the *Chikchi simch'e yojŏl*.[6]

Although these bhikṣuṇīs are all the students of Ch'an lineage, the names such as Myo___ (last character missing) and Myŏ___ (last character missing) are also found in the epitaph of the Hua-yen monk, Ch'ŏnhŭi (1307–1382).[7] In the late Koryŏ, considerable numbers of women from the ruling class were ordained.

In what follows, I examine the theory of women's enlightenment put forward by National Preceptor Chin'gak Hyesim, whose stela contains the oldest recording of the names of specific nuns in the history of Korea. To do this, I first examine the social status of nuns in the Koryŏ period and the practice of Hyesim's nun students, and then compare these nuns to the other nuns of early Koryŏ. The lack of records from Hyesim's nun disciples' point of view is a serious handicap in getting a picture of their practice, but we can obtain an indirect idea of what this practice may have been like based on the episodes recorded in his sayings where Hyesim offers guidance to nuns.

THE ORDINATION OF WOMEN IN KORYŎ AND THE SOCIAL STATUS OF NUNS

In Koryŏ, both men and women needed governmental permission to join a monastery. After obtaining permission from the government, they received a certificate.[8] The monk or nun was then entered in the register of his or her home temple, which was inspected once every three years by the Sŭngnoksa (Monastics Registry Office) and by the Yebu (Office of Rites). According to the *Sabun-yul* (C. *Ssu-fen lü*; Skt. *Dharmaguptaka-vinaya*; Vinaya of the Four Categories), and, in contrast to monks, women who received governmental permission and officially joined monasteries had to first be ordained by ten nuns in their home temple and then be ordained again by the ten nuns together with ten monks in a monks' temple. However, there were also women who were ordained "illegally," without governmental permission.

Reasons for women to join a monastery in the Koryŏ period included joining for the sake of chastity, carrying out Buddhist practice, searching for the truth, being punished or avoiding punishment, and acting out of yearning to be reborn in heaven or in Amitābha's Western Pure Land. Among these, the reason most frequently given was chastity—specifically, to pray for one's husband after his death, or to remain faithful to him after his death and not have to remarry. Queen Taesŏwŏn and Queen Sosŏwŏn became nuns after spending one night each with King T'aejo. After her death, the nun Sŏnghyo was extolled for "upholding fidelity through becoming a nun" and was given the title "Esteemed Great Mother of the Pyŏn Han Kingdom, Great Master Chinhye."[9] A woman known simply as "the wife of Munhwagun"[10] also became a nun for chastity. It is said that she "cut her hair with her own hands, swearing chastity to death." The widow of Milchik Hŏ Kang from the Kim family became a nun after the corrupt Sindon (?–1371, an ambitious monk involved in court politics and interested in her family background) forced her to marry him. In the cases of Hong Hyu's daughter and the two queens of King Kongmin (Queen Hye of the Yi family and Queen Sin of the Yŏm family), the reasons for joining a monastery are not known; however, based on the fact that both women joined after their husbands died, it seems clear that they also became ordained for chastity. That the phenomenon of becoming a nun to preserve chastity was not restricted to women of the ruling classes is confirmed by a statement made by the Ŏsadae (Royal Inspections Office) before the measures that forbade female ordination were put into place in the tenth year of King Kongmin's reign (1361). The Ŏsadae criticized monastics, saying that they "seduced widows and female orphans into becoming nuns by telling them about sin and happiness."[11] From this we can deduce that an important reason why common women of the time became nuns was to pray for the sake of their deceased parents or spouse.

Yet there were also cases when women became nuns because they were too poor to marry, like the two daughters of Kim Chisuk, who became nuns during the reign of King Ch'ungsŏn. For the nonruling classes, then, physical survival was another important reason to become a nun. This can also be inferred from an earlier law forbidding women's ordination, decreed in the eighth year of King Hyŏnjong's reign (1017). At the time, many men had been killed in the war with the Khitans, so quite a number of women who were widowed or orphaned would have turned to the monastic establishment as a means of survival.[12] The law forbidding new ordinations for women was meant to stem this tide.

Although women frequently used the pretext of chastity, in reality many of them became nuns to be able to pursue Buddhist practice and seek enlightenment. An example is the marchioness of Marquess Chin'gang (Ch'oe Ch'ung-hŏn) from the Wang family (also known as Chŏnghwa T'aekchu). As already mentioned, the reason given for forbidding women's ordination in 1361 was that men and women living together were spreading immorality. From this we can deduce that nuns were relatively free to travel, pursue and provide education, and so on. Further evidence of the relative lack of restriction that nuns in this period enjoyed are the facts that Hyesim's nun followers participated in the summer retreat at Susŏn-sa, and that the nun Sŏnghyo, after being ordained at the age of sixty-one, freely traveled around Kyŏngju and other places with the *śarīra* relics of T'ongdo-sa.[13]

Other reasons for becoming a nun included being forced to do so as punishment for an offense and choosing to do so to avoid other punishment. The slave-concubine of the crown prince of Myŏngjong and the wife of Yi Chip both had to shave their heads for committing adultery. Hwaŭi Ongju[14] from the Ki family suffered the same fate for secretly communicating with North Yüan during the punishment of Ki Ch'ŏl's insurgent group.

Also, widows who lived alone often became nuns just before death. The wife of Kim Ku from the Ch'oe family became a nun the day before her death at age eighty-three; the wife of Ch'oe Sŏ from the Pak family became a nun at seventy, only nine days before her death; and the wife of Yi Tŏk-son from the Yu family passed away after becoming a nun at the age of eighty as soon as she became ill.[15] These ordinations were not official, nor were they condoned by the state. These women clearly became ordained for the sake of being reborn in heaven or paradise in the next life.

Nuns engaged both in practices intended to assist in the attainment of paradise, or the Pure Land, such as reciting the name of Amitābha Buddha and reading sūtras, and in meditation and *hwadu* practice (C. *hua-tou*; J. *wato*; literally, "word-head"), in which they focused on the point, or key line, of a *kongan* (C. *kung-an*; J. *kōan*; "public case"). They also enthusiastically engaged—both individually and through associations such as the Manbul-hoe (Community of Ten Thousand Buddhas) or Manbul Hyangdo (Membership of Ten Thousand Buddhas)—in a variety of activities for the public good as well as in Buddhist works. They taught laypeople and actively participated in the creation of tombstones for their masters, the publication of anthologies, the creation of statues, and the building and renovation of temples, both donating their own money and asking others for donations. Occasionally, due to their mobility, nuns also reported news to noblewomen, as the daughter of Hong Hyu conveyed news of the outside world to Queen of King Ch'ungnyŏl.

Nuns had to live separately from monks. Chŏngŏpwŏn and Anilwŏn were built specifically for nuns in the capital, and most nuns from the elite class probably did live in these temples. However, some women who became Buddhist nuns to maintain their chastity and pray for the well-being of their deceased husbands (or who cited these reasons for doing so) built their own small temples next to their family homes. This was the case for the nun Sŏnghyo, posthumously named Great Master Chinhye, for example. This phenomenon was restricted to the ruling elites who could afford it; the vast majority of nuns lived in temples scattered all over the country.[16] This geographic decentralization made it easy to break official rules, and toward the end of Koryŏ nuns and monks sometimes shared temples, which led to the banning of new ordinations for nuns.

In Koryŏ, orders of nuns were subordinate to orders of monks. Nuns could only attend summer meditation retreats if they were sponsored by monks, and there seem to have been no nuns who took the exam to become nationally certified monastics. On the stela of Great Master Poje at Sillŭk-sa, erected in late Koryŏ, Myobong, who was the head of the nun's temple Chŏngŏpwŏn in the capital, is listed first among the nun followers of Naong Hyegŭn, from which we can deduce that she was considered the highest-ranked nun. Nuns were thus leaders in their own temples, although it seems that their terms of office and powers were not codified into rules by the state as they were for temples where monks lived.

After the Silla nuns' office Toyunarang disappeared, women were not allowed to take the national monastic exam or to assume a place in the official monastic rank, so it seems that their position within the religious establishment was weaker than it had been shortly after the official acceptance of Buddhism in Silla. Yet Buddhism was much more deeply ingrained in Koryŏ society than it had been in Silla, and monastics were even more highly respected than they had been then. The number of nuns increased, and they received the respect of both the general populace and the royal house. Together with monks, they were invited as guests of honor to a national event in honor of monastics in the first year of King Ch'ungsŏn (1308), as well as in the eighteenth year of King Kongmin (1369).

However, unlike the common practice for monks, when the names of nuns were recorded, the names they had used before ordination were given as well. For example, Great Master Chinhye is listed as "Esteemed Great Mother of the Pyŏn Han Kingdom, Great Master

Chinhye," Myoch'ŏl is listed as "Esteemed Great Mother of the Three Han Kingdoms, Myoch'ŏl from Yŏm family," and Myoryŏng is listed as "Sunsŏng Ongju Myoryŏng." Also, as we can see from the cases of Queen Hye and Queen Sin, queens and royal concubines received the same tribute and fees after ordination that they had in lay life. Thus, even after they became nuns, women of the ruling class remained affected by their relations to males in the lay world, namely, their husbands or sons. After ordination, nuns could also actively use their private property to do Buddhist works. A typical example is that of Myodŏk, who had the hermitage Yunp'il-am built and also contributed funds to the metal type printing of the *Paegun hwasang ch'orok pulcho chikchi simch'e yojŏl* (Essential Passages by Reverend Baegun Directly Pointing at the Essence of the Mind). Although the possession of private property is forbidden to monastics according to Buddhist precepts and rules, it seems that this rule was tacitly ignored in these cases.

In conclusion, it seems fair to say that the many restrictions placed on nuns that did not affect monks were primarily due to Koryŏ society's strong male focus. The fact that most nuns were ordained only after the death of their husbands—that is, relatively late in life—also limited the scope and scale of nuns' activities in Koryŏ.

THE SEARCH FOR ENLIGHTENMENT AMONG HYESIM'S NUN DISCIPLES

Among the followers of National Preceptor Chin'gak Hyesim, there are many examples of nuns practicing for the sake of attaining enlightenment. On Hyesim's stela at the Wŏllam-sa site, the four nuns—min (first character missing), Ch'ŏngwŏn, Hŭiwŏn, and Chŏngsim are listed as female followers. The first three also appear in the *Recorded Sayings of National Preceptor Chin'gak*, as follows:

> In the second year of Sunggyŏng, the year of Kyeyu, in the summer, Chongmin came with her sisters Ch'ŏngwŏn, Hŭiwŏn, and Yoyŏn and held a Dharma convocation, brought a scroll, and, asking for instruction, wrote down the conflict. In the summer of the second year of Sunggyŏng, the year of Kyeyu, Chongmin came with her sisters Ch'ŏngwŏn, Hŭiwŏn, and Yoyŏn for a Dharma ceremony. They brought a scroll and asked for instruction, so I wrote the meanings down for them.[17]

We can assume that the lost first character on the stela is "Chong" and that this nun is the same Chongmin mentioned in the *Recorded Sayings of National Preceptor Chin'gak.* We also know that Chongmin, Ch'ŏngwŏn, Hŭiwŏn, Yoyŏn (who is not mentioned in the stela inscription), and other nuns participated in the ninety-day summer retreat at Susŏn-sa in the second year of the reign of King Kangjong (1213).[18] Yoyŏn is probably not mentioned in the stela inscription because she died before it was erected. (Another nun, Chŏngsim, is mentioned in the stela inscription but not in the *Recorded Sayings.*)

In addition, the *Recorded Sayings of National Preceptor Chin'gak* mentions Sŏnan, Chŏngsin, Chŏnggyŏn, and Wang *toin* (Practitioner Wang), all thought to be Buddhist nuns.[19] The only one whose life we can glean anything about is Wang *toin,* who was the marchioness of Marquess Chin'gang from the Wang family, the wife of the military leader and ruler Ch'oe Ch'ung-hŏn, and the daughter of one of King Kangjong's concubines. Her older son was Ku, and her younger son, who was ordained under Zen Master Chigyŏm, rose to the level of Zen Master himself.[20] There is no record of her having become a nun in *Koryŏsa* or other historical records, and on Hyesim's stela inscription she is listed as Upāsikā Chŏnghwa T'aekchu of the Wang family. However, based on the fact that she is addressed as *toin* by Hyesim, it seems that she must have become a nun after the death of Ch'oe Ch'ung-hŏn in the sixth year of the reign of King Kojong (1219). She wrote the following letter to Hyesim:

> Although I have earnestly practiced Zen meditation ever since I was young, I was held back by bad deeds from my past lives and merely became more filled with an ardent yearning for enlightenment. Veteran monks from different places occasionally came and taught me, saying that when the heart opens, no matter where you go there are no boundaries. Despite this teaching, I could only see a trace of the Dharma and was never really awakened. I pray that you bestow on me even just a little bit of the fruit of your wisdom, that I may use it to gain the virtue needed to enter the path. I hope that my desire of a *kalpa* (incalcuable eon) will be fulfilled at this moment. This wish springs from the utmost devotion.

Hyesim replied:

> I did not know that you were in this situation. I truly hope that your wish will come true. It is clear that you are

> fervent. I received your letter. Since you ask me to bestow the fruit of my wisdom to help you gain the virtue needed to enter the path, fortunately there are the good teachings of the sages of ancient times. It will suit if you concentrate on those old *kongans* [C. *kung-an*; J. *kōan*; a catechetic question, dialogue, or story for meditation]. They expressed that Mind is nothing but the Buddha in eight letters, but in turn showed that it is neither Mind nor Buddha. Do not mind those words; just get enlightened as we are, then you can certainly see the appearance of the true heart of the ancient sages. . . . It is proper that you calmly study for a long time to break free from all illusions. If you meditate on Chao-chou's "letting go of attachment" *kongan* for a long, long time in your ordinary life, then you will automatically reach a stage where you do not doubt.[21]

Wang *toin* had devoutly meditated from a young age, but said she had made no true progress. So she requested a *kongan*, and Hyesim gave her Zen Master Chao-chou Ts'ung shen's (778–897) *kongan* known as "letting go of attachment." What could be the reason that she was so fervent about her meditation? To understand this, we should consider the fact that in the third year of King Kojong's reign (1216), when National Master Wŏnmyo Yose was erecting Paengnyŏn-sa, she commissioned an Amitābha statue for the main hall and financially supported the calligraphical writing, in ink mixed with gold powder, of the *Lotus Sūtra*.[22] According to the *Pŏphwa yŏnghŏm-chŏn* (Chronicle of *Lotus Sūtra* Miracles), she lamented that there is no such thing as peace in this world; power and influence melt away quickly, like ice, and the mundane world is like a house on fire. Thus, she wanted to practice in order to become able to leave life and death behind.[23]

The difficult position of being both the daughter of King Kangjong and the wife of General Ch'oe Ch'ung-hŏn, the most powerful man in the country,[24] must have made Wang *toin* painfully aware of the fickleness of political fortune and human life, causing her to lament that power in the mundane world is like an iceberg. That is how she must have come to wish to escape from the cycle of life and death, and to donate the Amitābha statue to Paengnyŏn-sa, practice meditation, and request a *kongan* from Master Hyesim, who also had a close relationship with her father, King Kangjong.[25]

As for the previously mentioned nuns Chongmin, Yoyŏn, Ch'ŏngwŏn, and Hŭiwŏn, we know that they participated in the summer retreat at Susŏn-sa in the second year of the reign of King Kangjong

(1213), received *kongans* from Hyesim, and practiced meditation. Their type of Buddhist practice was Zen meditation with *kongans*.

Although there are few extant records, it seems that the *kongans* given by Hyesim to his nun followers were Chao-chou's (1) "letting go of attachment," (2) *wu* (*mu* in Korean; literally, "no," indicating there is no inherent character of the Buddha, or of enlightened mind), and (3) *chuk-pi-ja* (in Korean; literally, "bamboo stick"; its deeper meaning is letting go of attachment and recognizing reality as it is), as shown in the following table.

Hwadu (Topic)	Nun's name	Source (*Chogye Chin'gak kuksa ŏrok*)
Letting go of attachment	Wang *toin*	"Tap Chin'gang hubi Wang toin munsŏbu"
(Chao-chou's) *wu* (nothingness)	Chongmin, Ch'ŏngwŏn	"Si Chongmin sangin," "Si Ch'ŏngwŏn toin"
chuk-pi-ja (bamboo stick)	Ch'ŏngwŏn, Chŏnggyŏn	"Si Ch'ŏngwŏn toin," "Si Chŏnggyŏn toin"

Why were *kongans* like these necessary? When Hyesim gave the nun Chŏnggyŏn hers, he said:

> The only way to be freed from the ties of the world is to awaken your mind. This mind is at the very root of all beings, but we are not able to see it because we block it ourselves through illusion. Therefore, if we break away from this delusion, the awakened mind appears before us. Thus there is nothing equal to *hwadu* practice in trying to break out of the world of illusion. If we say "*chuk-pi*," it is a contradiction, but if we do not say it, it is also a contradiction. Although we should add no words to that, we also cannot but say something. Therefore, do not try to understand it or even think of it.[26]

And when he gave the nun Chongmin her *kongan*, he advised:

> Hold onto this *hwadu* and always study it in your daily life without forgetting it for an instant. Trying to be enlightened without studying your *hwadu* in daily life is like searching for water while ignoring the waves, or like looking for gold

> while throwing away your pan. You will only get even farther removed from your goal.[27]

For Hyesim and his followers, *hwadu* practice was a very important method of achieving enlightenment "now," in this life. The fact that Hyesim had nuns participate in summer meditation retreats and urged them to include *hwadu* practice in their daily lives is closely related to his views on women's enlightenment.

HYESIM'S THEORY OF WOMEN'S ENLIGHTENMENT

Unique Aspects of Hyesim's Theory

Recommending meditation practice to the nun Hŭiwŏn, Hyesim said, "By making a sincere effort and practicing, I hope that you can quickly be liberated."[28] This statement shows that Hyesim believed that women could achieve enlightenment. In this section, I examine his other statements about women's enlightenment.

First, Hyesim referred to the *Kyŏn'gonyŏ-kyŏng* (*Sūtra of Lady Kyŏn'go*), when talking to the nun Yoyŏn. By the *Kyŏn'gonyŏ-kyŏng*, Hyesim meant the first fascicle of *Fo shuo Chien-ku-nu ching* translated into Chinese by Narendrayaśas in Sui. In this sūtra, the woman Kyŏn'go vows to be a guide in the Buddha's work to educate all beings, saying, "I have Supreme Enlightenment to steer beings who are following the wrong path onto the right path." Hyesim gave his female students the example of this enlightened woman to urge them to devote themselves to their practice.

However, the *Kyŏn'gonyŏ-kyŏng* also states the limits of women's enlightenment before and after the part that Hyesim quoted to Yoyŏn:

> If any female resolves to gain Supreme Enlightenment, first she must think of this: By resolving to gain Supreme Enlightenment, flattery, jealousy, covetous anger, wicked lies, and other bad deeds of women will not reappear in the future world. Because of this, all women must definitely resolve to gain the Supreme Enlightenment.[29]

> When this woman's life is over, she will throw away the body of a woman, become a man, and, in the eon of constellations, gain Supreme Enlightenment, and she shall be called a perfectly enlightened one.[30]

If we look at the first of these two excerpts in relation to the second, we can see that the reason women who resolve to gain Supreme Enlightenment can "avoid bad deeds of women" in future lives is that they are reborn as men before they actually achieve enlightenment. Thus, the scenario put forth in this sūtra is very similar to the story of the Dragon Girl in the *Lotus Sūtra*.

Since Hyesim quoted from the *Kyŏn'gonyŏ-kyŏng*, he must have been familiar with the idea that women must be reborn as men before they can be enlightened, although he seems to have disagreed with it, if his explanation to the scholar Kal Nam-sŏng is any indication:

> Just as, in the time when Śākyamuni was a monastic and preached the supreme truth, he was no different from a monk, and when Vimalakīrti lived as a layperson and explained the results of enlightenment, he was no different from a layperson, so when Lady Śrīmālā explained the Mahayana Buddhist law, her appearance as a woman did not change, and when the monk Shan-hsing became a bodhisattva to help his fellow creatures attain enlightenment, his appearance as a monk did not change. This is none other than the difference between the knowing and the unknowing mind: what relation could there possibly be to the appearance of the body, whether it be male or female, or well or badly dressed?
>
> If appearance changed due to knowledge, if shape was transformed due to enlightenment, then, as a holy person, Gautama's appearance would have changed before becoming Śākyamuni, and the face of Vimalakīrti would have changed into Chin-su Buddha. Therefore, since it is the mind that is enlightened, there is no change in the face. Since enlightenment is a matter of a change in wisdom, we can know that it is entirely unrelated to changes in appearance. To make a comparison, we could say that just as the appearance of an official who is promoted to a high-ranking office does not change upon his promotion, so the appearance of someone who becomes enlightened does not change.[31]

In this passage, Hyesim exhorts the layman Kal Nam-sŏng, who studied at home, to practice without being fixated on appearance, since enlightenment has nothing to do with the physical appearance of the body, be it in terms of gender or various marks of social standing. We can see Hyesim expressing the same opinion again in the following passage:

> If you know it, you will understand that whenever you move on the old path, you will not fall into loneliness, and that there is no trace of your move but only the essence of appearance beyond sound and color [i.e., beyond external forms]. Also, if a [single] mote of dust enters into *samādhi* (absorption) and many motes of dust arise from *samādhi*, then we can know that a man's body enters into *samādhi* and a woman's [body] comes from *samādhi*.[32]

The following passage may help us understand this elliptical teaching:

> Muŭija [Hyesim's pen name] spoke: How can the nun Yoyŏn be undeserving? In the old days, the name of Mo-shan-ni [literally, "Mo Mountain Nun"] was Yoyŏn (C. Liao-jan). The venerable monk Kuan-hsi Hsien asked, "What is Mo Mountain?" Mo-shan-ni replied, "It is something that does not show its peak." "What kind of thing is the owner of Mo Mountain?" "It is something that does not have the shape of a man, and does not have the shape of a woman." Monk Hsien quickly shouted at her and said, "Why does it not change?" Mo-shan-ni said, "It is not a ghost, so what should it change to?" The Venerable Hsien capitulated and became the gardener of a vegetable field for three years. . . . Muŭija spoke: Since the Yoyŏn of the old days did in this way, what will this Yoyŏn do?[33]

In the first quotation, the statement that women's bodies come from *samādhi* is related to the second volume of the *Chu-fo yao-chi ching* (Sūtra of Collection of Various Buddhas' Essential [Teachings]) translated by Chu fa-hu.[34] In this text, Mañjuśrī Bodhisattva, sitting near Sakyamuni Buddha, sees a woman named Li-i-nu in *samādhi* and asks the Buddha why this is the case. The Buddha tells Mañjuśrī to wake her out of *samādhi* and ask her himself. But although Mañjuśrī uses all kinds of methods, he fails to wake her. Wang-ming Bodhisattva (Ch'i-chu-yin-kai Bodhisattva), a less enlightened bodhisattva, then receives the command of the Buddha, snaps his fingers, and the woman wakes up. In Chinese Zen schools, the illogical fact that the less enlightened Wang-ming Bodhisattva succeeded where Mañjuśrī had failed became the essence of meditation on this *kongan*.[35] Hyesim quotes this passage stating that men only enter *samādhi* whereas women arise from *samādhi* to emphasize that discrimination according to gender or other physical characteristics is unrelated to enlightenment.[36]

This stance is confirmed by the second excerpt, in which Hyesim gives the Korean nun Yoyŏn the example of the Chinese nun Yoyŏn (C. Liao-jan). The Chinese nun Yoyŏn was a disciple of Zen Master Kao-an Ta-yü and practiced at Mo Mountain in Jui-chou. The story that Hyesim quotes is the Zen dialogue that Liao-jan had with the monk Kuan-hsi Chih-hsien when he came to see her.[37] The story explains that it is not correct to distinguish between male and female bodies. Following the passage previously quoted, Hyesim cites an ode of praise by the monk Hsin-wen-pen that says "the mountain does not expose its peak and there is no shape to people,"[38] leaving no doubt as to his point. Particularly remarkable in the story Hyesim quotes is the fact that a nun wins over a monk in a Zen dialogue. Furthermore, by asking, "Since the Yoyŏn of the old days did in this way, what will this Yoyŏn do?" Hyesim strongly encouraged the Korean nun Yoyŏn to exert herself. Thus, Hyesim emphasized his conviction that, depending on practice, a nun could become enlightened more quickly than a monk.

In that case, enlightenment should certainly be possible for women now, in this very life. An ode of praise that Hyesim gave the nun Chongmin talks about the moment of enlightenment:

> Stop your mind but do not lose your thoughts
> Take your mind and do not let it be fettered
> Take the *hwadu* that a dog has no buddha-nature
> Only watch the *hwadu* and be aware of it carefully and do not do it darkly!
>
> Do not form an opinion that there is or there is not
> Do not think that there is none
> Do not think of overcoming any obstacle
> Do not even think that you know everything!
>
> Do not follow the path of words or the path of reason
> Do not sit in an empty box doing nothing
> Do not try to know in the moment you take the *hwadu*
> Moreover, do not wait to break free from confusion!
>
> Reach the place where there is no way to use your mind and be satisfied
> Finally, do not retreat from there
> Suddenly hit the clothes barrel and smash it
> Happily be happy and be happy again![39]

While urging Chongmin to study the *wu-tza* ("no"-character) *hwadu*, Hyesim explains the obstacles encountered in *hwadu* practice, and in the last two lines he describes the extreme joy of breaking through the clouded mind and becoming enlightened. He is describing the joy of the moment of (not simply sudden but) sudden and complete enlightenment.[40] By giving the nun Chongmin this ode of praise, Hyesim presents her with the idea that, through *hwadu* practice, she can become enlightened today, at this very moment, without first changing into a man, and shows that he does not differentiate between men and women. In other words, Hyesim demonstrates his belief that all are equal in the face of the dharma, be they man or woman, lay or ordained.

Hyesim also quotes the words of the nun Yüan-chi, "All laws are but the mind; if there is no object, it is the enlightment of self-nature," and teaches that when you understand these words, you will understand that there is no difference between your mind and your karmic condition, no such thing as truth and no such thing as enlightenment.[41] Thus, we can see that Hyesim used examples of nuns who had gained enlightenment to energetically encourage his nun followers to seek enlightenment through practice.

Indeed, neither the Theory of Transforming into Men (before attaining enlightenment) nor the Theory of Five Obstacles (that prevent women from becoming buddhas) figures in Hyesim's view of women's enlightenment. The Theory of Five Obstacles says that a woman cannot become a Wheel-Turning Sage King, Indra Heaven King, King Mara, Brahman Heaven King, or Dharma King of the Three Realms. That "women face five obstacles" appears in the *Ti-p'o-ta-to p'in* (Devadatta chapter) of the *Lotus Sūtra*, the *Wu-fen lü*, and other texts.[42] If this is accepted as true, it also means that a woman cannot become a buddha, who is a Dharma King of the Three Realms. The theory that women must first turn into men to become enlightened is based on the account in the Devadatta chapter of the *Lotus Sūtra* in which the Dragon Girl becomes enlightened after turning into a man in the Southern World. If these two theories are true, then women cannot become enlightened here and now. Hyesim's theory of women's enlightenment, which ignores these theories, is characterized by his emphasis on the idea that women can become enlightened here and now by engaging in *hwadu* practice in everyday life.

The Significance of Theory of Women's Enlightenment

Hyesim's attitude toward women's enlightenment differed greatly from that of the monastics who preceded him. Citing the Theory of

Five Obstacles, Silla monastics argued negatively about the chances for women to be enlightened,[43] while an aspect of the theory that women must first turn into men to become enlightened can be seen in the beliefs of the monastics of early Koryŏ, especially those who concentrated on the study of texts.

In the following excerpt from the *Sŏk Hwaŏm-kyo pun'gi wŏnt'ong ch'o* (Perfectly Penetrating Commentary on Hua-yen Teaching), Kyunyŏ (932–973) discusses the enlightenment of the Dragon Girl.[44]

> Question. As is written in the *Ti-p'o-ta-to p'in* (Devadatta chapter) of the *Lotus Sūtra*, "At that time, the Dragon Girl had a treasure pearl which was worth three thousand galaxies. When she gave it to Buddha, Buddha took it immediately. She said to Chih-chi Bodhisattva and Saint Śāriputra, 'I gave the Buddha the treasure pearl, and he accepted it. Is this quick?' The answer was, 'This is very quick.' The Dragon Girl said, 'See that my achieving enlightenment is even quicker.' All the many people gathered there at that time saw the Dragon Girl suddenly turn into a man, take on the appearance of a bodhisattva, go to the Southern Paradise, sit on a sacred lotus blossom, achieve enlightenment, take on the thirty-two marks of Buddha, take on the eighty forms and lecture on the Dharma in all the ten directions, for all living beings." This story appears in the *Lotus Sūtra*, so why is this story quoted in the teaching about *i-sheng-ch'eng fo* (一生成佛, enlightment in this life), a part of the *wu-ch'eng fo* (五成佛, the five kinds of rapid enlightment), in the *Flower Garland Sūtra*?[45]
>
> Answer. Although this is discussed in the *Lotus Sūtra*, it is a quotation from the *Flower Garland Sūtra*. As is written in the first volume of the *Kong-mu zhang* [i.e., *Hua-yen kong-mu-zhang* by Chih-yen], "There naturally must remain some doubt about the case of the Dragon Girl. This episode where the body that someone was born with was changed by their mind shows the effective, rare, and outstanding practice, which proves that the teachings of the *Lotus Sūtra* are of an outstanding nature." So the *Lotus Sūtra* quotes this episode from the *Flower Garland Sūtra* to show its own outstanding nature.
>
> Question. The *Flower Garland Sūtra* does not mention the Dragon Girl's enlightenment, so why is the *Flower Garland Sūtra* quoted?

Answer. This is because in the *Ju-fa-chieh p'in* (Entry into the Realm of Reality chapter) of the *Flower Garland Sūtra*, all the Dragon Kings are mentioned. Actually, the story of Dragon Girl is explained here, but in this case it was left out.

Question. For what reason?

Answer. Because in the *Flower Garland Sūtra* Mañjuśrī taught a gathering that the Dragon Kings attended, and in the *Lotus Sūtra* he taught the Dragon Girl. The common factor of Mañjuśrī in these stories indicates there is a connection between two sūtras.

In this exchange, which is meant to elucidate the *Wu-chiao chang*, a commentary on the *Flower Garland Sūtra*, Kyunyŏ quotes the Theory of Transforming into Men at length from the *Lotus Sūtra* and explains why the text mentions the Dragons Girl's enlightenment even though it is not mentioned in the *Flower Garland Sūtra*.[46] To do so, he strictly cites the *K'ung-mu chang* and quotes the *Flower Garland Sūtra* to say that the Dragon Girl's enlightenment was sudden in the *Lotus Sūtra*. In addition, he is asked why the *Lotus Sūtra* quotes the *Flower Garland Sūtra* when the enlightenment of the Dragon Girl does not appear in this sūtra. To this he replies that in the *Ju-fa-chieh p'in* section there is a part about Dragon Kings, and that the Dragon Girl's enlightenment was omitted from this part. The reason for this, according to Kyunyŏ, is that both were taught by Mañjuśrī.

Although Kyunyŏ admits that the Dragon Girl's enlightenment was sudden, he does not comment on the fact that her body turns into that of a man. How can this silence be interpreted? Is it because he found the Theory of Transforming into Men too worthless to mention, or because this theory was so natural that he did not feel any need to comment on it? To answer this question, it is useful to consider the practice of Kyunyŏ's older sister, Sumyŏng. Sumyŏng asked to hear the teachings of a monk who had studied the *Lotus Sūtra* and also heard teachings about Samantabhadra and Avalokiteśvara, as well as the *Shen-chung ching* (Bodhisattva of the Protection of Buddhist Doctrine Sūtra) and the *Ch'ien-shou ching* (Thousand Eyes and Hands Sūtra), which her brother Kyunyŏ was learning. She secretly listened to him memorize the meaning of the sixth stage of the bodhisattva path taught in the *Flower Garland Sūtra* and became enlightened as a result. When asked to write about her enlightenment five years later, she was able to record every sentence that she had heard at the time of enlightenment without missing a single one.[47]

The *Kyunyŏ chŏn* (Book of Kyunyŏ) uses the term "sudden enlightenment," but this only means that Sumyŏng understood the words of the *Flower Garland Sūtra* after her enlightenment. Sumyŏng nevertheless succeeded even though her brother Kyunyŏ did not urge her to try to gain enlightenment, and her high degree of understanding of Buddhist texts is extolled. Considering this background, it is difficult to conclude that Kyunyŏ held that women could become fully enlightened in this very lifetime. Accordingly, the fact that he did not add his own comment to the account of the Dragon Girl having to change into a man before she could become a bodhisattva can probably be taken to mean that he agreed that women must become men before they can be enlightened.

Chegwan, a Korean monk who brought the classic texts of the T'ien-t'ai school to China in 960 and was an active T'ien-t'ai monk there, used the *Lotus Sūtra* as his basis to say the following about the enlightenment of Dragon Girl:

> Even if we say that a first religious resolution and deep awakening are not different from each other, knowing the reason for the relation, one must understand in detail that they are not two. The Dragon Girl became suddenly enlightened, and all the disciples of Buddha predicted their future enlightenment.[48]

In explaining the line from the *Ch'ŏnt'ae sagyo-ŭi*, "In the first abode [i.e., the abode of initial determination], the clouded mind is broken off and the enlightened mind arises, attaining release from suffering and the Dharma body of *prajñā* (wisdom)," Chegwan says that this has the same meaning as "At the time of first religious resolution, one immediately acquires true enlightenment" in the *Flower Garland Sūtra*, and names the Dragon Girl as an example of achieving true enlightenment.[49] This view of Chegwan's is less conservative than that of Silla monastics who held to the Theory of Five Obstacles and never even mentioned the Dragon Girl's enlightenment. But given that the *Lotus Sūtra*, which contains the Theory of Transforming into Men, is the basic sūtra of the T'ien-t'ai school,[50] it seems likely that Chegwan presupposed that the Theory of Transforming into Men is true.

This interpretation is corroborated by the following passage, which also reveals Chegwan's view of women:

> I will explain about the Three Incalculable Eons. If we take as the starting point the time when Śākyamuni was

> practicing the bodhisattva path, meeting one eon of 75,000 buddhas, the last of whom was called Shih-ch'i Buddha. From that time on, not taking a female body or the four evil destinies, and he always practiced the Six Perfections (*pāramitās*). But he did not know that he could become Buddha by himself. . . .[51]

Śākyamuni practiced the Six Perfections for three incalculable eons, or *kalpas*. In explaining Śākyamuni's practice for the three *kalpa*s, Chegwan emphasizes that Śākyamuni always avoided being born in a woman's body, just as he avoided the four evil destinies of being born as an *asura* (demigod), starving ghost, hell-being, or animal. This shows that Chegwan believed that enlightenment must follow Buddhist practice in a man's body.

Hyesim's recognition that women could be enlightened just as they were contrasted greatly with the views of these other early Koryŏ monks, and represents major progress. Hyesim recommended the same practice for women that he did for men, holding that the same practice would lead to enlightenment in both men and women.

It seems clear that Hyesim's attitude toward female enlightenment was related to his popularization of *hwadu* meditation.[52] Unlike his own teacher Chinul (1158–1210), who thought that *hwadu* meditation was only suitable for those with superior innate religious capacity, Hyesim held that progress in *hwadu* meditation was unrelated to innate religious capacity.[53] Furthermore, as we have seen, Hyesim recommended constant *hwadu* practice for his female followers because he emphasized seeking enlightenment in daily life. As already noted, most nuns of the Koryŏ period were ordained after being widowed and often built separate houses near those of family members, although some did live in nuns' temples. Emphasis on meditation retreats and the kind of practice that is only possible in a temple was not suitable for the types of lives most of these nuns led. By not being overly concerned about women's dwelling places or situations, but rather emphasizing *hwadu* meditation, Hyesim threw open the door of enlightenment to women.

In fact, neither the theory of Five Obstacles nor the Theory of Transforming into Men, originating in the *Lotus Sūtra* and repeated throughout the Mahayana Buddhist canon, actually state that women cannot be enlightened; rather, they are intended to aid in removing women's suffering (by pointing out the hindrances they face) and to reinforce the idea that it is not correct to be attached to being a woman.[54] But these theories were misused by a patriarchal society to limit the possibility of women's enlightenment. Considering these facts, Hyesim's emphasizing women's capacity for enlightenment was truly extraordinary, in contrast to the stance of early Koryŏ monks of the Ch'ŏnt'ae (C. T'ien-t'ai) and Hwaŏm (C. Hua-yen) schools.

CONCLUSION

Buddhist nuns of the Koryŏ period engaged in various practices, including chanting, sūtra reading, Buddhist works, and the education of laypeople. What is remarkable about the nuns in the line of Hyesim and Naong Hyegun is that they received *hwadus* and practiced meditation. In particular, Hyesim's disciples participated in the summer retreat at Susŏn-sa and received *hwadus* individually. Hyesim kindly urged nuns to always think of their *hwadu* in daily life in order to break free from illusion and gain enlightenment. Hyesim taught this way because his view of women's enlightenment was different from that of other monastics of his time.

Hyesim maintained that enlightenment is not related to gender, social standing, or ordination. He urged nuns to practice and try to gain enlightenment, and encouraged them by giving them examples of women who had achieved enlightenment, such as Kyŏn'go from the *Fo shuo chien-ku-nu ching*, Li-i-nu from the *Chu-fo yao-chi ching*, Śrīmālā from the *Śrīmālā-sūtra*, and the nuns Yoyŏn (C. Liao-jan) and Yüan-chi who appear in the *Recorded Sayings* of Chinese Zen masters.

Nowhere in Hyesim's views can the Theory of Five Obstacles or the Theory of Transforming into Men be found. Both theories amount to a statement that women cannot become enlightened now, in this lifetime. What is unique about Hyesim's theory of women's enlightenment is that it emphasizes that women can gain enlightenment here and now through the use of *hwadu* meditation in daily life.

We can see that Hyesim was a pioneer when we compare his view to the theories of other monastics active in Koryŏ. In the Silla period, the Theory of Five Obstacles was prevalent, while the Hua-yen monk Kyunyŏ and the T'ien-t'ai monk Chegwan, both active in the tenth century, had negative views of the possibility of women's enlightenment. Kyunyŏ recognized that, in the Devadatta chapter of the *Lotus Sūtra*, the Dragon Girl becomes enlightened very quickly. He quoted the account of her turning into a man before becoming enlightened in the Southern Paradise but did not himself mention the Theory of Transforming into Men, probably because he did not doubt that the Dragon Girl was enlightened only after turning into a man. Chegwan also explained that the Dragon Girl "became enlightened as soon as she set her mind to it," but also claimed that Śākyamuni was able to achieve enlightenment by avoiding being born either in a woman's body or in one of the four evil destinies and by practicing the Six Perfections. In other words, Chegwan thought that to achieve enlightenment one must be born as a man and then practice. The reason Hyesim had such a positive view of women's enlightenment is that, in contrast to his own teacher Chinul, he took the position that *hwadu* meditation is not related to any kind of innate ability.

NOTES

An earlier version of this chapter originally appeared in the Korean language in the journal *Ihwa sahak yŏn'gu* (Study of History at Ehwa Womans University), 30 (2003), as "Koryŏ Chin'gak kuksa Hyesim ŭi yŏsŏng sŏngbullon" (Koryŏ Master Chin'gak Hyesim's Theory of Women's Attaining Enlightenment).

1. The existence of Buddhist nuns in both Paekche and Silla has been confirmed. Although there has been no confirmation in the case of Koguryŏ, we can deduce that there were also nuns there from the fact that Buddhism entered Silla from Koguryŏ and that the first person to ordain as a Buddhist monastic in Silla was Lady Sa, the older sister of Morye); see *Memorabilia of the Three Kingdoms*, vol. 3, Hŭngbŏp section, "Adogira."

2. Min Hyeon-Ku (Min Hyŏn-ku), "Wŏllam-sa-ji Chin'gak kuksa pi ŭi ŭmgi e taehan il-goch'al" (A Study of the Reverse-side Inscription of the Stela of National Preceptor Chin'gak at the Wŏllam-sa Site), *Chindan hakpo* 36 (Chindan Hakhoe, 1973), 15.

3. Yi Saek, "Sŏch'ŏn Chenappakt'a chonja pudo-myŏng pyŏngsŏ" (Preface to the Inscription on Venerable Indian Chenappakt'a's Relic Stupa), *Tongmunsŏn* (Anthology of Korea Literature), vol. 119. Requoted from Heo Hung Sik (Hŏ Hŭng-sik), ed., "Wŏn-pimun kwa pi-ŭmgi" (The Original Epitaph and Reverse-side Inscription), *Koryŏ ro omgin Indo ŭi tŭngbul: Chigong sŏnhyŏn* (A Light of India Carried Over to Koryŏ: Chigong Sŏnhyŏn) (Ilchogak, 1997), 125–126.

4. Yi Saek, "Sillŭk-sa Poje sŏnsa sari sŏkchong pi" (1379 C.E.), in *Han'guk kŭmsŏk chŏnmun* (The Collected Texts of Korean Epigraphy; hereafter *HKSC*) 3:1211–1212. Yi Saek, "Yŏngbyŏn Ansim-sa Chigong Naong sari sŏkchong pi," *HKSC* 3:1226. "Poje chonja t'apchisŏk," *HKSC* 3:1243. Yi Sung-in, "Sillŭk-sa Taejanggak ki," *HKSC* 3:1218.

5. "T'aego-sa Wŏnjŭng kuksa t'appi," *HKSC* 3:1234. Myoan is recorded as a disciple, along with the Esteemed Mother of the Three Hans, at the end of the last volume of *T'aego hwasang ŏrok* (Recorded Sayings of Monk T'aego).

6. Kyŏnghan, *Paegun hwasang ch'orok pulcho chikchi simch'e yojŏl*, in Han'guk pulgyo chŏnsŏ (The Collected Texts of Korean Buddhism; hereafter *HPC*) 6:636; Kyŏnghan, *Paegun hwasang ŏrok* (Recorded Sayings of Monk Paegun), *HPC* 6:668.

7. "Ch'angsŏng-sa Chin'gak kuksa Taegagwŏnjo t'appi," *HKSC* 3:1237–1238, fails to record the names of those bhikṣuṇīs, which are, however, found on the epitaph.

8. This section, which intends to provide some basic understanding about the life of Buddhist nuns in the Koryŏ period, is a summary of the following papers: Kim Young Mi (Kim Yŏng-mi), "Koryŏ sidae yŏsŏng ŭi ch'ulga" (A Study of Women Entering the Buddhist Priesthood in the Koryŏ Dynasty), *Ihwa sahak yŏn'gu* (Study of History at Ewha Womans' University), combined vols. 25 and 26 (Ewha Womans' University, Sahak Yŏn'guso, 1999); and "Koryŏ sidae Piguni ŭi hwaldong kwa sahoe-chŏk chiwi" (A Study of the Activities and Social Status of Buddhist Nuns in the Koryŏ Dynasty), *Han'guk munhwa yŏn'gu* (Korean Cultural Studies), vol. 1 (Ewha Womans University, Han'guk Munhwa Yŏn'guwŏn, 2001).

9. "Esteemed Great Mother" was an honorary title given to a noblewoman whose son had contributed significantly to his country.

10. Munhwagun was an honorary title given to a nobleman who had contributed significantly to his country.

11. Tenth year of King Kongmin, May, *Koryŏsa chŏryo*, vol. 27.

12. In January 1016, the year before the decree forbidding nun's ordinations, the Khitans invaded Kwakchu, and tens of thousands of soldiers died in battle (seventh year of King Hyŏnjong, January, *Koryŏsa*, vol. 4, sega 4).

13. *Śarīra* are bead-like relics found in cremation ashes. For a portrait of the nun Sŏnghyo (posthumously named Great Master Chinhye), see chapter 5 in this volume.

14. Ongju was a title given to princesses in the royal harem, though in the Koryŏ dynasty it was also bestowed on the wives of government officials.

15. On the grave of Kim Ku's wife of the Ch'oe family is written: "by being ordained and practicing even for just one day, one could go to heaven." And the fact that Ch'oe Sŏ's wife from the Pak family chanted to Amitābha while facing death also shows that ordination was seen as a way of reaching the Pure Land. For more on these ordinations, see Kim Young Mi, "Koryŏ sidae yŏsŏng ŭi ch'ulga," 65–67.

16. Kim Young Mi, "Koryŏ sidae Piguni ŭi hwaldong kwa sahoe-chŏk chiwi," 79–82.

17. "Si Chongmin doin"(Admonition to Chongmin), *Chogye Chin'gak kuksa ŏrok, HPC* 6:25.

18. "Si Hŭiwŏn doin"(Admonition to Hŭiwŏn), *Chogye Chin'gak kuksa ŏrok, HPC* 6:28.

19. For the method of deducing that these were nuns, see Kim Young Mi, "Koryŏ sidae yŏsŏng ŭi ch'ulga," 61.

20. "Ch'oe Ch'ung-hŏn-chŏn," *Koryŏsa*, vol. 29, yŏlchŏn 42; "Ch'oe Ch'ung-hŏn myoji-myŏng," in Kim Yong-sŏn, ed., *Koryŏ myoji-myŏng chipsŏng* (Hallim University Press, 1993); "Ko Hwajang-sa chuji wangsa Chŏngin taesônsa ch'ubong Chŏnggak kuksa pimyŏng," *Tongmunseon* (Anthology of Korea Literature), vol. 118.

21. "Dab Chin'gang Hu Bi Wang toin" (Reply to Chin'gang Hu Bi Wang toin), *HPC* 6:45. The translation had been modified based on Kim Tal-chin, trans., *Chin'gak kuksa ŏrok* (Segyesa, 1993).

22. Chae Sang Sik (Ch'ae Sang-sik), "Koryŏ hugi ch'ŏnt'ae-chong ŭi Paengnyŏnsa kyŏlsa" (The Baekryeon-sa Community of the Late Koryŏ Ch'ŏnt'ae Sect), *Han'guk Saron*, vol. 5, 1979.

23. "Ch'ŏnje yogyŏng i ip chang Chŏnghwat'aekchu," *Pŏphwa yŏnghŏmchŏn*, *HPC* 6:551.

24. Kim Young Mi, "Koryŏ sidae yŏsŏng ŭi ch'ulga," 62.

25. For more on the relationship between Hyesim and King Kangjong, see Kim Kwang-sik, *Koryŏ muin chŏnggwŏn kwa Pulgyo-kye* (Minjoksa, 1995), 125–127.

26. "Si Chŏnggyŏn toin," *Chogye Chin'gak kuksa ŏrok*, *HPC* 6:36.

27. "Si Chongmin sangin," *Chogye Chin'gak kuksa ŏrok*, *HPC* 6:25.

28. "Si Hŭiwŏn toin," *Chogye Chin'gak kuksa ŏrok*, *HPC* 6:28.

29. *Fo shuo chien-ku-nu ching*, *T* 14:946.

30. *Fo shuo chien-ku-nu ching*, *T* 14:948.

31. "Si Kal haksa Nam-sŏng," *Chogye Chin'gak kuksa ŏrok*, *HPC* 6:37.

32. "Si Hagun sangin," *Chogye Chin'gak kuksa ŏrok*, *HPC* 6:29. The meaning of the teaching as a whole is that the external form is meaningless, whether that form is a single mote of dust or many motes, a man or a woman.

33. "Si Yoyŏn toin," *Chogye Chin'gak kuksa ŏrok*, *HPC* 6:26. For more on Mo-shan and this story, see Miriam Levering's papers "The Dragon Girl and the Abbess of Mo-shan; Gender and Status in the Ch'an Buddhist Tradition" (*Journal of the International Association of Buddhist Studies* 5.1:19–35) *and* "Nuns in the History of Chinese Buddhism" delievered in the HanMaum conference.

34. *Chu-fo yao-chi ching* appears in *T* 17.

35. *The Dictionary of Zen*, 991. This appears as "women awaken in *samādhi*" in the *Mumunkwan* (C. *Wumen guan*; Gateless Barrier).

36. According to Sahoe Kwahag-wŏn Minjok Kojŏn Yŏn'guso, *P'alman taejanggŏyng haeje* (Glossary of P'alman Taejanggŏyng), vol. 4 (Pyŏngyang: Sahoe Kwahak Ch'ulp'ansa, 1992), 514, the second volume of *Chu-fo yao-chi ching* says that men and women are not fundamentally different.

37. *Ching-te ch'uan-teng lu*, vol. 11; *Wudeng huiyuan*, vol. 1.

38. "Si Yoyŏn toin," *Chogye Chin'gak kuksa ŏrok*, *HPC* 6:26.

39. "Si Chongmin sangin," *Chogye Chin'gak kuksa ŏrok*, *HPC* 6:25, translation by Park Jae Geum (Pack Chae-kŭm), *Han'guk sŏnsi yŏn'gu: Muŭija Hyesim ŭi si segye* (A Study of Korean Zen Poetry: The World of Hyesim's Poetry) (Kukhak Charyowôn, 1998), 83–84.

40. Ibid., 85.

41. "Si Chŏngsin toin," *Chogye Chin'gak kuksa ŏrok*, *HPC* 6:35.

42. Chŏn Haeju, "Pyŏnsŏng sŏngbul-ron ŭi pip'an-chŏk kŏmt'o" (A Critical Review of the Theory of Transforming into Men), *Pulgyo sasang* 27 (Pulgyo Sasang-sa, 1986); Han'guk yŏsŏng Pulgyo yŏnhap-hoe, ed., *Pulgyo ŭi yŏsŏng-ron* (Pulgyo Sidae-sa, 1993), 72–75. Both sources show that the Theory of Five Obstacles appears in the *Lotus Sutra*, the *Fo shuo ch'ao-jih-ming san-mei*

ching, and the following sūtras and precept texts: the *Wu-fen lü, Chung a-han ching, Tseng-I a-han ching, Fo shuo Chü-t'an mi chi kuo ching*, and the *Fo shuo ssu-p'in fa-men ching*. They also suggest that the Theory of Five Obstacles was added to these sūtras and precept texts after the time of Śākyamuni's life.

43. For Silla monastics' position on the Theory of Five Obstacles, see Kim Young Mi, "Silla Pulgyo-sa e nat'anan yŏsŏng ŭi sinang saenghwal kwa sŭngnyŏ dŭl ŭi yŏsŏng-kwan" (The Religious Life of Women and Monks' Understanding of Women in the History of Buddhism in Silla), *Yŏsŏng sinhak nonjip* (Feminist Theology Review), vol. 1 (Ewha Womans' University, Yŏsŏng Sinhak Yŏn'guso, 1995), 144–145.

44. *HPC* 4:485. For more details on the enlightment of the Dragon Girl, see Yoshida Kazuhiko, "The Enlightment of the Dragon King's Daughter In the Lotus Sutra," Barbara Ruch ed., *Engendering Faith*, Center for Japanese Studies, University of Michigan, 297–324.

45. These two types of enlightenment are explained by the second Chinese patriarch, Hua-yen Chih-yen (602–668), in his *Hua-yen kong-mu-zhang*. The awakening of the Dragon Girl is given as an example of the *i-sheng-ch'eng fo* in the text; see *T* 45:585.

46. Fa-tsang, *Hua-yen i-sheng chiao-I fen-ch'i*, vol. 4, *T* 45:505.

47. Hyŏk Yŏn-chŏng, *Tae Hwaŏm sujwa Wŏnt'ongyangjung t'aesa Kyunyŏ-chŏn pyŏngsŏ, HPC* 4:511.

48. Chegwan, *Ch'ŏnt'ae sagyo-ŭi, HPC* 4:526.

49. Chegwan is expounding the following line in T'ien-t'ai Chih-i's *Mo-ho chih-kuan*, vol. 7.

50. Of course, there is also research that suggests that T'ien-t'ai Chih-i, in contrast to Chegwan, had a positive view of women's enlightenment. In the section of the *Fa-hua wen-chü* (*T* 34:117), Chih-i saw women's enlightenment as a matter of course, on the basis of the buddha-nature that all beings possess. Takahashi Rikū, "*Ryūjo Jōbutsu* ni tsuite," *Taishō Daigaku Daigakuin ronshū* (Taishō Daigaku Daigakuin, 1993), 17:101–106.

51. Chegwan, *Ch'ŏnt'ae sagyo-ŭi, HPC* 4:522.

52. Chinul presented the Sŏngjŏktŭngji-mun (gate of maintaining alertness and calmness equally), Wŏndonsinhae-mun (gate of fulfilled and sudden faith and understanding), and Kanhwagyŏngjŏl-mun (gate of *hwadu* meditation), but thought that Wŏndonsinhae-mun and Kanhwagyŏngjŏl-mun were only suitable for beginners with superior innate religious capacity. However, Hyesim advocated Kanhwail-mun (only one gate of *hwadu* meditation). Chinul's three *muns* are melded into Kanhwail-mun, but the most important difference is that in Hyesim's view, *hwadu* practice is not only for those with superior innate religious capacity but for anyone, monastic or lay, man or woman. The unique aspect of Hyesim's view is that, regardless of innate religious capacity, anyone can practice *hwadu* meditation in daily life. Therefore, after suggesting a *hwadu*, Hyesim kindly explained it again, and through his actions caused *hwadu* meditation to become more widespread among laypeople. See Yi Tong-jun, "Hyesim Kanhwailmun ŭi kujo wa kŭ ŭiŭi" (The Structure and Implications of Hyesim's Kanwhailmun), *Kuksagwan Nonch'ong* 42 (Kuksa

P'yŏnch'an Wiwŏnhoe, 1993) and Cho Myung-je (Cho Myŏng-je), *The Study on Koan Zen* (Kanwha Sŏn) *in the Late Koryŏ Dynasty*, Hye-an, 2004, 96–107.

53. Ibid.

54. Chŏn Haeju, "Pyŏnsŏng sŏngbul-ron ŭi pip'an-chŏk kŏmt'o," 79.

4

Koryŏ Ladies and the Encouragement of Buddhism in Yuan China

Tonino Puggioni

This chapter examines the activities of Buddhist laywomen in the fourteenth century. More specifically, it analyzes the activities of Koryŏ laywomen residing in Yuan China. What is striking is the high degree of religious fervor dedicated to building or repairing temples, promoting the activities of Buddhist monks, and helping the religious communities of their home country. In certain cases, these activities were by no means limited to the capital Dadu, but also encompassed, as we shall see, their country of origin.

In the course of my studies on the work of Koryŏ Pŏpsang monks in Yuan China, I came across several cases of Koryŏ women involved in promoting Buddhist initiatives. Almost all the available data concern the undertakings of court ladies. Putting them aside, there are several references to the activities of a few women married to high officials of the Yuan bureaucracy not necessarily residing in the capital. Most often, the activities of these laywomen also involve court eunuchs. I intend to dedicate a separate study to this subject in the near future.

In this period, for the first time in Koryŏ history, we find an abundance of epigraphical and literary information on the encouragement of Buddhism by women. The purpose of this chapter is to verify the ways in which Koryŏ women's religious activities took place, their role in promoting Buddhism in China, the character of the Buddhist faith they promoted, and, finally, the historical meaning of their undertakings.

Considering the important role laywomen had in the promotion of Buddhism in general, and especially within Koryŏ communities in China, it is curious that so far no study has been done on this subject.

HISTORICAL BACKGROUND

For around thirty years, Koryŏ experienced a war of resistance against the invading Mongol armies. The country was crushed, with a few symbols of national identity and pride destroyed, such as the collection of the Tripitaka at Puin-sa (1236), the pagoda of Hwangnyong Temple in Kyŏngju (1238), and numerous other temples and sites of historical interest that were burnt down. Hundreds of thousands of people had been killed or made prisoners of war while the land was ravaged and depleted. In 1259, Koryŏ managed to stipulate peace with the Mongols, when the heir Prince Chŏn (the future King Wŏnjong) traveled to China to meet Qubilay. Peace was sought from both sides, as Koryŏ wished to put an end to decades of warfare against the Mongol armies, while Qubilay was engaged in an internecine war with his brother Arigh Böqe, with the outcome of this war by no means certain. Qubilay felicitously welcomed the Koryŏ king. The conditions of peace were harsh, but not as harsh when compared to other countries that had such a long record of resistance against the Mongols.

For the first time since the end of the Tang dynasty, Koryŏ's frontiers were laid open to all outsiders: Koryŏ people could visit the rest of the continent, with foreigners visiting Koryŏ with much ease compared to the past. This openness must have conferred a special atmosphere both to the Yuan capitals and to Kaegyŏng, where many foreigners lived, as part of the entourage of the Mongol princesses, envoys of the Yuan court, part of military units, as Buddhist monks, merchants, and so on.

But more than Kaegyŏng, the Yuan capital itself was crowded with foreigners from all over, many of whom were on duty at the Yuan court as functionaries or as military personnel, while many others were engaged in the most disparate activities. Accordingly, foreign communities sprang up all over Yuan China, in particular in the capital and its surroundings, at ports, and at the most important communication centers. As today, and as it was in the recent past, one of the most important foreign communities in China was Korean.

As part of the peace agreement, on repeated occasions Koryŏ would send young women and boys to Yuan China, to take up duty at the Yuan court as court ladies, often being married off to Yuan court officials or provincial dignitaries. Boys were usually employed as eunuchs at court, and a kind of communal feeling developed accordingly among the court ladies and eunuchs, especially among people of the same country of origin.

From historical sources we know that most of the eunuchs and a good portion of the ladies attending the court were of Korean origin. Their numbers grew disproportionately compared to other nationalities, especially during Emperor Shundi's reign (1333–1368),[1] understandably due to the nationality of his empress who was from Koryŏ, Empress Ki, and her need to secure a solid power basis for herself and her son. She was also, thanks to her financial means, one of the foremost promoters of Buddhism, both in Dadu and in her home country.[2]

Buddhist temples were at the center of Koryŏ communities in Yuan China, catering to the needs of the Koryŏ people living nearby, and to travelers.[3] Temples were market centers, providing lodging and food for travelers, places where Koryŏ people could meet and exchange information, finding refuge and financial help when needed. Moreover, all sorts of shops selling Koryŏ goods, especially restaurants, must have sprung up around temple areas. At temples, people would encounter merchants going back to Koryŏ and hand them mail or presents for their relatives back home. Most of all, temples were places where Koryŏ people living in China could find their brethren and speak the same language, listen to religious functions in the Koryŏ tongue, and receive education from teachers of their homeland.

High court bureaucrats, students, monks, court ladies, eunuchs, soldiers, travelers, and all sorts of people met at these temples and, aside from some nearby Chinese city dwellers, the husbands of Koryŏ court ladies, no matter what their nationality, must have accompanied their wives or favorites to the temple. With the passing of time and the consequent increase in the presence of Koryŏ people at Dadu, the number of Koryŏ temples in the Yuan capital increased, so much so that Yi Kok observed that Koryŏ temples in Dadu were "so many as to face each other."[4]

KORYŎ LADIES AS PATRONS OF THE SAṄGHA

Koryŏ laywomen played a crucial role in financing Buddhist temples, quite often donating their own houses to the Buddhist community to be used as temples, as is the case of Lady Kim, wife of Chaghan Temür, or Lady Son, wife of the Great Officer in Palace Attendance

Kim Baianchai, a Koryŏ official on duty at the Yuan court. In other instances, they donated money and land to temples to finance religious functions, praying for the afterlife of their defunct relatives. Still others, like the wife of the King of Anxi, Ananda, and daughter of Han Son-su, must have had their husbands call the most eminent Korean monks, such as Haewŏn, to find comfort in a setting so unfamiliar as the Mongolian steppe. We have only scant literary references to the activities of Koryŏ ladies. Nonetheless, these scant resources aid us considerably in understanding the atmosphere of their time.

But why did Koryŏ ladies so fervently promote the development of Korean temples abroad? We can surmise that Koryŏ women, together with eunuchs and other displaced people (such as students and corvée laborers), developed each in their own group a mutual understanding and solidarity that tied them together. After all, they came from the same land, shared the same views and prejudices, spoke the same language, and were imbued with the same culture, all living in a foreign land, in a complex, multifarious, and somewhat hostile social milieu. Accordingly, they needed to recreate an atmosphere similar to their home country's, by wearing the same traditional garments and eating the same foods. With time, those who succeeded in court as musicians, artists, artisans, and court functionaries of high rank helped to spread the Koryŏ fashion among the Chinese and people of other nationalities.[5] This phenomenon must have become apparent when Empress Ki was at the apex of her political power.

This also allowed a greater popularity to Koryŏ Buddhist monks, who were often invited to court to provide lectures on the sūtras, possibly in the Chinese language, permitting the imperial entourage and all court dignitaries to understand them.[6] Likewise, the Indian monk Zhigong was repeatedly invited to lecture at the presence of the imperial family, possibly thanks to his relations with Koryŏ people in general.[7]

There are instances when Koryŏ people living in China concerned themselves with promoting Chinese temples, such as those at Fangshan,[8] Daqingshousi in Dadu,[9] Gaolisi in Hangzhou,[10] and, in the case of King Ch'ungsŏn, with the advocacy of the White Lotus Society.[11] However, it is fairly safe to assume that most of the energy and interest of Koryŏ people living in China was devoted to temples run by Korean monks for the interests of Koryŏ people.

In many cases, Koryŏ court ladies acted in accord with court eunuchs, with whom they were in constant relation at court, helping and sustaining each other, as in the case of Empress Ki. Moreover, there must have been many other instances of which we are unaware.

The cases of Singwang temple at Haeju, Fawang, Mito and Fayuansi in Dadu, Kyŏngch'ŏn Temple in the Kaegyŏng area, and Changan Temple on Mount Kŭmgang are all typical in this regard. The empress also sent Koryŏ court eunuchs to aid the poor and needy, to summon Buddhist monks to court, and so on. We shall now view a few of the instances that we can examine through epigraphical and literary sources.

When Ananda, King of Anxi, requested Emperor Chengzong (1294–1307) to send a messenger to Koryŏ to invite a monk of renowned conduct and high moral standing, the reason behind this must have been due to his Koryŏ wife's homesickness and her need of spiritual solace.[12] Ananda's wife was a daughter of Han Son-su.[13] The choice fell upon a Pŏpsang monk living at Pulchu Temple, Haewŏn. In 1305, he journeyed to the Yuan court, followed by an envoy and a few of his disciples. After a meeting with the emperor, Haewŏn followed King Ananda to his northern kingdom in the steppe. However, because he could not eat meat due to his strict observance of the Buddhist precepts, Haewŏn had to endure many hardships during this period, some caused by the scarcity of vegetables. Thanks to the strict observance of the Vinaya, Haewŏn gained King Ananda's respect. He must have lived in the steppe for about two years with a few of his disciples until the first months of 1307.[14] When Wuzong (1307–1311), the new emperor, ascended to the throne, he eliminated his most dangerous political adversaries, starting with Ananda, thereby ending Haewŏn's stay in the steppe.[15]

After marrying Han Son-su's daughter, Ananda called for other women from Koryŏ, though we do not know for what purppose. Regardless, from this we can infer that Ananda's interest in calling monks from Koryŏ was determined by the desire to please his Koryŏ wife, or wives. We can say this because, although Ananda might have been interested in striking a chord with the Buddhists as a king and as a possible candidate to the Yuan throne, he was actually a Muslim. In any case, after following Wuzong to Dadu, Haewŏn resided at Chongenfuyuansi in the capital for about thirty years, passing away in the same temple and without ever returning to his home country. In this instance, we can indirectly verify the involvement of one, or perhaps more, Koryŏ ladies in the support of Buddhism.[16]

Lady Im's case is a particularly interesting one. She financed the reconstruction of Xingfu Temple, and served at the Yuan court for many years while also becoming a favorite of Qubilay's empress. She received donations in great quantity, thereby being able to afford a high standard of living. Lady Im, referred to as the Dame of Changsŏng,[17] learned that a Koryŏ monk named Wŏndam had bought five *mou* of land in Dadu's southern section, Nancheng, and, together with his disciples Sungan, Pŏbun and others, had built a temple there.[18] The temple must have been in dire straits notwithstanding the donations of nearby dwellers. However, after a donation of money and the allotment of fifty *mou* of land by Lady Im, the temple was rebuilt on a considerable scale. A large number of artisans and workers gathered construction materials to prepare for the renovation of the temple. Construction went on from 1313 to 1317 and included of a hall, lodgings for the monks, a kitchen, and new Buddhist statues. Koryŏ monks were asked to hold lectures on the sūtras on a regular basis, thanks to their profound knowledge of the Vinaya. Wŏndam had a close relationship with Yi Che-hyŏn, whom he asked to write an inscription.[19] Thanks to this inscription, today we have some knowledge of their activities.

A similar example is that of a certain Lady Ki, a relative of Empress Ki and daughter of Sŏn'gyŏng Ongju.[20] She was married to Sharabal, a literary official of Uighur origin in service at the Yuan court as a member of the Classics Mat. Sharabal was a son of Alin Temür, who had also been in the service of Toghon Temür (Shundi) as a man of letters.[21] He seems to have been close to Empress Ki's political faction at court, and, after the death of Empress Danashiri, had proposed the crowning of Second Empress Ki as First Empress. Judging from the fact that Ki Ch'ŏl organized the religious function held at Pohyŏn Hermitage on Mount Kŭmgang in 1336, which Sharabal participated in, together with his Koryŏ wife, he must have also been quite close to Ki Ch'ŏl.

He came first to the Koryŏ capital on official duty during the Taiding years (1323–1328).[22] At the time, he went on a tour to Mount Kŭmgang and visited many temples, admiring the scenery. However, he was particularly impressed by the beauty of Pohyŏn Hermitage's natural settings. Its abbot Chigyŏn was in charge of renovating the temple. On that occasion, Sharabal had an interview with Chigyŏn, encouraging him with the reconstruction work by offering his financial support. Thus, in 1336, only ten years later, a monk of the hermitage, Master Talchŏng, was able to travel to Dadu and visit Sharabal. Sharabal greeted him amicably, donating over 5,000 *liang* in paper notes to the monk. He also assured continuous financial support to the hermitage. Talchŏng went back to Koryŏ, gathering about three hundred monks and providing them with robes and edibles. They celebrated a function that started on the eighth day of the fourth month, lasting until the fifteenth day of the seventh month. Talchŏng also vowed to hold a *Joy of Meditation* ceremony (Sŏnyŏlhoe) in the summer of the following year, to pray for the longevity of their rulers and the well-being of the people.

Lady Son's case is also worthy of attention. She is referred to as the Dame of P'ohae County and was Kim Baianchai's wife, a Koryŏ official who had been on duty as Great Officer in Palace Attendance for more than thirty years. In 1331, along with her husband, she purchased land in Wanping county, Zhishui village,[23] and built a temple there. The temple was called "Jinsun Mitosi" (Kim Son Mit'a-sa) from their family names. The reason for building the temple lay in the couple's gratefulness for having served at the imperial court for more than thirty years, starting with the first year of the Dade era (1297–1306). Following Kim's calling to the imperial court, all his relatives enjoyed welfare and prosperity at home in Koryŏ. The temple was founded during the first month of 1331, but on the eighth month of the same year Lady Son died. Her funeral was held at the north section of the temple. After her death, forty additional *mou* of land were donated to the temple in order to celebrate religious functions in her memory and support the livelihood of the monks. Kim also freed his servants and had them ordained as monks under the names of Kyehong and Kyemyŏng. However, he did not enjoy good health in his last years. Thus, after an understanding with his new wife, Lady Yun, he further donated 5,000 *liang* in paper notes and silver coins to the temple, to help with its administration. Thereafter, he sent his sons Nangp'al, Grand Master of Consultation, and Dorji (Duo'er'ji, ducongguan)[24] to the famous writer Yi Kok, requesting an inscription, which he wrote in 1336. In this case, we have seen the zealous support of the saṅgha by two Koryŏ ladies, Kim and Yun, both of whom were wives of Kim Baianchai.[25]

Also worth mentioning is Lady Ch'oe's support of the saṅgha. She was the wife of Cho Pun, a Koryŏ eunuch on duty at the Yuan court.[26] They actively supported the construction of Fawangsi, a temple in the Dadu area.[27] Cho Pun's brother, Cho Bayan Böqe, was also serving at the Yuan court as a eunuch, although he does not appear to be among the donors of the temple. In the beginning, Yi Sam-jin had donated his house at *Anfuli* to be used as a temple. Even earlier, the building had been the official residence of the Censorial Inspector Kuanyinnu and had an extension of about nine *mou*. Yi Sam-jin called on the monk Chasin to oversee the temple's reconstruction and administration. Some time later, however, a powerful family encroached upon the premises, and the land was closed and used as a stable. Nonetheless, Yi Sam-jin managed to receive compensation and intended to buy a piece of land in some other place where a temple could be built. He gathered the money with another court eunuch of Koryŏ origin named Sin Tang-ju, who donated 7,000 *ding*, and after collecting a sum total of 25,000 *ding*, bought nine *mou* of land at Jinchengfang in *Dadu*. They once more entrusted the temple's construction work and its administration to the monk Chasin. Unfortunately, Yi Sam-jin died without ever witnessing the completion of the works.

Following his death, Lady Ch'oe and her husband sold the best articles and clothes they had at home to donate the money to the temple. After Chasin's death, they called the Tiantai Master Irin to preside over its construction. Finally, the temple was built on three sides of the land for lodging, while in the center they later built a hall where a statue of the Buddha Sakyamuni was installed in the middle. Besides the statue of Sakyamuni, images of Samantabhadra and Manjusri' were mounted, together with those of the Tiantai masters, starting with Zhiyi, all of them gilded. Judging from the emphasis Yi Kok gave to this new arrangement, it is highly probable that the temple was not a Tiantai one from its inception. Around this time, the intervention of Empress Ki took place. She made many donations to the temple, as we shall see in the next section.

Lady Wi, wife of Yi Tae-sun, an official working at the Yuan court, had close relations with Chongren Temple (Sungin-sa). The location of the temple is not yet clear. She invited the famous Indian monk Zhigong, who was on his way back to Dadu from Yangzhou,[28] and received the Buddhist precepts (*kye*) directly from him. Lady Wi must have had a close relation to this temple and we cannot exclude the possibility that it was controlled by Koryŏ people.

Also close to Zhigong was Lady Kim, wife of the influential general Chaghan Temür (? –1362). She became a nun under Zhigong's tutelage, possibly after her husband's assassination. She offered her house in Chengqingli, Dadu, as a temple after having it enlarged and renovated. After Zhigong's saying that all rivers flow from west to east, the temple was named Fayuansi.[29] Zhigong must have used this temple as his main abode, which was mainly inhabited by Koryŏ monks. Monks from Koryŏ must have paid frequent visits to Zhigong at Fayuansi, thanks to the fame gained in Koryŏ by the Indian monk.[30]

In this context, the efforts of Yuan empresses to promote Koryŏ Buddhism, as well as the exchange of Buddhist culture are noteworthy, though they took place within the tributary framework. We can quote the cases of Empress Dowager Targi (Shuyuan Huang Taihou), who sent the Koryŏ eunuch Pang Sin-u to Kaegyŏng to oversee the calligraphy of a copy of the canon in gold characters in the sixth month of 1310. The empress had made a donation of sixty *ding* of gold leaves to finance the enterprise. The work was carried out at Minch'ŏn Temple, where Sin-u gathered about three hundred monks and laymen. At the same time, religious functions were held to pray for the longevity of the empress, and an amnesty was issued, where prisoners were freed to celebrate the event. Later on the sūtras were moved to Sinhyo Temple.[31]

In another instance, in 1338, the Grand Empress Dowager Budashiri sent the commissioner of the Directorate of Imperial Insignia Sin Tang-ju to celebrate the completion of Hŭnggyo-wŏn with a generous donation of incense and silk.[32] In 1337, she also helped the Koryŏ monk Kyemyŏng renovate Longquan Temple in Chongnang nanxiang, Daxingxian.[33]

The support Koryŏ ladies offered Buddhism follows the great flow of Koryŏ Buddhism at the time, where the Sŏn and Ch'ŏnt'ae sects were the mainstream. We have seen Lady Ch'oe and Empress Ki's involvement in the foundation of Tiantai Fawangsi, but many other women must have participated in the foundation of Guangjiao Temple, which also belonged to the Tiantai, though we do not have any direct proof of this. On the other hand, Lady Wi received the precepts at Chongrensi from Zhigong, which suggests a close relation on her part to the temple and its probable belonging to the Chan. Lady Kim, Chaghan Temür's widow, founded Fayuansi and called on Zhigong to stay there, which leads us to believe that this temple was also close to the Meditation sects.

After the end of the war, Susŏn Society, to whose tradition illustrious monks belonged, made a gradual recovery, thanks to the efforts of people like Manhang, Ch'unggam, and others, responsible for the diffusion of the Linzhi monk Mengshan Deyi's teachings in the country. His disciple Tieshan Shaoqiong was even invited to visit Koryŏ, and his master Mengshan's books were published repeatedly at Songgwang Temple, thereby propagating his Kanhwa Sŏn teachings throughout the country. From the relations Shaoqiong had with Hon'gu, one of the representatives of the Kaji-san stream, we can understand that the interest in Deyi's teachings was common to most Koryŏ Sŏn sects.[34] We do not have any clues as to the involvement of Koryŏ court ladies in promoting Mengshan's teachings but, as we have seen, their contribution has been great concerning the encouragement given to another great foreign monk of the time whose message was close to Sŏn, the Indian Zhigong. His teaching deeply influenced the greatest Koryŏ monks of the time, to start with Naong Hyegŭn, T'aego Pou, Paegun Kyŏnghan, aside from the ones mentioned previously.

EMPRESS KI'S SUPPORT OF BUDDHISM

Empress Ki, a Koryŏ lady whose family was from Haengju, played the most important role in promoting Buddhism. Thanks to her standing, her Koryŏ relatives received the same treatment as, if not superior to, the Koryŏ king himself. Her biography in the *Yuanshi* is the longest of the empresses' biographies and this is an indirect recognition of the important role she played in later Yuan history.

Lady Ki was introduced to Emperor Shundi (r.1333–1368) by the Koryŏ eunuch Tumandir and was sustained by a host of other Koryŏ eunuchs in service at the court, among whom Pak Böqe and Ko Yong-bo seem to have been closest to her. The emperor soon became fond of her, probably due to her uncommon beauty. She experienced some difficulties during the first years, mainly due to Empress Danashiri's jealousy, but when her party was eliminated, Lady Ki had no other political rivals. Although she could not immediately become First Empress due to political opposition from the powerful Minister Bayan, she bided her time until 1365, remaining in control of the inner affairs of the court for most of that time. In 1342, Lady Ki's political standing was enhanced after the birth of a son, Ayūshridar, and all her efforts were bent on the candidacy of her son to the Yuan throne, which she finally managed to secure.[35]

Empress Ki actively supported the Buddhist religion using funds she could draw from the Office of the Empress' Household Administration. The practical work was done for her by Koryŏ eunuchs in service at court, like the previously mentioned Pak Böqe, Ko Yong-bo, Sin Tang-ju, Yi Qutuq Temür, and others.

One of the first documented instances of her involvement in religious matters is the generous support of Fawangsi, mentioned earlier. Lady Ch'oe and her husband Cho Pun built the temple, whose land had been bought by Yi Sam-jin. Empress Ki first donated 10,000 in paper money to the temple, aiding the reconstruction work. In October of that same year, when the emperor was in the western side of the palace, he was offered a manuscript of the *Lotus Sūtra* written in gold characters. The emperor ordered it to be preserved at Fawangsi. Empress Ki then visited Fawangsi and made donations of incense and precious articles to finance the chanting and reading of the sūtras, doing so the following year as well. The temple earned so much money that the abbot, Master In, donated 5,000 *kuan* of his own and, along with the Associate Commissioner of Administration of Civilian Artisans Pak Swe Nooldae and the Grand Director Zhu Yuanze Temür, contributed 2,000 *kuan* each, to light long-life lanterns and chant the sūtras. Local people also joined in the initiative, which was repeated every year for a period of almost ten years, starting in 1334 until its end in 1343. Thanks to the donations of Empress Ki, two temple halls were built to the west and east of the temple, while corridors were built to the south, and to the north new lodgings for monks were provided; in the central corridor a gate was opened, and this gate substituted the traditional three gates. They also added lodgings for guests on both sides. The following year, they built a new apartment for the abbot on the southeast side of the temple and, to the south, a kitchen to store goods. In all, the money used for the reconstruction amounted to 140,000 *kuan*, and the buildings were over 80 *kuan*.[36] This also allowed the temple to purchase all paraphernalia and instruments needed for the life of the monastic community and the performance of temple rituals.[37] Empress Ki's intervention could be established in the last years of this period. In fact, judging from the timing and the amount of money donated, we can surmise that it must have occurred in connection with the birth of her son Ayūshridar.

To thank the Buddhist divinities for her son's birth, which took place in 1442, she also heavily funded the reconstruction of a temple in Koryŏ, the Changan-sa, on Mount Kŭmgang. Convinced as she was that her present status was due to the *karma* accumulated in her previous lives, she wished to make an offer to the Buddhas to secure a long life for the emperor and their son. According to the inscription, she was told that no place could be better than Changan Temple on Mount Kŭmgang for this purpose. Mount Kŭmgang had been traditionally considered sacred, and temples and stupas dotted its slopes since time immemorial. According to the *Flower Garland Sūtra* (*Avataṃsaka-sūtra*), to the northeast there is a mountain called Kŭmgang, the abode of the Bodhisattva Dharmodgata who had been preaching the *Prajñāpāramitā-sūtra*, together with 12,000 Bodhisattvas. At the time that Yi Kok wrote the inscription, Changan Temple was the most important religious center on the mountain.[38]

After a request from the monk Kwengbyŏn, who had visited the Yuan court to secure some funds for this reason, she sent the eunuch Ko Yong-bo to Mount Kŭmgang with a donation of 3,000 *ding* of gold as a token of gratitude. She made her contribution in several installments within a span of three years, while the temple was renovated. Besides the money, she also donated four sets of the *Tripitaka*, one of which was a manuscript in silver characters. The temple already had three versions of the *Avatamsaka* in golden characters and eight copies of the *Lotus Sūtra*, all handwritten. The person in charge of the whole operation on her side was Ko Yong-bo, one of the highest officials in the Office of the Empress' Household Administration. He was assisted by another Koryŏ eunuch, the Commissioner of the Empress' Household Administration Yi Qutuq Temür. The names of the donors are listed on the back of the inscription, and among them is Yi Qutuq Temür, probably followed by Ko Yong-bo and nobles of the Koryŏ court.[39] Kwengbyŏn and a group of five hundred monks celebrated the inaugural ceremony.

It is important to note that Changan Temple owned land in several parts of Koryŏ, among them a few *kyŏl* in the Haengju area, which was the place of origin of the empress herself. This helps us understand the reason that brought her to finance Changan Temple. In the inscription, Yi Kok tries somewhat to embellish the relation between Empress Ki and Changan-sa, but it is clear that between her family and the temple there was a long-standing relationship. Ko Yong-bo, following her orders, asked Yi Kok to write the inscription to commemorate the event.

Empress Ki also financed the reconstruction of Chijang Temple on Pogae-san, which had been destroyed in a fire in 1361. The monk Chahye visited the Yuan court to ask for her support. He already had the temple repaired in the past but, due to the fire, two-thirds of the buildings had been destroyed. She made a generous donation to the temple and, following this, the Koryŏ royal house and nobility emulated her example, not only by rebuilding the temple, but making it more magnificent. Among Koryŏ nobles, Queen Hŭi, Ch'oe Maeng-son, Ch'oe Ch'ung, Pak Hu, and many others participated in the donations.[40]

The empress and her eunuchs must have been behind the reconstruction of Singwang Temple at Haeju, the family temple of the Yuan imperial house. Each emperor of the Yuan used to build a temple in Dadu to celebrate his reign and invoke the protection of the Buddhas for their longevity and peacefulness.[41] Shundi, however, did not have any temple built in the Yuan capital as far as we know, but instead had Singwang Temple built on a massive scale near Haeju, in today's North Korea.[42]

Shundi's relations with Koryŏ date back to his early youth, as he had been exiled to Taech'ŏng Island, off Haeju, for about one year during Emperor Wenzong's reign (1329–1332). At the time, he had promised to rebuild the temple if he gained back his freedom and the throne. The period he spent on Taech'ŏng Island must have familiarized him with Koryŏ customs and people, and perhaps even the sounds of the language. This possibly also played a role in the blossoming of his relationship with Lady Ki. In any case, the emperor must have attributed great significance to his relation with the temple. The Koryŏ king, Ch'ungsuk, underlined the importance of such a relationship when he paid a visit to the temple in 1333, the year of Shundi's ascension to the throne, to celebrate the event and pray for the longevity of the new emperor.[43] This is clear evidence of the symbolic importance the temple held for the emperor, and the fact that the Koryŏ court readily understood it is further proof of this. Moreover, because the Koryŏ king did not pray for the emperor's long life at a temple in the capital, but instead journeyed far off to Haeju to celebrate the event testifies to the symbolic importance of Singwang Temple at the time in Koryŏ–Yuan relations.

The temple was rebuilt in 1337, when the emperor sent Kim Temür with a donation to reconstruct the monks' living quarters, side halls, and so on. The temple's most important parts were the Pogwang and Lohan halls. The Lohan cult had always occupied a central role in the temple since its origins, which date back to the Silla dynasty.[44] In 1341, the emperor again sent Songqur to oversee the reparation works. Songqur traveled to Koryŏ to oversee thirty-seven foreign artisans and artists. Koryŏ's prime minister Kim Sŏk-kyŏn helped superintend the work, along with the vice commissioner of the Bureau of Military Affairs Yi Su-San. The temple must have acquired an international and unique look, thanks to the intervention of artists and artisans from different countries.

Emperor Shundi's family temple was rebuilt in Koryŏ to invoke protection for the imperial family and guarantee the continuity of the dynasty. For this reason, it must have received the highest priority and attention not only from the Yuan imperial house, but also from the Koryŏ royal family. The attention of the Yuan imperial house is testified, among other reasons, by the fact that the duty of writing an inscription was given to the most outstanding Yuan scholars of the time; first to the Hanlin academician Jie Xisi (1274–1344) and, after his demise, to Wei Su (1303–1372). They were both brilliant writers, having received official recognition not only through their rank, but also because they both participated in writing the official histories of the Song, Liao, and Jin dynasties. Recognition not inferior to that of the Yuan was also bestowed on the temple by the Koryŏ court, which invited the most important Sŏn monks of the time, such as Naong Hyegŭn and Paegun Kyŏnghan, to preside over it. It is then visible just how important Empress Ki's role must have been in the decision to reconstruct the temple. It is not a case that was decided after the deaths of El Temür and Empress Danashiri, in the sixth month of 1335.

However, while Shundi rebuilt Singwang-sa from a national point of view, as it was the official temple of the imperial family during his reign, Empress Ki was not satisfied with this arrangement, and built her own private temple in Koryŏ, the Kyŏngch'ŏn-sa. The temple was on Puso Mountain, in the Kaegyŏng area. The temple's history can be traced back to the Middle Koryŏ period, as the *Koryŏsa* reports frequent visits by Koryŏ kings starting from the reign of Yejong (thirteenth year tenth month, 1118). Thus, Empress Ki actually renovated Kyŏngch'ŏn-sa. We know that she donated precious articles to the temple, among them a treasure of pearls and a beautiful pennant made of gold strings. On that occasion, a beautiful stupa was erected in white marble, among its donors the Prince of Chinnyŏng Kang Yung, the eunuch Ko Yong-bo, the Dahuazhu Sŏnggong, and the monk Yug'i. This is the famous stupa of Kyŏngch'ŏn Temple that we can admire even today in the gardens of Kyŏngbok Palace. Empress Ki's name does not appear amongst those of the donors. Regardless, the stupa was built and engraved by foreign artists within the framework of Empress Ki's adoption of the temple as her own. From this we can surmise that foreign technicians and artists probably also took care of the reconstruction of the temple itself. One of the temple halls contained a portrait of the great Yuan Prime Minister Toghto, possibly placed there after his death in the twelfth month of 1355. The son of the Prince of Chinnyŏng and Director of Political Affairs Kang Yung, C'hŏn-yu must have brought the portrait to the temple. In fact, Kang Yung's sister was Toghto's wife, and this helps us understand Toghto's relation to the temple.[45]

As mentioned earlier, Empress Ki also invited many Koryŏ monks to preach at the Yuan court. Famous examples are those of T'aego Pou, who was invited to hold a lecture on the *Prajñāpāramitā-sūtra* upon his arrival in Dadu in the year 1346, to celebrate the prince's birthday. He was invited again the following year to hold a religious function at Yongning Temple and was later appointed abbot of the temple itself.

Naong Hyegŭn also held religious functions at Yongning Temple, to which many court nobles participated. He was later appointed abbot of both Yongning and Guangji Chan temples, in Dadu.[46]

Furthermore, the Indian monk Zhigong was close to the Koryŏ monastic community. He preached at court and held several interviews, both with Empress Ki and the heir-prince. Being close to the Koryŏ people, he was highly esteemed and treated with great reverence by the Koryŏ communities in China.

All these cases demonstrate that Empress Ki favored Buddhism, in particular Koryŏ Buddhism, in a world politically dominated by Tibetan Buddhism. She opposed the influence exerted on her son's education by Tibetan priests, advocating the importance of a Confucian upbringing. However, aside from an obvious sincerity of faith, her favor of Koryŏ Buddhism had strong political implications. In fact, she tried to pack the imperial court with eunuchs and ladies from Koryŏ, and she also probably favored officials from her home country, many of whom perhaps were also her relatives, in order to gain a firmer grasp on Yuan court politics. Her unswerving efforts were directed to enthrone her own son if necessary, even before the demise of Emperor Shundi, and the favor she showed to Koryŏ's Buddhist community must be studied in the light of her political objectives.

FINAL CONSIDERATIONS

In this chapter, we have observed a typical case of cultural exchange between two distinct cultural traditions, those of Koryŏ and China during the period of Yuan rule. Mongol domain provided the necessary political conditions for these exchanges to take place to such an important extent.

Koryŏ ladies patronized the foundation of many Buddhist temples in the Yuan capital. We have observed the cases of Lady Im, who financed the reconstruction of Xingfu Temple, Lady Son, who gave her support for the founding of Jinsun Mitosi, Lady Ch'oe and Lady Yun, who built Fawang Temple together with their husband Cho Pun, Lady Kim, the widow of Chaghan Temür, who offered her house to the saṅgha under the name of Fayuansi, and so on.

Koryŏ ladies gave a fundamental contribution to the internationalization of Koryŏ Buddhism, especially through the encouragement provided to foreign monks, the construction of temples, the donation of sūtras, and so on. We need to further our research in the future in order to better appreciate Koryŏ's contribution in this field because here lies the historical importance of the activities of Koryŏ women in China at this time.

However, if their religious activities in China are relatively significant, certainly no less important is the role they must have played in introducing Koryŏ Buddhism to outsiders. We have observed just a few instances, but many more must have taken place that remain undocumented. Many foreign monks, perhaps not as illustrious as Zhigong, must have visited temples in Koryŏ and many foreign artists and artisans must have traveled to Kaegyŏng to boast their talents.

However, the activities of Koryŏ ladies living abroad did not stop with the founding of temples. They were assiduous in calling monks from their homeland, or foreign monks related to Koryŏ communities, like Zhigong, to preside over temples attended by Koryŏ residents in China. Empress Ki was especially prominent in this field. They financed all sorts of initiatives, such as religious ceremonies, the reading of the sūtras, the lighting of lanterns, regularly attending temples to pray and practice meditation, helping the poor, and building a strong social community. This is reminiscent of Empress Ki, who sent eunuchs to distribute food during famines and natural calamities. Many even became nuns, especially when some calamity struck their families, like Lady Wi and Lady Kim, who embraced religious life under the tutelage of Master Zhigong after their husbands had passed away.

The materials accessible to us concern almost exclusively the nobility, but no doubt commoners were deeply involved in giving their contribution to renovating temples as well, helping directly in daily chores at temples and in social work, both in favor of the monastic community and ordinary people in times of need. Unfortunately, we have no material concerning this at present, but this is certainly a field that needs to be further explored.

On the one hand, Koryŏ continued to draw all kinds of information and cultural elements from China. Particularly strong were its traditional relations with South China, to which Koryŏ had always looked to as the cultural inheritor of the Tang. To all this a very important element was added, that of the peculiar character of Mongol rule, which, together with territorial expansion, was bent on the diffusion of new cultural patterns and values. This was felt in the religious field, especially through the official adoption of Tibetan Buddhism as the state religion, also influencing Buddhism in Koryŏ to a certain extent, mainly in its artistic expressions. We also have records of Tibetan monks coming to Koryŏ to proselytize. Again, Koryŏ court ladies played no small role. Their participation was sometimes direct, like Empress Ki, at other times indirect, as we have no clear references, like in the case of Lady Ki, the wife of the Hanlin academician Sharabal.

On the other hand, Koryŏ culture made an important contribution to the enrichment of Yuan court life and, in the religious field, it exported its own version of Buddhism to China, directed not only to the Koryŏ communities in China, but also to the Yuan court, and to those who entered into any kind of relation with Koryŏ expatriates. Also noteworthy are the Buddhist religious functions held at the presence of the Yuan court, especially during Shundi's reign, as we have already seen.

Observations have been made on how Koryŏ court ladies actively sustained the Buddhist religion not only in Yuan China, acting as a bond for Koryŏ communities abroad, but also encouraging the development of Buddhism in their home country. They both financed initiatives to build temples, stimulating international exchange through the activities of Koryŏ monks in China, and also foreign monks like Zhigong in Koryŏ. Aside from that, they promoted the introduction of Koryŏ's ancient Buddhist traditions to Yuan China through several means, such as the diffusion of handwritten copies of the canon—probably both esoteric and exoteric, in gold, silver characters, and in fine print—Buddhist images, both in sculpture and painting, paraphernalia used at temples, local products like paper, wood articles, and so on. By doing so they not only they enriched Yuan culture, but also contributed to the enhancement of Koryŏ's prestige abroad and its international standing at the Yuan court.

NOTES

1. Quan Heng, *Gengshen waishi*, Zhizheng eighteenth year, quoted in Chang Tong-ik, *Wŏndae Yŏsa charyo chimnok* (Collected Records of Koryŏ Historical Materials of the Yuan Period) (Seoul: Seoul National University Press, 1997), 90.

2. Tonino Puggioni, "Wŏndae Ki Hwanghu ŭi Pulgyo huwŏn kwa kŭ chŏngch'ijŏgin ŭiŭi" (Empress Ki's Patronage of Buddhism and Its Political Meaning during the Yuan Dynasty), *Pojo Sasang* (Seoul: Pojo Sasang Yŏn'guwŏn, 2003) 17: 94–183.

3. After the end of the war, many people from Koryŏ went to China to look for their relatives who had been taken prisoner to work as soldiers, artisans, or as peasants; others traveled to China for trade, study, or to visit famous places; some were part of the following of important monks, or princes, courtiers, eunuchs; still others went to China looking for fortune, and so on.

4. Yi Kok, "Koryŏ Ch'ŏnt'ae Pŏbwang-sa gi" (Record of Koryŏ's Ch'ŏnt'ae Pŏbwang-sa), *Kajŏng-jip* (Collected Works of Kajŏng), Book 4.

5. See note 1. We can understand how seriously contemporaries judged this phenomenon from the request of the inspectorate in 1342 to reduce the number of ladies-in-waiting and eunuchs because the majority of eunuchs were from Koryŏ; Quan Heng, *Gengshen waishi*, Zhizheng second year, quoted in Chang Tong-ik, *Wŏndae Yŏsa charyo chimnok*, 89–90.

6. See T'aego Pou, *T'aego Hwasang ŏrok* (Records of the Sayings of Master T'aego), and Naong Hyegŭn, *Naong Hwasang ŏrok* (Records of the Sayings of Master Naong), in *Hanguk Pulgyo chŏnsŏ* (Collected Works of Korean Buddhism) (Seoul: Tongguk University Press, 1984), 6:669–701 and 6:702–729, respectively.

7. Yi Saek, "Sŏch'ŏn Chenappakt'a chonja pudomyŏng pyŏng sŏ" (Stupa Inscription and Preface to Venerable Dhyna bhadra-Sunyadiya), *Mogŭn mungo* (Collected Works of Mogŭn), Book 14.

8. "Zhongxiu Huayantang jingben ji" (Record of the Restoration of the Sūtras' Copies in the Avatamsaka Hall), *Fangshan Shijing tiji huibian* (A Collection of Dedications in the Fangshan Stone Inscriptions) (Beijing: Beijing National Library, 1987), 33–34.

9. King Ch'ungsŏn donated a set of the Tripitaka to Qingshou Temple; Cheng Wenhai, "Daqingshou-si Dazangjing bei," *Chuguo Wenxiangong Xüelou Cheng Xiansheng wenji* (Collected works of *Wenxiangong Xüelou Cheng* of Chu Kingdom), Book 18, quoted in Chang Tong-ik, *Wŏndae Yŏsa charyo chimnok,* 131–133.

10. Li Feihou, *Yucenshan Huiyin Gaoli Huayanjiao sizhi* (Records of the Huayan Huiyin Gaoli Temple on Mount Yucen), 1627; Tonino Puggioni, "Ch'ungsŏn wangdae ŭi Yŏ-Wŏn Pulgyo kwan'gye wa Hangju Koryŏ-sa" (Buddhist Relations between Koryŏ and the Yuan during the Reign of King Ch'ungsŏn and Gaoli Temple in Hangzhou), *Hanguk Sasangsahak* 18 (2002): 301–332. Gaoli-si was a Huayan temple, but we cannot exclude that a reevaluation of the figure of Ŭich'ŏn, the fourth son of King Munjong (1046–1083), actually took place during a time when the royal family strongly supported the Ch'ŏnt'ae sect in Koryŏ, with the foundation of Myoryŏn Temple in Kaegyŏng and the reconstruction of a few other temples belonging to Ŭich'ŏn's tradition. It seems that the Koryŏ royal house wanted to reassert its central role at home after a hundred years of military rule and enhance its prestige abroad by portraying the figure of Ŭich'ŏn as a saint of international standing.

11. Yi Kok, "Kyŏngsa Poŭn Kwanggyo-sa gi" (Inscription of Kwanggyo Gratitude Temple in Dadu), *Kajŏng-jip*, Book 2; Pudu, *Lushan Lianzong Baojian* (Precious Mirror of the White Lotus Tradition of Mount Lu), 1305 (reprint Taipei: Dajue jingshe, 1988); Chang Tong-ik, *Wŏndae Yŏsa charyo chimnok.*

12. Yi Kok, "Taesungŭn Pogwŏn-sa Koryŏ Cheil Taesa Wŏngong pi" (Inscription of Wŏngong of Taesungŭn Pogwŏn-sa), *Kajŏng-jip*, Book 6.

13. Ibid.

14. Ibid.

15. *Yuanshi* (History of Yuan), Book 22, 477–479; Book 24, 535–536; Book 1134, 2873–2874. See also H. Franke and D. Twitchett, eds., *The Cambridge History of China*, Vol. 6, *Alien Regimes and Border States 907–1368* (Cambridge: Cambridge University Press, 1994), 505–507, 533; J. W. Dardess, *Conquerors and Confucians: Aspects of Political Change in Late Yüan China* (New York and London: Columbia University Press, 1973), 12–17; Ko Pyŏng-ik, "Koryŏ Ch'ungsŏnwang ŭi Wŏn Mujong ongnip" (The Enthronement of Yüan Wuzong on Part of the Koryŏ King Ch'ungsŏn), *Tongbin Kim Sang-gi kyosu hwagap kinyŏm* (In Memory of the Sixtieth Birthday of Professor Tongbin Kim Sang-gi), *Sahak Nonch'ong* (Seoul: Yŏksa Hakhoe, 1962).

16. Yi Kok, "Taesungŭn Pogwŏn-sa Koryŏ Cheil Taesa Wŏngong pi," *Kajŏng-jip*, Book 6.

17. Changsŏng was a county in the northwestern area of South Chŏlla Province.

18. Yi Che-hyŏn, "Taedo Namsŏng Hŭngbok-sa kal" (Stone Tablet of Xingfu si in Dadu's Nancheng District), *Ikchae Nango*, Book 6.

19. Ibid.

20. Lady Ki's name does not appear in any other literary sources, so it is difficult to establish her exact identity. She is not to be confused with her more famous relative, who later became Shundi's empress.

21. Dardess, *Conquerors and Confucians*, 201, n. 10.

22. Yi Kok, "Kŭmgang-san Pohyŏn-am pŏphoe gi" (Record on the Buddhist Ceremony Held at Pohyŏn Hermitage on Mount Kŭmgang), *Kajŏng-jip*, Book 2.

23. "Wangpingxian" was the name of the provincial administration overseeing the western section of Dadu and parts of its surrounding areas; Susan Naquin, *Peking: Temples and City Life, 1400–1900* (Los Angeles: University of California Press, 2000), 172–173. See also Nancy Shatzman-Steinhardt, "The Plan of Khubilay Khan's Imperial City," *Artibus Asiae*, no. 44, and idem, *Chinese Imperial City Planning* (Honolulu: University of Hawai'i Press, 1999).

24. *Ducongguan* means "chief commander." The *Ducongguan* shared control of military forces in Dadu Route (*lu*) with a chief military commission headed by a commander-in-chief. Charles O. Hucker, *A Dictionary of Official Titles in Imperial China* (Stanford: Stanford University Press, 1985), 544.

25. Yi Kok, "Kyŏngsa Kim Son Mit'a-sa gi" (Inscription of Jin Sun Mitosi in Dadu), *Kajŏng-jip*, Book 2.

26. Quite unexpectedly, eunuchs had wives, and some of them more than one, as was the case with Pang Sin-u, who was married to the daughter of the prefect of Kaesŏng Yi Kwang-si; Cho Pun, who was married to a Lady Ch'oe; Yi Tae-sun, who was married to a daughter of Wi Tŭg-yu; Ko Yong-bo, who was son-in-law of Sin Ye's sister; and so on. It seems that there were even eunuchs who preserved their sexual power after castration.

27. Yi Kok, "Taedo Ch'ŏnt'ae Pŏbwang-sa gi" (Inscription of Tiantai Fawang Temple in Dadu), *Kajŏng-jip*, Book 4.

28. This must have happened between the years 1324 and 1325 because Zhigong was traveling to Shangdu upon an invitation from Emperor Jinzong (r. 1324–1327). If we consider that Zhigong visited Koryŏ in the year 1326 and was allowed to stay in Shangdu, we can surmise that he must have stopped in Dadu sometime in 1325 at the latest. Yi Saek, "Stupa Inscription and Preface to Venerable Dhyna bhadra-Sunyadiya," *Mogŭn mungo*, Book 14. See also Hŏ Hŭng-sik, *Koryŏ ro omgin Indo ŭi tŭngbul—Chigong Sŏnhyŏn* (The Indian Lamp That Moved to Koryŏ: The Meditation Master Zhigong) (Seoul: Ilchogak, 1997), 32–45.

29. Yi Saek, "Stupa Inscription and Preface to Venerable Dhyna bhadra-Sunyadiya," *Mogŭn mungo*, Book 14.

30. Hŏ Hŭng-sik, *Koryŏ ro omgin Indo ŭi tŭngbul*, 57–58.

31. *Koryŏsa*, Book 122, Biographies, Pang Sin-u.

32. *Koryŏsa*, Book 33, Ch'ungsŏn second year.

33. Yi Kok, "Taedo Taehŭng-hyŏn chunghŭng Yongch'ŏn-sa bi" (Stone Inscription on the Reconstruction of Longquansi in Dadu's Daxing County), *Kajŏng-jip*, Book 6.

34. In'gyŏng, *Mongsan Tŏgi wa Koryŏ hugi Sŏn sasang yŏn'gu* (A Study on Mengshan Deyi and Buddhist Thought in Latter Koryŏ) (Seoul: Puril Ch'ulp'an-sa, 2000), 85–91; Ch'oe Yŏn-sik and Kang Ho-sŏn, *"Mongsan Hwasang Posŏl* e

nat'anan Mongsan ŭi haengjŏk kwa Koryŏ hugi Pulgyogye waŭi kwangye" (Mengshan's Activities as Reflected in the *Mengshan Heshang Pushuo* and His Relations with Later Koryŏ Buddhist Circles), *Pojo Sasang* (Seoul: Pojo Sasang Yŏn'guwŏn, Seoul, 2003), 19:163–206; Kang Ho-sŏn, "Wŏn kansŏpki Mongsan Tŏgi wa Koryŏ Pulgyogye ŭi kyoryu" (The Relations between Mengshan Deyi and Koryŏ Buddhist Circles during the Period of Mongol Control), presented in Korean, abstract in English, *Proceedings of the 21st Conference of the Association for Korean Studies in Europe*, Rome, 2003, 283–288.

35. Yi Kok provides the year of Ayūshridar's birth in the beginning of his "Kŭmgangsan Changan-sa chunghŭng gi" (Inscription on the Reconstruction of Changan Temple on Kŭmgang Mountain), *Kajŏng-jip*, Book 6, when he says that the excellent emperor, after seven years of reign, had a son with Queen Ki. Soon after the birth of her son, Queen Ki was given the title of empress and moved to Xingcheng Palace.

36. 1 *kan* was 1.818 meters; therefore, 80 *kan* were 145.44 square meters.

37. Yi Kok, "Taedo Ch'ŏnt'ae Pŏbwang-sa gi" (Inscription of Tiantai Fawang Temple in Dadu), *Kajŏng-jip*, Book 4.

38. Yi Kok, "Kŭmgang-san Changan-sa chunghŭng gi" (Inscription on the Reconstruction of Changan Temple on Kŭmgang Mountain), *Kajŏng-jip*, Book 6.

39. The rear side of the inscription is not extant, and for this information we have relied on a reference contained within the inscription itself.

40. Yi Saek, "Pogae-san Chijang-sa Chungsu gi" (Inscription on the Renovation of Chijang Temple of Pogae Mountain), *Mogŭn mungo*, Book 6.

41. Chen Gaohua, "Yuandai Dadu de Huangjia Fosi" (Imperial Buddhist Temples in Dadu during the Yuan), *Shijie Zongjiao Yanjiu* 2 (1992): 2–3.

42. Wei Su, "Gaoli Haizhou Shenguang-si bei," *Wei Taipu Wenxüji*, Book 3, *Yuanren Wenji Zhenben Congkan*, Vol. 7; quoted also in Chang Tong-ik, *Wŏndae Yŏsa charyo chimnok*, 99–103. An article by Chang Tong-ik also addresses this subject: "Wi So ŭi Singwang-Pogwang-sa pimune taehan kŏmt'o" (An Analysis of Wei Su's Stone Inscriptions on Singwang and Pogwang Temples), *Kyŏngbuktae Nonmun-jip*, no. 51 (Taegu, 1991).

43. Singwang-sa cho (Singwang Temple Entry), *Chōsen jisatsu shiryō* (Historical Materials on Korean Temples) (Keijō: Chōsen Shōtokufu, 1911; reprint Seoul: Chungang Munhwa Ch'upl'an-sa, 1968), 309.

44. According to Wei Su, who wrote the inscription with the aid of a copy of the temple records given to him by the monk Kwengyŏn, Singwang-sa had been founded during the Silla dynasty after Master Taejing sailed back from the Liang (502–557), bringing with him a picture of the Five Hundred Lohan (Skt. *arhat*). The rough seas wrecked the ship, and only the box containing the sealed copy of the Lohan picture was recovered. Thereupon the Silla king ordered a Lohan hall to be built on Puksung Mountain, and the place became a pilgrimage site due to the miracles the picture was believed to have performed; Wei Su, "Gaoli Haizhou Shenguang-si bei."

45. Probably taking into account what is recorded in the *Sinchŭng Tongguk Yŏji Sŭngnam* (Newly Enlarged Survey of the Geography of Korea), Book 13 (P'ungdŏk County, Temples, Kyŏngch'ŏn Temple) and in the *Sok Tongmunsŏn* (Supplement to the Anthology of Korean Literature), Book 21, the *Chunggyŏng-ji* (Records of the Middle Capital), Book 6 states that the temple was Toghto's family temple. However, given the scale of the work and the mobilization of foreign artists, it seems more appropriate to think that Empress Ki had founded the temple, as stated in Ch'ae Su's *Yu Songdo-rok* (Record of a Trip to Songdo), Part 1. Besides, it would make little sense for the Empress to donate so lavishly to a temple built by a foreign prime minister in her own country of origin. The contrary is much more plausible. See also Chin Hong-sŏp, ed., *Hanguk Misulsa Charyo Chipsŏng (1) Samguk Sidae—Koryŏ Sidae* (Collection of Materials on the History of Korean Art (1) Three Kingdoms to Koryŏ) (Seoul: Ilchisa, 1987; 3rd ed. 1996), 45, 156–157.

46. The fact that Koryŏ monks were regularly appointed abbots to these temples makes us surmise that Koryŏ residents in Dadu may have founded or renovated them.

5

Two Female Masters of Two Eras

Differences and Commonalities in Roles

Heung-sik Heo
Translated by John Jorgensen

The word *yŏdaesa* means a female master. Epitaphs and stupa stelae survive for them. Although bhikṣuṇī is a term that encompasses female master, "master" had the sense of "eminent cleric," and so *yŏdaesa* meant a model bhikṣuṇī (nun) who excelled in practice and behavior. Many nuns were unable to leave their names to Korean history, but there are a fair number whose names have been transmitted. However, compared to the numbers of monks known to us, there are only a few nuns, and comparatively little material exists about them. Even fewer were titled "female master"—in fact, only two: Chinhye (1255—11 February 1324), and Chŏngyu (1717—15 November 1782). Thus, Chinhye was active in the late Koryŏ dynasty (918–1392), and Chŏngyu in the late Chosŏn (1392–1910) period. The secular background to their lives differed, but they deserve attention as special women. Their lives were separated by five hundred years.

Master Chinhye was granted a posthumous title,[1] whereas Master Chŏngyu is referred to as "the Master" only in a stele inscription written by a famous literatus-official.[2] Yet the fact that the term was recorded in the collected works of this scholar, who later became famous as a prime minister, implies an evaluation the equivalent of official approval. Although there are no grounds for claiming that there were royally approved cloisters for the exclusive use of nuns from the time Buddhism was adopted in the Three Kingdoms period through most of the Koryŏ period, the Chŏngŏpwŏn (the palace nunnery) was established at least from the end of the Koryŏ.[3] Since 1945, there has been a tendency for the numbers of nuns building or leading meditation cloisters or nunneries to increase. To understand this tradition, it is necessary to take note of the examples of Chŏngyu and Chinhye.

Our study of Chinhye and Chŏngyu will be advanced in three perspectives. First, the lives of these two model nuns are thoroughly analyzed. I begin with Chŏngyu rather than Chinhye because Chŏngyu's life and achievements are more significant, given that in the Chosŏn dynasty Confucianism was a state ideology oppressing Buddhist activities, and yet she left an inscription, whereas Chinhye lived in late Koryŏ when a number of nuns' grave inscriptions survived. Second, the life and achievements of each female master are valued on the basis of the universal values of the period rather than her particular features as a nun. Finally, I highlight the differences in their social backgrounds and in their lives.

Even though human achievements are evaluated as models, when examined from different time periods, it is common for them to become the object of criticism. The values of each age differ, and it is possible that the human environment that made that age what it was also functioned as a restraint on values. For the evaluation of humans in general, it is difficult in any age to achieve a consensual objectivity. However, if a person has maintained model conduct with a noble character, he or she will be esteemed even in another age, and the prejudices of the age making the evaluation will be abandoned. Even though there is a tendency for history to reflect the values of that age in which it is written, sometimes one can propose hypotheses presenting universal values that overcome the limits of the times.

MASTER CHŎNGYU OF THE CHOSŎN

Confucianism was the culture of the ruling class in Chosŏn-dynasty Korea. It was applied as a method of government and education from the Three Kingdoms period on. In the Sung dynasty in China, Confucianism was transformed into neo-Confucianism through an expansion of its intellectual bases. Neo-Confucianism was adopted in Korea in the later Koryŏ period, and strengthened in the early Chosŏn as the leading concept of government, gradually merging with state rituals and expanding into religious functions. In the latter half of the sixteenth century, royally chartered Confucian academies were formed, and as policy shifted from the oppression of Buddhism to its abolition, Confucianism secured a base even in regional society.

The seventeenth century was the zenith of neo-Confucianism. In the latter half of the eighteenth century, Catholicism—called Sŏhak

(Western Learning)—began to appear, but this was restricted to one part of the intelligentsia and so was insignificant. Thus, the glory days of neo-Confucianism continued. Buddhism was officially recognized for its role in countering the Hideyoshi invasions (1592–1598), with Chŏnghŏ Hyujŏng (Master Sŏsan) leading a monk army in defending the state. Moreover, in the first half of the seventeenth century, in the transition period between the Ming and the Ch'ing courts, the monk army built fortresses in the Pukhan and Namhan mountains to protect the northern and southern approaches to the capital, Hansŏng. Buddhist monks continued to support and repair these forts. With the expansion of the *yangban* clans, there was a reduction in the number of ordinary commoners (*yangin*) responsible for military service, so the role of the monk-soldiers, who were despised just like the *ch'ŏnin* (outcastes), increased in importance. From the time of Hideyoshi's invasions, the commanders of the monk army received official posts from the state.

In the Silla and Koryŏ periods, when Buddhism prospered, state academicians wrote stele inscriptions for eminent monks. Examples of such writings were commonplace, but from the early Chosŏn they suddenly shrank in number and became almost nonexistent. This was the mark of a different age. Beginning in the seventeenth century, however, stele inscriptions by academicians who practiced Confucianism reappeared on the stupas that were the graves of eminent monks. Again, in the eighteenth century, the numbers of inscriptions for eminent monks written by neo-Confucian scholars increased. At the end of the eighteenth century, the Confucian scholar Pŏnam Ch'ae Che-gong (1720–1799), who held the post of prime minister for a decade, wrote a number of inscriptions for eminent monks. In this he was not unusual.

At this time, aside from a small minority of eminent monks, most monks were held in contempt. Thus, for the Confucian scholar Ch'ae Che-gong to write a stele inscription for a nun was indeed uncommon. The inscription for a female master that is recorded in his *Pŏnamjip* (Collected works of Pŏnam) is also found in collections of inscriptions.[4] Because this inscription has not been translated before, it is given here in its entirety:

The Stupa Inscription for the Female Master Chŏngyu, together with a Preface

> The Master's lay surname was Kang. She was the daughter of a commoner family of P'yŏngyang. Her character was calm and pure, and she had none of the desires of ordinary people. From a young age she placed her faith in the Buddhas and patriarchs, and onions, garlic, and meat did

not touch her lips. From early in the morning until night she intoned the Buddhist scriptures, unaware of the passing of time. She made up her mind to visit famous scenic sites and went there as often as she went outdoors. She broke the night by worshipping the Big Dipper (Ursa Major), then she would enter her room and quietly close her eyes and sit in meditation, but she would not go to sleep.

In 1775, I had finished up as Inspector of P'yŏngan Province and was returning to Hanyang when one day the Master visited me. I asked, "What is your aim in coming from afar to visit me? Where do you live?" She answered, "I am a peasant from Kwansŏ (P'yŏngan Province) and your eminence's grace [the good administration of the Inspector while in office] was endless. Although I only have a woman's body, I had to come and visit to give my thanks." Then she stayed at my house, helped my wife and served my mother, staying for several months before departing. She did the same the next year and again the following year, and she never appeared to be the slightest bit tired.

I lost my wife, and when I dwelt on Mount Myŏngdŏk, the Master sought me out. She said, "I have formed a link with the monk K'waeho like that of a mother and child, and he is supporting this elderly person." Following this, she had K'waeho introduce himself. I had the Ch'unsŏng Hall cleaned and had the Master and K'waeho live there. Late at night I would walk around the lotus [pond] supported on a cane, and when I looked up through the thicket, I would see the light of a single lamp shining in the window, and I could hear her voice reading the Buddhist sūtras, sometimes low and sometimes distinct, carried on the breeze through the pines and gullies, and so I would know that the Master had not gone to sleep. I was suddenly aware that this is a joy of living in the mountains.

Not long after, the Master came bringing her good clothes, saying, "I am going to Hwajang Hermitage at Changdan[5] to have my hair shaved and become a nun." When she said this, she was already over sixty years of age. I consoled her, saying, "Do you really need to do this?" politely trying to dissuade her. The Master said, "Death is not far off, and I wish to go and enter nirvana. If I do not take the tonsure, I fear I will not be able to achieve my desire." Then, with tears streaming down, she said, "I am sad that I cannot promise to meet you again."

Several months after she left for Hwajang Hermitage, a letter arrived, informing me that, "On a certain day my head was shaved. My Dharma name is Chŏngyu. My Dharma master is Yuram Sik'wal." On the fifteenth of the eleventh month in 1782, the Master died at the age of sixty-six *se* (years). When she was cremated, *śarīra* beads were produced.[6] K'waeho and I transported her relics to Ch'ilsŏng Hermitage in Kwansŏ, where we erected a stupa, and K'waeho requested that I write recording the facts in her memory.

In the summer of 1778, when I was returning from a mission to Yen-ching, I crossed the Ch'ŏngch'ŏn River at night. The Master had walked 200 *ri* (80 km) from P'yŏngyang and crossed the river to meet me. When we saw each other, we were very happy. When she got into the boat, she cut up a watermelon and gave it to me. How can I forget such sincerity? In later days, when I faced a disaster, she entered deep into the mountains to purify herself with ablutions, and she prayed to the gods until dawn. When she had finished one hundred days [of these austerities], I wondered who could be more sincere than her. When I die, no one will be able to convey this, so because I cannot forget the Master, I have engraved this in my mind:

Why is it that this world suffers and the other world is a Pure Land?
Although she disliked the [burial in a] tomb, and wished for cremation,
Whether one is buried in the ground or burned
It is the same, as one reverts to nothingness.
What difference is there, then, between them?
I will say,
Because you had no desire or dislike for anything in the world,
If you see Śākyamuni,
Please use my words to ask [about this].

The peculiarity of "The Stupa Inscription for the Female Master Chŏngyu" is that it consists almost entirely of Chŏngyu's connections with its author, Ch'ae Che-gong. It is clear that the Master's lay surname was Kang, that she was from P'yŏngyang and was the daughter of a commoner family. Beyond that, her life after she met the author is divided into the three stages of (1) her ties with the author, (2) her entrance into the Buddhist order, and (3) her death, as shown in the following table.

Chronological Comparison
of the Lives of Master Chŏngyu and Pŏnam Ch'ae Che-gong

Chŏngyu	Ch'ae Che-gong
Surname Kang; daughter of a P'yŏngyang commoner.	Member of the Ch'ae clan of P'yŏngyang.
1717 Born.	1720 Born and raised at Hongsŏng. Takes Yaksan O Kwang'un as a teacher, studies under Kang Pak.
	1735 Passes the provincial exams.
	1736 Marries daughter of O Hong'un.
	1751, 1st month. Wife dies; exiled to Samch'ŏk [Kangwŏn Province].
	1752 Remarries a woman of the Kwŏn clan of Andong. There were no children to look after.[a]
	1758 Shifts to O Kwang'un's home.
	1762 In mourning for mother.
	1764 In mourning for father.
	1767 The death of Chang Tŏg'yang, who had lived for ten years as a housewoman.[b]
1775 Visits Ch'ae Che-gong, gives thanks, and resides with him for several months.	1775 P'yŏng'an Province Inspector, incident of assault by secondary son.
1776 As above.	1776 Birth of secondary son, Honggŭn.
1777 As above.	
1778 Encounter with Ch'ae Che-gong at Ch'ŏng-ch'ŏn River on his return from mission to Ch'ing.	

1779 Resides at Ch'un-sŏng Hall on Mount Myŏngdŏk. Ordained as a nun by Dharma master Yuram Sikhwal. Dharma name Chŏngyu.	1779 Dismissed from official post, moves to Mount Myŏngdŏk.
1782, 15 November Dies, aged sixty-six years.	1782 Rises to post of Chief of the Board of the Military, shifts to Map'o.
	1786 Secondary son Hongsin dies at age of eight.[c] His mother was a concubine of the Kim clan of P'yŏngyang.
	1787 His wife of the Andong Kwŏn clan, Lady Chŏnggyŏng, dies.[d]
	1792 His eighteen-year-old secondary son, Honggŭn, dies.[e]
	1799 Dies.

[a] *Pŏnamjip* fascicle 38, "Che mangsil Chŏnggyŏng Puin Kwŏnssi mun" (*Han'guk munjip ch'onggan* 236:558).

[b] *Pŏnamjip* fascicle 37, "Che Kyŏm'in Chang Tŏg'yang mun" (*Han'guk munjip ch'onggan* 236:162).

[c] "Sŏja Hongsin yeji," *Pŏnamjip* fascicle 54 (*Han'guk munjip ch'onggan* 246:517). Hongsin was born when Ch'ae Che-gong was sixty years old, and died of smallpox on the seventeenth day of the second month at the Myŏngdŏk residence.

[d] *Pŏnamjip* fascicle 35, "Che mangsil Chŏnggyŏng Puin Kwŏnssi mun" (*Han'guk munjip ch'onggan* 236:182). Lady Chŏnggyŏng lived for thirty-five years after marrying Ch'ae Che-gong. She raised as her own (1) the five offspring of Ch'ae Che-gong's sister, who had been married to a Mr. Yi, and also (2) Ch'ae's two secondary sons, one each born to his two concubines. When Hongwŏn became his heir, he recalled that she did not eat and yet said she was full (probably meaning that she was satisfied that he was the heir). When Ch'ae's secondary son Hongsin died of smallpox (see note *c*), she grieved as if he was her own son, even suffering an illness due to excessive grief. Ch'ae Che-gong had previously prepared a tomb for himself and his first wife, and buried Hongsin nearby, saying that he wished to make the secondary son welcome. Lady Chŏnggyŏng died at the age of fifty-four, when Ch'ae Che-gong was sixty-eight years of age.

[e] *Pŏnamjip* fascicle 38, "Che mang sŏja Honggŭn mun" (*Han'guk munjip ch'onggan* 236:188). Ch'ae Che-gong's secondary son Honggŭn was eighteen at the time, and had been married the previous year. Ch'ae then adopted the seven-year-old son of Hongdŭk, his second cousin (via a concubine), and arranged for the support of both Honggŭn's wife and Honggŭn's mother (Ch'ae's concubine)—worrying, while he grieved, about whether this would split up the family. In this text, Ch'ae Che-gong states that he was fifty-six years old when his son Honggŭn was born, and although Hongsin was born later to another concubine, it is certain that he died earlier. The text also says that to find out whether Hongwŏn, Ch'ae's heir (see note *d*), had made it onto the list of 1792 exam passers, Honggŭn had waited outside the palace gates from dawn on, but that in the evening his horse bolted at the sound of the announcements and he fell off and fractured a bone, making him even sorer than before at Ch'ae Che-gong's designating Hongwŏn his heir. When Ch'ae Che-gong composed the plaque for Honggŭn, he wrote that he regretted having left his property under his heir Hongwŏn's control. According to the list of successful graduates in the higher civil service exams compiled by the state, Ch'ae Hongwŏn's natural father was Min'gong, and Hongwŏn passed the 1792 palace exams in the last place in the third category.

The ties between Ch'ae Che-gong and Master Chŏngyu began when Ch'ae went to take up a new post after having been Inspector of P'yŏngan Province. Besides the fact that Chŏngyu was the daughter of a commoner who lived in P'yŏngyang, we know nothing about her secular connections except that she had a deep connection with Ch'ae. The human relationship she had, before she was ordained and after, with the monk K'waeho—described in the inscription as akin to the ties between a mother and son—may have involved complications that were difficult to resolve in terms of Confucian ethics. Yet in the inscription only her life and her relationship with the author are recorded. The dramatic space for the master is directly related to the public offices of Ch'ae Che-gong. When Ch'ae resigned from the post of Inspector and went home, the master sought him out to thank him for his good administration, and for the next three years returned for several months at a time to assist in his domestic affairs.

In the fourth year, Ch'ae completed his duties as an envoy to Yen-ching, and on his trip back, the master crossed Ch'ŏngch'ŏn River and came out to greet him. The next year he had problems in his official career and so retired to Mount Myŏngdŏk, and it seems that he had the ordained monk K'waeho and the master reside in Ch'unsŏng Hall. The next turning point is when the master left Ch'unsŏng Hall and took holy orders.

Ch'ae Che-gong's chronological history and his genealogy have not been compiled. An official's chronological history mainly records his public life and the setbacks to his career, in which family ordeals can be crucial. Ch'ae was raised in Hongsŏng, Ch'ungch'ŏng Province. His guide (or original teacher), Yaksan O Kwang-un, was the cousin of his father-in-law, O Hong-un. He was married when he was seventeen, and fifteen years later, when he was thirty-two, his wife of the O clan died. The next year he remarried a woman of the Kwŏn clan, but despite that, six years later he moved to the home of O Kwang-un. The love for his first wife must have been deep and persistent.

Because Ch'ae and the master were a man and a woman in a period when men and women were thoroughly segregated, their age difference and family relationships are very important. Ch'ae had no children with his first and second wives, though he had two sons, one with each of two concubines, beginning at the age of fifty-six. In 1750, he received a post in a southern district. When he left to go there, his wife of the O clan was six or seven months pregnant.[7] In 1751, she was unable to produce an heir and died. In 1752, Ch'ae married a woman of the Andong Kwŏn clan, but he had no children with her, either.

Ch'ae's younger sister lost her husband, who left her with five children. Ch'ae took care of them by joining forces with his parents, but his sister also died soon after. His wife of the Kwŏn clan, Lady Chŏnggyŏng, looked after the five children as her own. Among them was a handicapped child. Ch'ae's *kyŏmin* (housewoman), Ms. Chang, who had let her hair hang down her back until her parents passed away, died three years later. Ch'ae had a son with each of his two concubines—concubine Kim from P'yŏngyang and another. Lady Chŏnggyŏng was not jealous and brought the two boys up as if they were her own children.

In 1775, when the master first visited Ch'ae, he had resigned from his post. The master filled the place left by housewoman Chang due to her death and assisted Lady Chŏnggyŏng. Lady Chŏnggyŏng was forty-two at the time, and the other concubine had given birth to Ch'ae's secondary son Hong-gŭn. Ch'ae was fifty-six. At fifty-nine, the master was of an age when she had no sex appeal.

When Ch'ae was sixty, he retired onto Mount Myŏngdŏk, and the next year the master, at the age of sixty-three, came to live in the Ch'unsŏng Hall within the compound where Ch'ae resided. It is uncertain whether the master stayed there for as long as one season. The master is known to have joined the Buddhist order three years before she died. She went to Hwajang Monastery, where dharma master Yuram Sik'wal was her ordination master. Hwajang Monastery, like Mount Myŏngdŏk, is in Kyŏnggi Province.

The master was ordained when she had only a short span of life remaining, and although Ch'ae Che-gong writes in his stupa inscription that he tried indirectly to dissuade her, he could not block her intention to be ordained. The master, after she was ordained, offered her heartfelt thanks by praying for Ch'ae for one hundred days. In 1782, when she died and was cremated, the monk K'waeho saved her *śarīra* beads and prepared a stupa for her at Ch'ilsŏng Hermitage on Mount Myohyang, close to her hometown. K'waeho visited Ch'ae, who then composed the stupa inscription, which is found in his collected works. In the same year, the author unexpectedly revived his official career with a post as the Chief of the Board of the Military. Later he also held the post of prime minister for ten years concurrently.

MASTER CHINHYE OF KORYŎ

Master Chinhye's deeds have come to us through a tomb inscription. The late Chosŏn Sirhak scholar An Chŏng-bok deciphered and transmitted various tomb inscriptions from the vicinity of Kaesŏng, and this inscription is among them.[8] The master's story was recorded only because of her husband's eminent lineage.[9] Although these tomb inscriptions have been translated and recorded a number of times—because they can be used to fill in the lives of people who were related in the broad sense, including relatives by marriage[10]—no articles to date have noticed that Chinhye was a woman who was posthumously honored with the title of master.

Although attention has been drawn to writings on the aristocratic lineages of relatives by marriage that included Chinhye,[11] they have only noticed her as one of a number of nuns.[12] The master's dharma name was Sŏnghyo. Chinhye was the posthumous title granted to her by the state. Her father and mother both had pedigrees belonging to first-rank Koryŏ aristocrats who intermarried with the royal house. She was married when she was fourteen to Kim Pyŏn of Ŏnyang. Her parents' lineages, plus that of her husband, were those of distinguished clans that produced examination graduates for generation after generation—clans that even had members who had risen to the level of prime minister. Although she lost her husband when she was forty-seven, she had produced four boys and three girls.

Around the time she was married, she was so distinguished by her beauty and character that she was sought in marriage by a house that was among the final power-holders of the military regime, which made her parents anxious. Even before she joined the order, this woman had deep faith, and, after her husband died, she became even more devoted to Buddhism and assisted Buddhist services by offering her devotion and property. She joined the order at the age of sixty-one, and until her life ended at the age of seventy, she explored Buddhist sites and lived a pure life. The author of her stele inscription praised her as an excellent female master, the likes of whom appeared but once in a thousand years. The master's life can be organized simply in a chronological list, as follows:

1 *se*	1225	Born the eldest daughter of Hŏ Kong.
14	1268	Married to Kim Pyŏn of Ŏnyang; later gave birth to four boys and three girls.
47	1301	Husband died.
48	1302	When Mugŭk was returning from Chiang-Huai (a region in southeastern China), she admired him and listened to his sermon.

50	1304	When Ch'ŏlsan Sogyŏng came from Kiangnan (a region to the southeast of the Yangze River in China), she received the Mahayana precepts from him.
57	1311	Visited Mi-lo Great Cloister, explored Mounts Nieh-p'an and Ch'ing-liang.
61	1315	Joined the Buddhist order. Dharma name Sŏnghyo. Precepts master Pai-hsiu.
62	1316	Visited T'ongdo monastery, received twelve *śarīra* beads; visited Kyerim (Kyŏngju).
66	1320	Obtained a place on Namsan in Kaegyŏng (Kaesŏng) and built a thatched hut there.
70	1324	Fell sick on the eleventh day of the second month. Died on fourth day of the third month. Grave inscription erected in the fourth month.

As mentioned earlier, the master was born in an aristocratic clan and was married at fourteen. At the time her husband died when she was forty-seven, she had four boys and three girls. Her husband, Kim Pyŏn, was born in 1248. He was seven years older and died at the age of fifty-four. The average life span calculated for the later Koryŏ population, including the outcastes, was forty-three; for commoners it was forty-six.[13] This means that he lived beyond the average life span.

In her natal home, there were five siblings of the same mother and four children of her maternal aunt. Her husband's siblings and her own offspring by chance coincided in numbers: four boys and three girls. (As members of distinguished clans, both groups gave birth to as many children as possible, having been raised not to lose such a good environment.) She was married for thirty-four years, and lived for another twenty-three years after her husband died. Her personal history as a nun at the end of her life led to her receiving the posthumous title of Master Chinhye.

The Master's life can be divided broadly in two stages: (1) her life as a woman in the secular world, and (2) her life as a nun after joining the Buddhist order. The clerical life was only the last decade, though her lay life after her husband died was enhanced by her life of faith, her support for Buddhist services, and her exploration of Buddhist sites, which were good preparation for joining the order.

After setting out the careers of members of the master's natal home, details about her husband and their children, and their marriage relations, the tomb inscription describes her character and deeds.

Chinhye's genealogy—and, of course, the lineages of her father, mother, husband, and siblings—possessed all the requisites of an influential clan. Described simply, they are as follows:

Father's lineage	Father, Hŏ Kong, meritorious subject, worshipped at the royal shrine. For generations, members of this lineage were graduates of the civil service exams, prime ministers, and held literati positions.
Grandmother's lineage	Yi clan of Inju, at times the most distinguished clan after that of the royal house.
Mother's lineage	Descendants of Yun Kwan, one of the greatest of the noble lineages. Meritorious subjects and exam graduates produced generation after generation.
Husband	Prime Minister Kim Pyŏn of Ŏnyang, held posts of academician and military minister concurrently.
Nine siblings	The majority of the males passed the exams; the son of the third younger brother and the sixth younger sister married into the royal house.
Seven children	Eldest son, Yun, passed exams. Second son, U. Third son, Master Ch'ŏngo, Hyŏnbyŏn, abbot of Kamŭn Monastery. Fourth son, Yŏch'an, highest marks in the monastic exams, Sŏn Master of Mount Kaji. First daughter, husband Yi Kye-ham. Second daughter, selected as a palace lady offered to the Yüan court. Third daughter, husband Wŏn Sŏnji.

In the Koryŏ, the conditions for the formation of a distinguished clan were (1) many descendants in the father's lineage, (2) the continuous production of examination graduates, (3) the existence of meritorious subjects, and (4) the broadening of appointment by privilege as far as possible to descendants. Next, one had to have relatives by marriage who were examination graduates, and it was helpful if they inherited property and status. The noblest members of the distinguished clans married into the royal house and were incorporated as royal clansmen. This was the ultimate level. After the submission to the Yüan, while suffering from having to present court ladies and hostages (*chilja* or *tongnohwa*) to the Yüan, one could use the foreign power to achieve results that added to real power-holding in Koryŏ. Buddhist monasteries indirectly assisted the clans by being places where the clergy had social exchanges and engaged in financial and cultural activities. The master herself possessed all of these without exception, being a woman who was positioned in the core of the aristocracy.

At the time of her husband's death, he was in the first rank of meritorious subjects. Having held the posts of prime minister, academician, and senior general concurrently, while she was a noblewoman of middle age left with seven children, riches, and honors. The author of the tomb inscription, Kim Kaemul, was a relative by marriage. When her husband died, the master did not stint but inaugurated Buddhist services in honor of her late husband and, about the time she joined the order, continued to provide Buddhist services and visit Buddhist sites.

The tomb inscription is a biography that praises virtues, not an objective narrative, and so is limited. It tends to embellish the life story with descriptions of character and sponsorship of Buddhist services. Since there were many cases of people trying to gain indulgences by making small donations to monasteries, there are records that sound a warning by highly valuing donations like the master's, which came from the heart, such as those from impoverished believers that are recorded in the Buddhist sūtras and the *Samguk yusa* (Memorabilia of the Three Kingdoms). Records about the character of a child raised in a wealthy family are even easier to embellish, and so it is necessary to freshly and critically study them in light of the family environment and the time period in which the child was born. The tomb inscription has the following to say about the master's birth and her character before she was married at fourteen:

> She was born in 1255. Her character was modest and trustworthy, and she was pretty and circumspect. From a young age, even when she played, her attitude was extraordinary, and in her childhood her character was conspicuous, and on a number of occasions it surprised people.

It was in the period of Ch'oe Hang's power when she was born as the first daughter of her father who was then twenty-three. When she was four, her father Hŏ Kong passed the examinations, with Ch'oe Cha as the official examiner, and it seems this was another happy event in the family. When she had grown up, her family attempted to marry her to Yumu, the son of Im Yŏn. However, worrying about the prospects of the powerful minister, they married her off instead to Kim Pyŏn. The fact that the family had faced this crisis as a consequence is not recorded in the master's tomb inscription.[14] From 1268, when she was married, until 1270, Im Yŏn held real power and eliminated many of the military officials he disliked. The master's father Hŏ Kong, who was a target for elimination, had left the capital to conduct funeral services for his late wife, barely escaping this purge. From the time of her marriage until her husband's death, the master displayed a disposition to lead her family. This can be seen in the following passage from the tomb inscription:

> When she was married at fourteen, she ably tended to her husband, devoted her efforts to meals and weaving, and fulfilled the propriety of a wife. When she worshipped the ancestors in the home, she knew not a little of the regulations, and there was no occasion when she did not assist. When she became a mother and gave birth to her children, and they were infants who still lacked the power of discrimination, she taught each of the children the basic duties. Early on she counseled, "If a male is not restrained and vigilant, he will become treacherous and unjust, and be useless; if a female is not restrained and vigilant, she will be unreasonable and biased toward that to which she is already partial." When the wife has integrity and encourages [the children] like this, she becomes a model for the whole clan and the family will prosper.

Her characteristics are revealed from her activities related to the funeral and sacrifices for her late husband, and the Buddhist services in his honor, as described in the tomb inscription:

> In 1301, when her husband predeceased her, she was very sad, but she declined a state funeral. She prepared the funerary equipment herself and prepared a grave site on the southern slopes of Mount Taedŏk. When the funeral was over, she built a house to the southwest that could be seen from the grave site, and she also built a monastery less than 1 *ri* (400 m) distant, making it a place to pray for his happiness in the afterlife. She named it Kamŭng Monastery. She donated all the goods and treasures of the household,

> and requested the monks to copy out the *Wŏndon Sūtra*[15] in ink mixed with gold and silver. Besides this she initiated not a few Buddhist services.
>
> Although she became a widow at forty-seven, she went to the grave personally on the first and fifteenth days of the month to perform sacrifices, and while observing the three years of mourning, no matter how cold or hot it was, she did not neglect [these sacrifices]. Even after this, on the days for the offer of sacrifices, she abstained from going on outings, and although there were no occasions on which she did not go [to the tomb] like at the very first, after she became a nun she stopped doing so.

Following the completion of some of the Buddhist services in her husband's memory, the master became even more fascinated with Buddhism. She personally attended the dharma assemblies of eminent monks and listened to the sermons, and, while receiving the precepts, she deepened her faith. Through praying to the Buddha, going on pilgrimage to visit Buddhist sites, and, training herself, she finally joined the order and became a nun. Her tomb inscription records her activities up until the time she joined the order:

> In 1302, when Sŏn Master Mugŭk[16] was coming back by boat from Chiang-Huai, she met and venerated him, and heard his sermon for the first time. In 1304, when Master Ch'ŏlsan came from the south and was proselytizing, she went out and received the Mahayana precepts. In 1311, she packed up her bags and went to Mi-lo Great Cloister, and offered up worship to the sixteen-foot stone Buddha. While making pilgrimage to various mountains and rivers, she even went to the holy ruins on the two mountains, Nieh-p'an and Ch'ing-liang. In 1315 she had her hair shaved off and became a nun. Her Dharma name was Sŏnghyo, and the precepts-platform Master Pai-hsiu was her teacher.
>
> In 1316 she went to T'ongdo Monastery and obtained twelve *śarīra* beads, and when she went to the past eastern country of righteousness of Kyerim [the capital of Silla], because of its many glories, she went around there looking to her heart's content. Although she had been sightseeing to innumerable mountains and rivers, here ends mention of it. In 1320 she chose a site on the south side of Namsan

> in Kaegyŏng, built a thatched hut, and lived there. Because her eldest son's house was on the west side, when her husband died, she followed the son, because she obeyed the examples of the [Confucian] moral precepts.

This widow supported Buddhism and participated in Buddhist services, and we can suppose that the monk who returned from Chiang-Huai was the Koryŏ native, Hon'gu, who had the style Mugŭk. There is evidence that Ch'ŏlsan was the Koryŏ native who was heir to Meng-shan, who was an eminent monk in Kiangnan. Meng-shan's fame spread from Hsiu-hsiu Hermitage; later he exercised a great influence on Korean Buddhism, though in the Chinese Buddhist world he was rather unknown.[17] The master's death and the posthumous grant of the title of Master Chinhye by the state are described in the tomb inscription as follows:

> On the eleventh of the second month of 1324 she fell ill, and on the fourth day of the third month she departed this world in the thatched hut at the age of seventy. Even when she was about to die, her speech was untroubled and her actions were as normal. Since the office in charge was informed of her obituary notice, and in her integrity she constantly obeyed the state system, she was praised. She was posthumously granted the titles Lady of the Pyŏn Han Country and Master Chinhye—a rare event. On the fourth day of the fourth month of this year, when they held the funeral together at the ancestral graveyard, they followed the intentions of a wife who followed after a husband, [burying her] a few paces to the west [of his grave] in the graveyard.

DIFFERENCES BETWEEN THE TWO LIVES

The stupa inscription of Chŏngyu and the tomb inscription of Chinhye are the main records for these two female masters. They are concise because they had to be in a literary style appropriate to the limited space for recording on stone. The historical narratives that use epigraphy are called *myŏng* (inscriptions), and are further restricted by the fact that one has to read between the lines of the prefaces that explain the condensed verse. Furthermore, there were close relationships between the authors of such inscriptions and those praised. If the author had received a commission to write them, the inscriptions also have the limitation of concealing unfortunate facts.

The two female Buddhist masters studied here lived five hundred years apart. Besides the fact that Chŏngyu was born the daughter of a commoner, nothing of her family background is known. The fact that, as a laywoman, she had a mother–son relationship with the monk K'waeho is not explained, though he may have been a distant relative. We also lack a concrete explanation of the good governance of the inspector, Ch'ae Che-gong, made in relation to Chŏngyu.

Chinhye, in contrast, was born into a distinguished aristocratic clan. This may seem fortunate, but the reality was a bit different. Her father had lost his first wife; the second wife was the daughter of his first wife's younger sister—his niece-in-law who had been brought up in the household. This was a marriage custom related to the tradition that a man married his late wife's younger sister. It is likely that this had a severe impact on the family relationships of Master Chinhye. Later, her father declined a request for Chinhye's hand from a powerful member of the military regime, placing his own life in danger. Such an atmosphere provided a further opportunity for Chinhye to be a model for the family.

As is seen in the tomb inscription, there were nine children in all in Chinhye's natal home, four by her father's first wife and five by the second. Her sixth younger sister was married off to the son of King Wŏnjong, Hyŏn, Duke of P'yŏngyang, but he died, so she then became Queen Sun, consort of King Ch'ungsŏn. Chong, the son of her third younger brother, Sung, married Princess Such'un, and so produced a parallel marriage relationship with the royal house.

However, after her husband died, Chinhye had to raise their seven children alone, and her second daughter was selected as a palace lady to be presented to the Yüan, and so was separated from her. Although her two sons' marriages seem to have been splendid, we can conjecture that these were not unrelated to the unhappiness of the severe trials of an aristocratic clan. Her efforts to overcome this unhappiness through faith may also have had the potential to advance the marriages of her two sons.

Chŏngyu's stupa inscription, in contrast, is silent about her family. It only lists her relations with the author of the inscription, Ch'ae Che-gong. This was because Chŏngyu was only the daughter of an ordinary peasant. The greatest difference between the two eras is revealed precisely through such points concerning the two masters. In the Koryŏ, the tendency was for aristocrats to put their faith in Buddhism, which was the state religion. Chŏngyu's status was that of a commoner, not an aristocrat, and, in the period when she lived, aristocrats had distanced themselves from Buddhism, reflecting the fact that it was no longer the state religion.

There is no record that Chŏngyu was ever married, whereas Chinhye of course was married and gave birth to seven children. Chinhye's relatives by marriage were of a prominent clan, and her younger siblings and nephews married into the royal house, so she had close connections even with the palace. Thus, her life was full for many years, and she later cherished the memory of her husband and family. Chŏngyu, in contrast, may even have refused marriage, and had no warm retreat in children or in relatives by marriage.

Although Chŏngyu frequently explored scenic sites, we have no concrete details as to which ones she visited. From the fact that her stupa was prepared at Ch'ilsŏng Hermitage on Mount Myohyang, it is possible that she had visited Mount Myohyang frequently. Of course, Hwajang Monastery in Changdan, where she joined the order, was also a famous monastery. If we take into account that it, together with Pohyŏn Monastery of Mount Myohyang and Oeho Cloister of Hoeam Monastery, were places where the memory of the Indian monk Chigong was cherished,[18] we might conjecture that she visited these places. It is difficult to judge whether or not Chŏngyu's appreciation or selection of Buddhist sites was poorer than Chinhye's: not being an aristocrat, Chŏngyu would not in any case have been able to visit as wide a range of Buddhist sites or contribute to as many Buddhist services as Chinhye.

It is difficult to conclude that the Mi-lo Great Cloister, Mount Nieh-p'an, and Mount Ch'ing-liang that Chinhye packed her bags to visit in the third year of the reign of King Ch'ungsŏn were inside Koryŏ; rather, there is a great possibility that these were in the broad territories ruled by the Yüan.[19] Chinhye's second daughter was a palace lady presented to the Yüan and so was separated from her, and her sixth younger sister was Queen Sun, consort of King Ch'ungsŏn; thus, while participating in the Buddhist services of King Ch'ungsŏn, who was residing in Yen-tu, the Yüan capital, it is probable that Chinhye visited various places in Yüan territories.[20] Chinhye also received twelve *śarīra* beads at T'ongdo Monastery. This acquisition would have been difficult without the support of the state, though we have no records about the Buddhist services that would have followed to preserve these relics.

It is not clear what Buddhist services Chŏngyu practiced. She offered a hundred days of prayer to alleviate the difficulties of her benefactor Ch'ae Che-gong who had practiced good administration, and it is possible that she considered the Buddhist practices of reading Buddhist sūtras, praying to the seven stars of the Big Dipper, and even meditation to be less worthy because they were only for herself. In contrast, Chinhye supervised the sacrificial rites for her family, and even before she joined the order built Kamŭng Monastery, which was close to the grave of her late husband, as a prayer chapel. Besides this, she invited sūtra-copying monks and had them make copies of sūtras in gold lettering.

Both women were humane through their Buddhist ideals and overcame personal trials through the medium of Buddhism. If Chŏngyu was zealous in her meditation and sūtra reading, Chinhye had decisiveness of character, exploring broad territories, performing sacrificial rites and Buddhist services, and educating her children. Thus, in the compressed inscription at the end of her tomb, she is evaluated as having the temperament of a gentleman.

Although Chinhye's ordination dharma master, Pai-hsiu, has not been identified, we know that she listened to the sermons of Sŏn Master Mugŭk when he returned in 1302 from Chiang-Huai; two years later, when Ch'ŏlsan Sogyŏng came from Kiangnan, she received the Mahayana precepts from him. Mugŭk and Ch'ŏlsan Sogyŏng were eminent monks who were important enough to be noted in Buddhist history. And it is possible that the *śarīra* beads Chinhye acquired from T'ongdo Monastery were intended for use in state-level Buddhist services for her second daughter who had been taken to Yüan as a palace lady, and for her younger sister and nephew who were connected with the royal house. She was posthumously granted the title of master not only because of her Buddhist practice, but also in all probability because she was an aristocrat related by marriage to the royal house and because the Buddhist services she supervised had state support.

In contrast, the literatus-official Ch'ae Che-gong is the only eminent person we know of in Chŏngyu's life of Buddhist service and faith. The monk K'waeho, who was like a son to her, and the dharma master Yuram Sik'wal of Hwajang Monastery, who ordained her, are not mentioned in the extensive materials on Buddhist genealogies.

COMMONALITIES IN THE ROLES

As female masters of the Koryŏ and Chosŏn dynasties who lived five hundred years apart, Chinhye and Chŏngyu nevertheless share a number of aspects in common. They both joined the Buddhist order late in life, were linked to their families, and took care of domestic matters. Chinhye was born at the end of a military regime in which powerful ministers dominated, and before she was married at the age of fourteen, her father had declined a request for her hand, which placed his life in danger. There is a distinct possibility that Chŏngyu was born into a family that was caught up in the troubles between the children of a legal wife and those of a concubine. To overcome family misfortunes, the two female masters both seem to have practiced self-denial, diligence, and self-control.

Although they did not join the order and obtain dharma names until after the age of sixty, both women had a forthright faith in Buddhism from a tender age. From childhood on, Chŏngyu did not eat onion, garlic, or meat. Chinhye also had a pure character and was cautious in her conduct, and after marriage devoted herself to cooking and weaving. It is said that she knew the regulations for the ancestral rites and could practice them accordingly. When her husband died, she declined the state's offer to celebrate the rites and instead set up the funeral and completed the rites in her home. So sincere was Chinhye that she even supervised the follow-up rituals herself. In this we can glimpse a character thoroughly versed in the culture and training of the Buddhist rituals of the times. The fact that in Koryŏ women supervised rites can be confirmed from the material found in the body of a Buddha statue,[21] and is clearly proved in Chinhye's life.

Chinhye devoted great financial resources to constructing Kamŭng Monastery as a prayer chapel for her late husband, and before she joined the order she invited a monk to be the abbot there. After she had joined the order, she prepared a thatched hermitage near the home of her oldest son on Namsan, but was not permitted to take charge of the cloister. Although she was not an ordinary nun and was posthumously titled master, the limits were clear-cut. In Chŏngyu's case also, although Ch'ae Che-gong called her master, a title he attached to her because he respected the extent of her practice, she could not take charge as abbess of the cloister.

Both women lived much longer than the average life span of the times. Chinhye lived nine years after joining the order and died at seventy; Chŏngyu lived to be sixty-six. Since they had lived pure lives, we can speculate that as they aged their minds remained serene, just like those of eminent monks, and they were not disturbed as they were dying. Chinhye approached death in the thatched hermitage close to where her eldest son lived. Mount Myŏngdŏk, where her protector had retired to, and the small hermitage of Hwajang Monastery, where Chŏngyu died, were both in Kyŏnggi Province.

Chŏngyu's funerary service and cremation were supervised by her surrogate son, the monk K'waeho. He asked her lay benefactor Ch'ae Che-gong to write a stupa inscription, which was done. Chinhye's son supervised her cremation, and he had the son of the person who had written her husband's tomb inscription compose hers also. The tomb inscription for Chinhye was buried in a grave site close to her husband's grave on Mount Taedŏk. The stupa for Chŏngyu was at the Ch'ilsŏng Hermitage on Mount Myohyang, where she had connections with lay society.

The lives of these two female masters had stronger secular features than those of the average eminent monk. They joined the order only in their twilight years, in preparation for death. Their activities as masters were merely extensions of their lives before joining the Buddhist order. They faithfully fulfilled their secular and familial duties, yet were obviously devoted to Buddhism long before they joined the order. For example, once Chinhye had raised her seven children in accord with the standards of her relatives by marriage, who were aristocrats with ties to the royal clan, she donated her lay riches to Buddhist services and other activities.

Although Chŏngyu was a commoner, she passed her life in an upright way, constantly helping for several years in the household of her benefactor Ch'ae Che-gong without the slightest blemish on her conduct in order to repay that official for his kindness. One of Chŏngyu's motives for joining the order was no doubt to avoid placing the burden of her funeral on her benefactor. In the later Koryŏ, when Chinhye lived, the ties of eminent monks with their parents became stronger than in the early Koryŏ. Nuns generally maintained even stronger family ties than monks did, living in nunneries close to their secular homes. Thus, close ties with benefactors and family were shared by the two female masters.

Compared to Chinhye, Chŏngyu's activities in Buddhist services were much more limited, for she had grown up in a commoner family and had no financial resources of her own. Chŏngyu, who originally had a character that was quiet and composed, also had a narrower range of human relationships than Chinhye, who had nurtured and educated many children. Yet in the later Chosŏn period, when the status of ordained nuns had collapsed socially, along with Buddhism itself, Chŏngyu in some ways had greater opportunity to live an exemplary life than did Chinhye in the later Koryŏ, when Buddhism was the national religion.

Chŏngyu's friend and benefactor Ch'ae Che-gong, a Confucian scholar who later became a famous prime minister, transcended the limitations of the late Chosŏn period when he wrote a stupa inscription for Chŏngyu in which he consistently refers to her as master. He broke through the burdensome barriers called Tohak (neo-Confucianism) that established the moral principle of separating male and female, and even threw off the complications that deemed Confucianism superior and Buddhism inferior. Indeed, the *śarīra* beads that appeared in the ashes after Chŏngyu's cremation illuminate and eternally ornament the nirvana of the inspiring woman he called master.

CONCLUSION

From the outset of the adoption of Buddhism on the Korean peninsula, women are recorded as having supported it. For example, Ado's mother, Kodoryŏng, and the sister of Morye, Sassi, who supported Muk'oja, provided a huge support for Buddhism in the fifth century. In the religion of high antiquity, women had been high priests, and even in antiquity women converted to Buddhism, such as the sister of King Yuri, the women who were vestals of the Shrine to Heaven, the tiger woman who met Kim Hyŏn at a stupa domain, and the sisters of the king of Paekche who supervised the state ancestor worship. Thus, the female rulers of antiquity had experience in supervising the state ancestor rituals that would have assisted in their practice of government after taking the throne.

No material has been left giving figures that compare the numbers of monks and nuns. In the Silla period, there was an officer with jurisdiction over nuns, and there is a possibility that the person responsible was a nun.[22] From the late Koryŏ until the early Chosŏn, Chŏngŏpwŏn (palace nunneries) were established, where women of the aristocracy and royal clan, widowed by war, disease, and political changes, could join the order and live as nuns. Since these nunneries were called *wŏn* (as in Chŏngŏpwŏn), they had a lower status as cloisters than the usual *sa* (monasteries) where monks resided. Yet the idea was strong that these were holy precincts where nuns could lead a pure life even as they risked oppression by literati-officials advocating the abolition of Buddhism.

In the Buddhist world of late Koryŏ, the role of cloisters in protecting women increased, and their ties with the secular world strengthened. National teachers Pojo Chinul, Chin'gak Hyesim, and Pogak Iryŏn are examples of monks who cared for their aged mothers, and these women were nuns or sincere believers. Master Chinhye herself is an example of an aristocratic female believer of the late Koryŏ period.

It is a common phenomenon that in prosperous regions female believers give support to cloisters. In the Koryŏ, for example, we know that Chin Ŭi-gŭm helped with the publishing fee for Pojo's works,[23] and Myodŏk was the donor for the printing of the oldest extant text in metal movable type.[24] The names of numerous laywomen (*upāsikā*) and nuns are recorded in the stele inscriptions of eminent monks and in monastery records of the late Koryŏ,[25] though it was rare indeed for a nun to have been posthumously titled or to have had her own tomb inscription, as Chinhye did.

With the establishment of the Chosŏn state, the religious role of Buddhism was gradually coopted by neo-Confucianism. National Precepters and King's Teachers were abolished, and from the mid-Chosŏn period on, the *sallim* (independent Confucian scholars) spoke for neo-Confucianism and were venerated as the models for teachers.[26] The number of stele inscriptions written for eminent monks by literati-officials also lessened in the early Chosŏn and the erection of stelae for them eventually disappeared—reviving only after eminent monks, beginning with Ch'ŏnghŏ Hyujŏng, organized monk armies to supplement the flimsy defenses of the late Chosŏn state. This was a huge change in Buddhist history.

By the latter half of the eighteenth century, when Ch'ae Che-gong lived, it was again standard practice for well-known literati to write inscriptions for eminent monks. However, it is difficult to find a case besides his of a Confucian scholar writing a stupa inscription for a female master. As we have seen, Chŏngyu originally sought out Ch'ae to thank him for practicing good government in her home district, and for several months at a time over three years helped him with domestic matters. The next year, when he was on the road back from a mission, she walked more than 200 *ri* to meet him. She also sought him out when he had gone into retirement in the quiet mountains, where he had her live in a separate hall he had prepared in his own compound and could hear her chanting scriptures when he strolled along the edge of a pond late at night. In her stupa inscription he writes, "When we saw each other, we were very happy," and wonders, "Who could be more sincere than her?" Such expressions were possible only because they had first met in their late fifties and Chŏngyu was three years older. It remains remarkable, however, that in an ethical milieu that maintained an ironclad distinction between Confucianism and Buddhism—and between men from women, regardless of their ages—Ch'ae Che-gong and Chŏngyu managed to discard such limitations and develop a true student–teacher relationship, as well as a friendship evidently based on mutual respect and affection.

In Koryŏ and Chosŏn times alike, there are no examples of a nun—even one with the title of master—being made abbess of an officially recognized cloister. Nuns were abbesses of the Chŏngŏpwŏn, the Anilwŏn, and the Greater and Lesser Sŏwŏn, but these were only hermitages (*nanyak*), not officially recognized monasteries (*karam*), and were meant to function primarily as nuns' old age homes. In the case of Chinhye of the late Koryŏ, we have evidence that she fully supported her family and led a model life of faith long before she became a nun. In the case of Chŏngyu of the late Chosŏn period, although there are insufficient records about her early life in the secular world, we know from her stupa inscription that despite her low social status she had a natural disposition the equal of any ordained nun, in that she was pure in conduct, frugal, honest, sincere, and diligent even before she joined the order.

Thus, these two female masters of different eras were faithful to Buddhist virtues in their early and middle-aged lives in the secular world, and after they joined the order in old age, they remained closer to family and friends than monks generally did. They thus showed themselves to be models as both as laywomen and, of course, as nuns. Their joining the Buddhist order was the final arrangement to manage and support this. The two women took the tonsure to prepare for their own land of bliss, thus attempting, through the medium of Buddhism, to take care of themselves in their old age.

In premodern societies, women were much more strongly tied to the role of family support and childbirth than at present, while men concentrated on social activity and defense. Because women joined the Buddhist order much later than men, most of them being tonsured late in life,[27] the period of activity as a nun was only a few years in old age, as preparation for nirvana. Today there are many examples of young, unmarried women around the age of twenty joining the order. These women hold offices of responsibility in the Buddhist world, including the position of abbess at large independent monasteries. This indicates a generation that has bettered itself beyond those of the traditional age.

In the traditional period, women devoted themselves to burdensome domestic affairs and to a life of faith before they joined the order, prizing the opportunities that lay life gave them to cultivate their innate character and to serve others without distraction rather than looking after themselves. This could certainly be called bodhisattva conduct (*posal haeng*). Although Chinhye and Chŏngyu had only a short period after ordination to make an impression, their pure lives in the secular world prompted Chinhye to be called Great Teacher by the state and Chŏngyu to be called master by a prime minister, just as they both deserve to be called bodhisattvas by today's monks and nuns.

NOTES

This chapter originally appeared in the Korean language in the journal *Chŏngsin munhwa yŏn'gu* (Study of Intellectual Culture) 27, no. 4 (2004 Winter), as "Chosŏn ŭi Chŏngyu wa Koryŏ ŭi Chinhye."

1. Yi Nanyŏng, *Han'guk kŭmsŏk mun ch'ubo*, appendix, 278–279; *Han'guk kŭmsŏk chŏnmun*, chungse, ha, 1128–1130.

2. Ch'ae Che-gong, *Pŏnamjip*, fascicle 57, "Yŏdaesa Chŏngyu Pudo pimyŏng" (*Han'guk munjip ch'onggan* 236:558).

3. Yi Ki-un, "Chosŏn sidae wangsil ŭi piguniwŏn sŏlch'i wa sinhaeng" (The Beliefs and Foundation of the Palace Nunneries in the Chosŏn Period), *Yŏksa hakbo* 122 (2003).

4. Yi Chi'gwan, comp., *Han'guk Kosŭng pimun ch'ongjip* (Kasan Pulgyo munhwa yŏn'guwŏn, 2000), 554–555.

5. Hwajang Monastery was a representative monastery in Changdan, Kyŏnggi Province. It held a portrait of King Kongmin (1351–1374) and leaves of Sanskrit text brought by Chigong (Śūnyadiśya, d. 1363). I infer that Chŏngyu, as a woman, could not have lived in Hwajang Monasty, but rather in a hermitage belonging to the monastery.

6. *Śarīra* beads are bead-like relics found in cremation ashes; they are believed to be an indication of a highly accomplished Buddhist practitioner.

7. *Pŏnamjip* fascicle 38, "Mangsil chŭng Chŏnggyŏng Puin O ssi ch'ŏnjang p'amyo koyu mun" (*Han'guk munjip ch'onggan* 236:180).

8. An Chŏng-bok, *Chaptongsani* (Asea munhwasa, 1981), 257.

9. Yi Nanyŏng, comp., *Han'guk kŭmsŏk mun ch'ubo*, 278–279.

10. Kim Yongsŏn, *Yŏkchu Koryŏ myoji chipsŏng, ha* (Hallim Taehakkyo Asamunhwa yŏn'guso, 2001), 736–741.

11. Pak Yong'un, "Koryŏ sidae ŭi Chŏng'an Im ssi Ch'ŏlwŏn Ch'oe ssi, Kongam Hŏ ssi kamun punsŏk—Koryŏ kwijok kamun yŏn'gu (2)," *Han'guksa nonch'ong* 3 (1978).

12. Kim Yŏngmi, "Koryŏ sidae piguni ŭi hwaldong kwa sahoejŏk chiwi," *Han'guk munhwa yŏn'gu* 1 (Ihwa Yŏdae Han'guk munhwa yŏn'guwŏn, 2001).

13. Heo Heungsik, *Koryŏ sahoesa yŏn'gu* (Asea munhwasa, 1981).

14. *Koryŏsa* 103, biography of Hŏ Kong.

15. *Wŏndon* is a collective name for the *Avatamsaka* and *Diamond Sutras*.

16. Although the text has the character *mu*, either the first editor dropped the character or, when the tomb inscription was being engraved, it

is possible that a mistake was made. Mugŭk is the style name that Hon'gu received from Master Meng-shan.

17. Nam Kwŏnhŭi, "Pilsabon *Chegyŏng ch'walyo* e surokdoen Mongsan Tŏg'i wa Koryŏ inmuldŭl kwa ŭi kyoryu," *Tosŏgwanhak nonjip* 21 (1994); Heo Heungsik, "Koryŏ e namgin Ch'ŏlsan Gyŏng ŭi haengjŏk," *Han'guk hakbo* 39 (Ilchisa, 1985); "Mongsan Tŏg'I haengjŏk kwa yŏnbo," *Han'guk hakbo* 71 (Ilchisa, 1994); "Mongsan Tŏg'i ŭi yŏmbul-hwadu—Yŏmbul kwa hwadu ŭi chŏmmok," *Munhŏn kwa haesŏk* (T'aehaksa, 1999); "Mongsan Tŏg'i ŭi chosul kwa saeng'ae," *Sŏji hakbo* 15 (1995); "Mongsan Tŏg'i wa Chogyejong pŏpt'ong," *Nam P'unghyŏn Kyosu hwa'gap ki'nyŏm nonmunjip* 71 (Ilchisa, 1994).

18. Heo Heungsik, *Koryŏ ro olmgin Indo ŭi tŭngbul* (Ilchokak, 1997).

19. See Kim Yongsŏn, *Yŏkju Koryŏ myoji chipsŏng, ha*, 739–740 for each place.

20. It is difficult to list all the articles that deal with King Ch'ungsŏn's reform government, his activities in the Yüan empire, and relations with Yi Chehyŏn and the Man'gwŏn Hall (library). It has recently been noticed that when King Ch'ungsŏn was on the throne while residing in Yüan, he zealously devoted himself to Buddhist services. There is much material collected in the tomb inscription of Wŏn Kwan, the *Hui-yin Ssu chih* (Gazetteer of Hui-yin Monastery), the histories of the Yüan, and collected essays. See Chang Tong'ik, "Sin charyo rŭl t'onghae pon Ch'ungsŏn Wang ŭi chae Wŏn hwaldong," *Yŏksa kyoyuk nonjip* 23–24 (Kyŏngbuk University, Yŏksa kyoyuk hakhoe, 1999); Kim Sŏnghwan, "Koryŏ sidae myojimyŏng sinyŏl—Wŏn Kwan myojimyŏng," *Han'guk munhwa* 25 (Seoul University, Han'guk munhwa yŏn'guso, 2000); Tonino Puggioni, "Ch'ungsŏn Wang dae Yŏ-Wŏn Pulgyo kwan'gye wa Hangju Koryŏ Sa," *Han'guk sasangsa hak* 18 (Han'guk sasangsa hakhoe, 2002). The queen who accompanied King Ch'ungsŏn while he resided in Yüan was Queen Sun, and Wŏn Kwan's younger brother Kyŏng also went as a hostage (*tongnohwa*), so we can guess that he served as a palace guard, a military official. There is a great possibility that from 1311 to 1314 Queen Sun (Chinhye's sixth younger sister) and the palace lady presented to Yüan who was Chinhye's second daughter arranged for Chinhye to visit Buddhist sites and added their support to her sponsorhip of Buddhist services.

21. Onyang Minsok Pangmulgwan, *1302 nyŏn Amilta Pulbokjangmul ŭi chosa yŏn'gu* (Kyemong munhwa chaedan, 1991).

22. Kim Yŏngt'ae, "Paekche ŭi nijung sugye wa nisŭngjik kwan'gye; Ilbon saryo wa Silla mit Namcho ŭi sarye chungsim," in *Munsan Kim Samyong Paksa hwa'gap ki'nyŏm Han'guk munhwa wa Wŏn Pulgyo sasang* (Iri, Wŏngwang Tae ch'ulpanguk, 1985).

23. Kim Chi'gyŏn, comp., *Hwa'ŏm non chŏryo* (Poryŏn'gak, 1968), 459.

24. Heo Heungsik, *Koryŏ ro olmgin Indo ŭi tŭngbul* (Ilchogak, 1997); Yi Seil, "Chikji wa Piguni Myodŏk e kwanhan yŏn'gu," *Chungwŏn munhwa nonch'ong* 4 (Ch'ŏngju Taehakkyo Chungwŏn munhwa yŏn'guso, 2000).

25. Of the materials I have surveyed, those stele inscriptions with the greatest numbers of names of nuns inscribed in them are *Hoeam-sa Chigong Hwasang pi* and *Ansim-sa Chigong Naong sari sŏkchong pi*. Even though the

numbers of names are few in *Sillŭk-sa Taejanggak ki* and *T'aego-sa Wŏnjŭng Kuksa pi*, they are recorded there. These are from the end of the Koryŏ period.

26. Yi Usŏng, "Han'guk Yugyo ŭi myŏngbun chuŭi mit kŭ chŏngchijŏk kinŭng e kwanhan il kochal—Yicho hu'gi ŭi 'sanrim' e taehayŏ," *Tongyanghak haksul hoeŭi nonmunjip* (Sŏnggyungwan Taehakkyo, 1976).

27. Kim Yongsŏn, *Koryŏ kŭmsŏkmun yŏn'gu* (Ilchogak, 2004), 343.

6

Marginalized and Silenced

Buddhist Nuns of the Chosŏn Period

John Jorgensen

Except for the names of some queens and female members of the royal clan who became nuns in palace cloisters inside the capital, the prose records of the Chosŏn period reveal virtually nothing of the lives of Buddhist nuns collectively or as individuals.[1] This is a result of the anti-Buddhist policies of the neo-Confucian establishment, of the patriarchal and even misogynist attitudes of the Confucian ministers and students, and of the generally lower level of female education and status in the Chosŏn period, which meant that nuns left no writings.

The background to this lies in the previous Koryŏ court and its collapse. The Koryŏ was a period of great prosperity for Buddhism. Buddhism was virtually the state religion, with elaborate Buddhist rituals conducted at the court, and huge expenditures, both state and private, were lavished on Buddhism. As the Koryŏ state was weakened by invasions and infighting, Buddhism benefited as private resources were increasingly sequestered from taxation by being placed officially under the control of the Buddhist order but in reality were under the control of the monk relatives who acted for the aristocratic clans. Certain monasteries, often wealthy in land holdings and slaves, were really the domains of these clans.[2] This was resented by Confucians and those who wished to strengthen the state. Eventually these forces joined to overthrow Koryŏ.

The Chosŏn project had three aspects that had an impact on Buddhist nuns. One was the removal of Buddhist supremacy and participation in state or public ceremonial. The second was to reclaim for the state the resources that had been alienated to Buddhism.[3] Third, the introduction of a neo-Confucian orthodoxy aimed to strengthen the patriarchy and diminish the autonomy of women.[4]

This project meant Buddhist nuns were doubly marginalized and silenced, leaving very few traces in the written record until the Chosŏn court began to lose its grip. Therefore, only one nun is mentioned in the two Buddhist hagiographical collections compiled in the Chosŏn period, the *Tongguk sŭngni rok* (Biographies of Monks and Nuns of Korea) and the *Tongsa yŏljŏn* (Serial Biographies of Eastern Masters) by Kakan (1820–1896) of 1894. Kakan's collection contained 198 hagiographies, not one of a nun. The *Tongguk sŭngni rok* has only a brief notice of a nun from the Silla period, and she was probably included because she was the widow of a famous Silla hero, Kim Yusin (593–673).[5] Again, of the approximate 198 biographies or notices of Chosŏn Buddhist clergy known, only one is about a woman and not one was written by a woman.[6]

The available sources that remain are the court records and the monastic gazetteers; the first from the metropolitan center, the latter from the provinces. The court records chiefly demonstrate the nature of the antagonism of the Confucian elites to Buddhism, and to women becoming nuns in particular. This suggests these Confucian men feared the Buddhist faith of women and worried about their women's chastity in the all-male monasteries, something likely encouraged by the trope in popular Chinese (and Korean) literature of the randy monk. The gazetteers, on the other hand, are products of the faithful, and are almost the only Buddhist sources that mention nuns. They thus tend to praise the nuns, unlike the court records that provide only a negative image as they were restricted to recording debates over the major crimes nuns allegedly committed and restrictive legislation aimed at Buddhism.

THE COURT RECORDS

The major state record, the *Yijo sillok*, is concerned mostly with appeals to the throne by officials requesting that the Buddhist order be restricted or dissolved, and that elite women be prohibited from becoming nuns or even visiting monasteries outside the palace grounds. The Confucian state needed able-bodied males for military service, corvée labor, and agricultural production, and women for bearing children, weaving, and domestic work. To these fundamentalists, elite women becoming nuns set a bad example to the commoner population. Above all, these Confucian petitioners display paranoia about the chastity and purity of their women, so that elite women were separated into women's quarters accessible to only a few male relatives, where they were protected from the gaze of the general population by burqa-like clothing that covered the entire body, and by attendants.[7] The segregation of the genders (*taebang*) and class boundaries were prime topics.[8] It would not do to have elite women visiting monasteries, much less staying overnight where men lived, which such visits would often necessitate given the time it took to travel from place to place.

Thus, the first entry in the *Yijo sillok,* besides those petitioning for restrictions on the size of the order or the cleansing of its members, is a 1404 rule severely prohibiting all women from going to monasteries. The reason given is that the "core of Buddhism is to be separate from the worldly and secular, and for women the most important duty is to be properly modest, chaste, and self-controlled. . . . If women [are permitted] to go to monasteries and be involved in a Way that spreads debauchery and the loss of virtue, these will be the regulations of a very unenlightened age."[9] The misogynist element motivating this restriction can be seen in the prohibition of elite women and men from associating with *mudang,* the female shamans, although here there was a concern about the low social status of the *mudang.*[10] It was also part of the grinding down of Koryŏ values and mores, for Koryŏ women and Buddhists had greater freedom, which was now being curbed. Koryŏ women had freely interacted with members of the opposite sex, traveled in open palanquins, visited Buddhist temples and *mudang* shrines, inherited prosperity, and even when married lived with their natal family.[11]

Driven by the Confucian ideology of the subordination of women, and the perceived need for women to maintain a purity of customs in the household for the state be kept secure,[12] women were gradually deprived of their status and the relative autonomy they had possessed in the Koryŏ.[13] This Confucian ideology also implied that women should not become nuns.

Thus, some years after the above prohibition of women going to the monasteries, in 1413, it was ordered that all virgins of good families who had become nuns were to be laicized and married, "in order to correct human morality."[14] This was probably connected with Confucian ideas about the subordination of women, for, in the same year, legislation was passed that made women more dependent on their husbands and less able to maintain inherited property in their own right.[15]

Of course, the process of subordination of Buddhist women was gradual, with King T'aejo (r. 1392–1398) permitting a daughter to become a nun, but he still placed restrictions on Buddhism. The third king, T'aejong (r. 1400–1418) placed even more restictions on Buddhism, partly because he was the first of the Chosŏn rulers to have received a full Confucian education, and because he needed the support of the bureaucracy. T'aejong disestablished over two thousand monasteries, leaving only 242, which probably meant few were left for nuns to live in.[16] Of the eighty-two monasteries named as surviving this purge, only one has the slightest possibility of being a nunnery—Kunni-sa—simply because it has the character *ni* or nun in its name.[17] Even under the reign of the more liberal King Sejong, in 1428, the seemingly innocent activity of attending the Lantern Festival on the eighth day of the fourth month to celebrate the Buddha's birthday came under the scrutiny of the remonstrators (*saganwŏn*), who complained that "men and women gathered in crowds and watched and played all night," something that had been an evil custom of the Koryŏ period. This celebration had already been stopped in the palace grounds, but if the "vagabonds of the villages and streets"—a code for monks—could follow old customs, flying flags and beating drums to gather crowds and beg in the villages for the expenses of the lanterns, that would revive bad practices. Although this appeal was not approved, the remonstrators persisted, and soon afterward a prohibition was issued forbidding women to light lanterns and travel to see them at Hŭngch'ŏn Monastery.[18] Soon after, in 1431, women were forbidden to go to the houses of shamans because of their "corrupting influence."[19]

Such calls intensified, even in Sejong's time. Thus, in 1434, complaints were made that elite women were staying overnight in Hoeam Monastery to the north of Seoul, a criminal offense. Women may be ignorant, it was argued, so it was the fault of the family head for permitting such a threat to the chastity of these women. Since other monasteries were also involved, this was debated at court and reports were called for. One said that court women (*taebuin*), seven nuns, and more than ten women of *yangban* status had visited Hoeam Monastery. It was claimed that adult men and women had mixed together in the Dharma Hall, and that three monks had uninhibitedly played games with the women. All this was deemed a violation of the great gender boundary. Several monks from Hoeam Monastery were brought to court and interrogated about the numbers of women and their names. More than twenty laywomen and nuns were given eighty strokes of the rod and lectured on the protection of their virtue, the senior monk responsible received seventy strokes, and the three others who had sported with the women received fifty strokes; the others involved had to pay fines.[20]

In 1444, a report was made concerning the practices of nuns who disturbed the court. It stated, "The widows of good families who become nuns deeply fear the alienation of their feelings and wish to be entirely chaste. Now there are nuns who wear bamboo hats and shamefacedly walk in the streets. If one wishes to love the Buddha and be a nun, how could one shamefacedly walk the streets? If one wishes to keep chaste and be a nun, how can one shamefacedly walk the streets?" Therefore a prohibition was issued forbidding such women from wearing the bamboo hats or decorations, and from walking and showing their faces in the streets.[21] This illustrates the paranoia of elite males over female virtue and the alleged dangers of exposing the female face, for it was about this time that women had to be screened from public view and dress regulations were imposed on women.[22]

As time went on, there were attempts to halt elite and *yangban* women from becoming nuns or going to monasteries; petitions requesting the abolition of palace nunneries; torture of people with respect to women visiting monasteries (e.g., in 1451); and a prohibition on monks and nuns entering the capital (in 1487). This anti-Buddhist policy made it especially difficult for nuns to survive because they were cut off from sources of donations and from opportunities to recruit elite women, who had some education. The anti-Buddhist atmosphere became so poisonous in the capital that in 1495 Confucian students there went in to monasteries, beating up the monks and stealing items. When they saw monks in the streets, they injured them severely.[23]

Buddhism, at least in public, was almost extinct. The kings Sŏngjong (r. 1468–1494) and Yŏnsan'gun (r. 1494–1506) were fiercly Confucian and anti-Buddhist. However, there was an attempt to revive Buddhism during the reign of King Myŏngjong (r. 1545–1567) due to the influence of the queen mother, Munjŏng (1501–1565), who supported the monk Hŏung Pou (1515–1565). When she died, the Confucian backlash was furious and violent. Four hundred petitions were filed for the execution of Pou for working with the Dowager Queen Munjŏng (she made her brother the effective ruler from 1545) to promote Buddhism. He was beaten to death in 1565.[24] Buddhism only recovered again, albeit fitfully, due to the heroic defense of the realm by a Buddhist-monk army led by Sŏsan Hyujŏng (1520–1604) against the Japanese invasions of Hideyoshi from 1592.[25]

Thus, the state records on Buddhist nuns are always negative, depicting nuns as deceptive or lecherous, or as criminals. Yet it was the court women and the palace nuns who promoted Buddhism and assisted nuns in keeping their order alive. Because Professor Yi Ki-woon (Yi Ki-un) has studied the palace nunneries, I concentrate here on the nonroyal nuns whose deeds appear in the *Yijo sillok.*

NUNS IN THE *YIJO SILLOK*

The first nun to appear in the record for misdeeds was Chungbi, in 1463. By cutting off his hair, a certain Sabangji pretended to be a nun and traveled back and forth to Chungbi's place, where she lived with Chiwŏn and a female minor. Sabangji debauched the three females. Chungbi, fearing she was pregnant, claimed someone else had raped her. The court's decision pardoned her.[26] This is rather surprising, given that in 1423 the wife of a high official was beheaded for adultery. However, the trial of Chungbi took place in 1463 during the reign of King Sejo (r. 1455–1468),[27] who supported Buddhism, providing a short-lived respite from the relentless oppression of Buddhism.[28]

The second nun was named in a case that reached the court in 1469. It involved inheritances. "The nun Tamjŏng was the concubine mother of Kim Kyŏng-dal and the concubine of the late judge Kim Chŏn. Kim Chin favored Tamjŏng's mother, and therefore he was fond of Tamjŏng, and most of the slaves, lands, and prized possessions were given to Tamjŏng. The eldest son of the legal wife, Samno, received only a minute portion," and so he appealed this, but Tamjŏng tried to bribe the judge with a slave.[29]

The background to this case has a long history. During the Koryŏ, because women were able to inherit full or equal shares of family property, it seems that women who became nuns may have taken movable property at least with them. In one case, a nun had a slave who made the most exquisite cloth.[30] In Chosŏn, as early as 1397 in the reign of T'aejo, the issue had been raised of inherited property and slaves being transmitted inside the monasteries under the pretext that the slaves were dharma heirs and that the property was attached to them.[31]

The favoring of a child, here a nun who was the daughter of a concubine, over the eldest son of the legal wife, violated the Confucian norm of primogeniture. This case occurred just when the issue of inheritance was coming to a head, with primogeniture being preferred in the law code of 1471, which overturned Koryŏ practice.[32] The rules on inheritance stated that the oldest son of the primary wife was to receive the greatest proportion of the inheritance,[33] but here Tamjŏng was a daughter of a concubine and received the greatest share. It is not surprising then that Samno appealed. Yet this entry shows that a former concubine became a nun when her master died, but she still inherited considerable property. This may explain how some nuns were able to sponsor expensive rituals and donate land and slaves to the order. It also shows that state regulations were sometimes flaunted.

A most serious case was that of the nun Chŏngin, who killed her original superior, the nun surnamed Hong. This case was debated in front of King Sŏngjong (r. 1469–1494), a decidedly Confucian ruler, in 1475. Pertinently, the reason that all these nuns appear in the court record is that monks (and nuns), and the wives and daughters of noble families, could not be imprisoned without the king's knowledge and approval. However, monks did not have this "protection in cases of murder, theft, rape, or personal injury," and no one had it in death-penalty cases.[34] Indeed, the king reviewed all controversial death-sentence cases.

In the debate, Chŏngin was accused of being extremely crafty and of becoming pregnant so that she could not be interrogated under torture, which during Chosŏn could even be fatal.[35] She claimed that she only wished to harm the nun Hong by putting arsenic in her gruel. When Hong ate it, she sought cold water, but Chŏngin deliberately and tardily brought warm water. Realizing she had been poisoned, Hong tried to notify her elder brother, Hong Kyŏngson (1409–1481), a high civil official and distant descendant of the Koryŏ royal clan. She tried various remedies but died that day.[36] On the seventeenth day of the fifth month, the monk Hagyun was questioned and gave evidence saying that he had been debauching Chŏngin for fifteen years. Chŏngin's superior Hong was then still middle-aged. Not long after the affair began, Hong also had sexual relations with Hagyun. This became a subject of rumor. Hagyun was tortured by flogging, but did not confess. The discussants concluded they would have to wait until Chŏngin gave birth, when she could be questioned under torture.[37] Therefore she feared imprisonment. A debate was held on the legalities of this proposal, but it was approved. On the twenty-sixth day, the king was told that Chŏngin's intercourse with Hagyun had led to the killing of her superior Hong, a most serious violation. This event became a catalyst for various proposals affecting the nuns of Seoul and nearby villages, making it evident that Chŏngin was from the metropolitan region.

The royal lecturer said, "Many nuns live in the wards and streets of the capital and mix in the villages and hamlets. Therefore it is desirable they live separately in one district so they cannot mix. What about this?" An opponent said:

> Since the Chŏngŏpwŏn (the palace nunnery) already exists inside the city, why have yet another location? The Chŏngŏpwŏn also has a very poor reputation, and ordinary monks and nuns are not distinguished by the color of their robes, and so they come and go without suspicion, and it is easy for them to engage in indecency. If one wishes to eliminate the source of this, build a new, small residence in a ward street, and all can be removed there.

A remonstrator said:

> The women of the elite (*sajok*) are not permitted to become nuns, and yet recently the investigators have been lax, and so young virgin girls are ordered and pressured to shave off their hair. This injustice is widespread and serious. Moreover, they go to and fro with the monk crowd, and wilfully commit indecent acts. Recently, the monk Sŏlcham basically did not even know the precepts, and on the pretext of teaching the scriptures[38] went in and out of the Chŏngŏpwŏn, staying over a series of nights, and during that time there were possibly obscene events. It would be convenient to completely remove nunneries from the capital.

Another said:

> I have heard that the nun Hong enticed her niece to become a nun. When there was a recent questioning of her whereabouts, it was said she was travelling in the mountains of Kyŏngsangdo. When asked how her father allowed her to become a nun, they said, "As a young child she was ill, and therefore she was tonsured. Now that the nun Hong has been poisoned to death, and the girl is fully grown, he wants her to return and to marry her off." If one can thus delude and incite a girl to become a nun, how many can there be? I request that the newly built nunneries all be removed.

The king, Sŏngjong, then said, "The removal of the nunneries should be an order of the queen." The queen, who was a devout Buddhist,[39] approved that all nunneries inside the city and outside be moved to a separate site, and that the lumber and tiles be used to construct one large nunnery where all the nuns would reside. But there was opposition to this on the basis that there was no need to add another Chŏngŏpwŏn. The debate raged on, with the king still maintaining that this was the queen's decision. The queen said that because the nuns were also her people, all the nunneries should not be removed. She asked whether a nunnery in Inwang-dong, which had been built on the orders of the pro-Buddhist King Sejo, should be removed.

On the fourteenth day of the sixth month, it was argued that it was the violation of the nun Chŏngin by the monk Hagyun that had led to the murder of the senior nun Hong by Chŏngin, so Hagyun should not be released. Chŏngin, who was in prison, wished to see Hagyun and was in tears, but she would not divulge any information. A request was made that, after her baby was born in the tenth month, she be questioned under flogging. The king questioned whether Hagyun deserved imprisonment merely on suspicion of a crime, and suggested that he be pitied, but an official said he should not be released, remarking, "I have heard nuns say that they would not begrudge Chŏngin's death, but they feared Dharma Teacher Hagyun would also die. In light of this, it is clear that Hagyun's violation of nuns was not restricted to Chŏngin alone."

On the twenty-third day of the sixth month, a debate was held to decide on Hagyun's crime, and there was a division of opinion. The decision stated, "It was none other than Chŏngin who poisoned her superior to death. Hagyun had secretly violated her, and there is no harm in waiting until Chŏngin can be interrogated." But others said that Hagyun had not been told a murder had been committed, and that he did not confess to knowing about it, even under torture. The final word on the subject appears on the twenty-sixth day of the seventh month, with the determination that Chŏngin, fearing that her superior knew about her pregnancy and wished to punish her, used arsenic to poison her. The punishment was death by slicing, which the king approved.[40] This was the ultimate punishment, savage even by the standards of the day, for *yangban* women sentenced to death for crimes were normally only made to wear the cangue and were not executed, while commoner women convicted of murdering their husband were beheaded.[41] The punishment of Chŏngin was so severe probably because she was a nun.

This long-running and notorious case not only resulted in the most savage of punishments for Chŏngin but also threatened the very existence of nunneries in the capital—even the venerable palace nunnery, the Chŏngŏpwŏn. It also prompted inquiries into the fate of the younger nun, the niece of the murdered superior Hong, who was a member of an eminent clan.

In 1477, the case of the virgin Kwŏn, who had been tonsured, was raised. Almost immediately preceding this, in the second month of the lunar calendar, the tonsuring of monks had been forbidden.[42] The king, Sŏngjong, ordered that the investigation into Kwŏn be halted, but the officials wished to continue with it. The king said, "It must be thirty-three years since her mother died. If she was not ill, why did her mother not marry her off when she was of age? Female doctors have examined her and found many moxibustion scars, which is why I ordered an end to the questioning." But an official said that there was a severe prohibition on virgins taking the tonsure, and that virgins in the women's quarters did not take kindly to the fact that after women became nuns they could unashamedly show their faces wherever they went. Others claimed that Kwŏn's relatives had schemed to make her a nun in order to consolidate the family lands. The Confucians reiterated that the law stated a virgin should not become a nun, no matter what the circumstances.[43]

Here again, it was King Sŏngjong, a staunch Confucian, who tried to aid the nuns, and who argued against Confucian hardliners upholding the letter of the law. The case also demonstrates the Confucian concern that upper-class women not be seen in public and paranoia about the motives of the female population.

Preoccupation with the chastity of nuns continued, for, in 1495, the case of the crime of intercourse between the monk Chisŏn and the nun Chiho, which "violated the constant Way," was raised. The punishment was a fine in lieu of sixty strokes of the rod. A request was made to also laicize them, but the new ruler, King Yŏnsan'gun (r. 1494–1506), maintained that monks and nuns are also people, and that the pair had already languished in jail. If they were to be further interrogated, they would fear death by flogging in the process. Moreover, Chisŏn was elderly, and there was no benefit in returning him to the laity, so the initial fine remained.[44]

Yet the same ruler, the despotic Yŏnsan'gun, did not always side with accused nuns. In 1504, when the tomb of a woman of the Kwŏn clan was opened and found to be empty, it was reported that her corpse had been cremated by the nun Hyemyŏng of the Chŏngŏpwŏn.[45] The Lady Kwŏn had been a palace lady of the former honorary king, Tŏkjong (a.k.a. Wŏlsan Taegun, 1469–1494, father of Sŏngjong) and had been made a noble. A Buddhist, she had prevailed on the nun Hyemyŏng to follow Buddhist practice and secretly cremate her corpse. King Yŏnsan'gun had canceled Lady Kwŏn's noble rank and reduced her to commoner status because she had been involved in a certain incident. He then leveled her grave and split open the coffin. Furious at not finding a corpse to be punished, he ordered an interrogation.[46] Indeed, interference in any of the court matters of Yŏnsan'gun was not tolerated and no mercy was shown. Thus, when two nuns had tonsured one of the palace women of the late King Sŏngjong, Yŏnsan'gun had said that all that the palace women of a late monarch needed to do was be chaste, not become nuns and follow a perverse teaching. He had the nuns brought outside the palace gates and interrogated under torture immediately. Yŏnsan'gun then ordered that the Chŏngŏpwŏn be abolished, and all nuns expelled from the capital.[47]

A few years later, in 1509, the name of Hyemyŏng—possibly the same nun who had so angered King Yŏnsan'gun—appears in the petition of some Confucian university students, describing a nun who had lived in the Chŏngŏpwŏn between 1473 and 1494.[48] The students requested that the anniversaries of kings and the two schools of Buddhism be abolished, and that the monk Hakjo, who had been close to King Sejo,[49] and the nun Hyemyŏng, who were building and repairing monastery structures, be executed for deluding stupid people. These executions would warn their followers. The young King Chungjong (r. 1506–1544) turned the petition down.[50] The next day the students petitioned again, labeling the two Buddhists long-active evil wizards who would continue to delude the people. However, the king rebuffed them again.[51]

For the next 135 years, the court records are silent on the deeds of named nuns. Buddhism had been almost entirely deprived of influence and had become almost invisible until the fifteen-year revival under King Myŏngjong and the dowager queen. Sŏsan Hyujŏng, who began his Buddhist career under the reign of Myŏngjong, began another revival from 1592 with a defense of Chosŏn against the Japanese. However, in 1636, the Manchus invaded and captured King Injo, despite a defense attempted by Buddhist monk-soldiers. The confidence of Chosŏn was sapped, which provoked a search for a new, stronger, more orthodox Confucian identity. Moreover, court politics were split between pro-Manchu and anti-Manchu factions when two princes, captured in 1636, were returned from Manchu captivity in 1645. One of them, the heir apparent Sohyŏn, was sympathetic to the Manchu Ch'ing dynasty, but was poisoned soon after his return. His wife's family, the Kang clan, were persecuted ruthlessly. In 1646, Princess Kang, his wife, was executed.[52]

Part of this tragedy involved a nun. In 1646, during King Injo's reign (r. 1623–1649), the records state that an order was given to shift Lady Kang (the wife of Sohyŏn) and three female slaves of the outer palace, and also the nun Hyeyŏng of Mount Pogae, Ch'ŏlwŏn, from the court prison to the interrogation center. But one of the female slaves had already been tortured four times and, when she arrived, she could not speak and died under torture. The other two slaves said that much silver treasure in the palace had been discovered and buried, but another person of the inner palace had seen this and dug it up. Later, Lady Kang had taken a longish package and had the slaves send it to Hyeyŏng. Lady Kang said she had presented over 200 *yang* of gold and embroidery to Hyeyŏng. Their testimonies concurred after continuous torture, but one of the slaves died and the other was exiled to Kilju. Hyeyŏng testified that the previous year she had received a parcel from Lady Kang, unaware of its contents. When she looked inside she found the corpse of a newborn babe. She concealed it and took it to the sandbanks of Yangju to cast it into the water. A party of more than seventy fishermen and others were sent to search the waters but could not find the body. Hyeyŏng was tortured repeatedly but still said there was nothing in the parcel except the corpse. Her shinbones were shattered from the *churi* torture,[53] and in a deranged state she said there were letters on the baby's chest about the dragon king, god of the waters, rescuing the child, and a small bag of red embroidery that held a piece of carved jade, but nothing else. Under flogging, she gave a short shout and died. Hyeyŏng's hired servant, Yŏnhwa, said that Hyeyŏng had only looked at the package with great surprise when she was transporting it on horseback. The servant then stole a glance and confirmed that the contents were as the nun had confessed. The package was thrown in the water. Seven nuns of Mount Pogae were then arrested; they testified that when Hyeyŏng first entered the mountain, she formed attachments with the monks and was involved in lustful perversity.[54] This case involved the theft of treasure from the court and the disposal of a presumably illegitimate child. The action of the nun made her an accomplice to the crime. The severity of the interrogation was not because Hyeyŏng was a nun, but because she was associated with the target of a court vendetta. The unstated allegation was perhaps that Lady Kang was scheming against the throne and trying to provide an heir, a potential pretender. Moreover, as this event was involved in a search for a new Chosŏn identity, it points to a further degradation of Buddhism. The ritual controversy and murder of the prince for Manchu, read "barbarian," sympathies, led Confucians to claim Chosŏn had to be more Confucian than China, that it had to purge all barbarian influences,[55] which included Buddhism and shamanism.

Lastly, in 1762, the eunuch Pak P'il-su and the nun Kasŏn were executed because, at a picnic with the heir-apparent, the eunuch had incited the heir-apparent to make virtuous women of the harem and the nun Kasŏn of Anamdong, who was disguised with long hair, often entered the palace. King Yŏngjo (r. 1724–1766) ordered Pak, Kasŏn, and five singing girls (*ki'nyŏ*) of the western town beheaded.[56] Clearly, the reputation of the court was at stake again, especially after requests made in earlier years. In 1704, it was stated, the court had forbidden monks and nuns to enter the capital in order to prevent obscenities, and had ordered the destruction of monastic dwellings. However, a complaint pointed out that in recent years the nuns had proliferated again and were living in groups not far from the eastern suburbs, where they had built six large, resplendent complexes within 10 *ri* of the city. Village women from near and far opposed their husbands and masters to live there, and those who had committed misdemeanors or been widowed early flocked to the nunneries in waves. These, the complainant stated, became nests of iniquity, delusion, and disorder. The request to destroy all the nunneries and return the nuns to their homes was, however, denied.[57] The complaint does show some of the perceived motives for women to become nuns at the time.

Such cases always depict nuns in a bad light, and mostly deal with nuns of the metropolitan region or those who had contact with the court. Especially with the help of queens and dowager queens, palace nuns could ameliorate the lives of nuns throughout Chosŏn Korea. Despite all the restrictions placed on palace nuns, the Chŏngŏpwŏn—the nunnery in the palace grounds that accommodated the harem and concubines of former kings who wished to devote themselves to Buddhism because they were lonely and had no political life—existed from 1398 to 1448, and from 1456 to 1504, and then from 1522 to at least 1661.[58] Several other cloisters also existed at various times inside the palace, for most of the kings, possibly under pressure from their womenfolk or due to personal belief, managed to maintain these cloisters in the face of vehement opposition from the Confucians. For example, during the time of King Myŏngjong (r. 1546–1567), the queen supported the monk Pou, and by 1554 the Chasuwŏn cloister in the palace had become the largest nunnery in the country, with more than five thousand nuns. In the reigns of Sŏngjong (r. 1470–1495) and Myŏngjong, these nunneries played a major role in the restoration of Buddhism, and at other times in resistance to the anticlerical policies. However, the prohibition on monks and nuns entering the capital, issued during the time of Injo (r. 1623–1649), and the abolition of the nunneries in 1661 meant that their role became extremely limited.[59]

NUNS IN MONASTIC GAZETTEERS

Other records provide some balance to those of the court, and show the role of nuns and women donors in the building and refurbishment of monasteries in some regions, especially in the last reigns of the Yi dynasty when the court was less powerful in the provinces. These records are the monastic gazetteers, mostly written in the late Chosŏn or under Japanese colonial rule. They display considerable regional variation, with some gazetteers lacking even a single mention of a nun or female donor. This could be due to the locations of some monasteries, or to their strict observance in maintaining as complete a separation from women as possible, whereas others clearly supervised nunneries and welcomed donations from women. The monastic gazetteers of Chikji-sa, Taedun-sa, Songgwang-sa, T'aean-sa, Kŭmsan-sa, and Mandŏk-sa contain nary a mention of nuns or even of female devotees. Others, such as Unmun-sa, have only one mention of nuns, possibly of recent times, and several only mention female donors. For example, a woman of Tongnae donated paddy fields to T'ongdo-sa in 1790 in order to benefit her ancestors, and a woman and her daughters made donations of land to Pŏm'ŏ-sa for the same reason in 1804.[60] Several queens and palace ladies gave donations to refurbish the Buddha Hall of Pulguk-sa in 1564 and 1681, and another palace lady had a *t'aenghwa* (traditional Buddhist painting) of Vairocana made for Pulguk-sa.[61]

In contrast, the gazetteers of Taesŭng-sa, the branch monasteries and nunneries of Chŏndŭng-sa and Pongsŏn-sa, Kŏnbong-sa, and Yujŏm-sa contain many mentions of nuns and female donors. Unfortunately, most of these records date to the end of the Chosŏn period, for the gazetteers were mostly compiled in the 1920s and 1930s (which explains the headquarters and branch system that had been introduced by the Japanese), and the decay of monasteries led to the destruction of much evidence. Nevertheless, in the *Taesŭng saji*, the records of two hermitages (*am*), Sabul San Yunp'il-am and Myojŏk-am in Kyŏngsang Pukdo,[62] contain the lists of names of donors of buildings, ritual implements, and rice fields, including both nuns and lay female devotees. These date to 1832 (?), 1859, 1887, and 1911,[63] and the partial lineages of some nuns can be reconstructed from these records.[64] One nun, Sŏng'ŭn, was active from 1887 to at least 1911.[65]

Monastic gazetteers are invaluable sources for discovering the roles of nuns in Chosŏn Buddhism, despite their generally late compilation and sketchy details of earlier times. However, except for the names of nuns listed as donors, they rarely give any detail.

Unusually, the *Yujŏm-sa ponmal saji*, compiled in 1942, contains a record of the nun Sasin (1694–1765), of Sin'gye Monastery, transcribed from a funerary inscription for her dated 1767[66]. Surnamed Kang, from the capital, she tired of the secular world at an early age and took her tonsure from her nun-superior Pŏpch'an in Mit'a Hermitage on Chongnam-san (present-day Namsan, inside Seoul), then outside the capital. Her superior encouraged her to chant, she made donations for construction, and she gained merit from the reconstruction of the Buddha Hall of Sin'gye Monastery. In this she was said to be the equal of any elite monk. She died in 1765, and her pupils T'aehŭi and others cremated her on the eastern peak of Mount Chongnam. Her bones were gathered and buried in a stupa to the east of the monastery.[67] The monastery, in the Kŭmgang Mountains in Kangwŏndo, was reconstructed in 1711 by Soyo tang Ch'ŏnghwi,[68] so the activities of Sasin, an elite nun from the metropolitan region, probably postdate these events.

On the other coast of Korea, in the nineteenth century, nuns and laywomen made major contributions to the building of monasteries and hermitages on Kanghwa Island. The *Ch'ŏngnyŏn saji* of 1937 records that the nun P'o'gyŏm, together with the abbess Chŏnghyŏn, reconstructed Ch'ŏngnyŏn-sa in 1821, and that a mountain god hall (*sansin'gak*) was built there by a number of nuns, including Kŭnhun, in 1908.[69] P'o'gyŏm also appears as a donor in 1848, along with the chief nun Pŏpjin, for the repair of the Dharma Hall of Chŏngsu-sa at the foot of Mount Mani.[70] Later, in 1888, the chief nun, Kŭnhun, repaired this monastery.[71] Other nuns installed paintings on altars or gilded statues. For example, in 1892, Chŏngil made a statue of Kwan'ŭm and a backing *t'aenghwa*. An 1896 inscription shows that the funds were raised for the refurbishment of the Dharma Hall by means of Chŏngil and the assembly tramping all over the countryside seeking donations, and in 1902 and 1904 Chŏngil refurbished the Dharma Hall and rebuilt the mountain spirit hall (*sannyŏnggak*). The 1904 inscription indicates that this nunnery was very poor, and had only six or seven nuns in residence. They had to beg to survive.[72]

Another hermitage, just above Ch'ŏngnyŏn Monastery, was founded in 1807 by the nun Ch'aehwa. This nunnery, Wŏnt'ong-am, beneath Mount Koryŏ on Kanghwa, was rebuilt by the nun Ch'ukhŭp in 1854. She purchased the land and all the movable goods. In 1897, the nun Ko Inbok renovated the nunnery and lived there until 1935.[73] In nearby Kaep'ung-gun, as part of Hwajang Monastery, there was Mit'a Hermitage. This was rebuilt in 1878 by Hyesin, a virtuous nun who constantly chanted the name of the Buddha. She had the help of another nun and an elder monk, yet she had to travel and beg for donations.[74]

In the account of Wŏnt'ong Monastery, on Mount Sŏnggŏ, again part of the Chŏndŭng Monastery group, and in Kaep'ung-gun, at least thirteen nuns participated in the reconstruction of the monastery in 1798. Two of them, Kyehŭn and Sinhaeng, are also named as having been involved in the reconstruction of the Ten Kings Hall (*sibwangjŏn*) of Taehŭng Monastery in 1814 or 1824.[75] Another nun, Sŏnmyŏng, constructed the Hall of Bhaisajyaguru (*yaksajŏn*) of Wŏnt'ong Monastery in 1870. The preface to the inscription for this building states that a statue of Bhaisajyaguru had been left exposed to the elements when the monastery had fallen into ruins. A monk, Yŏngbong, had lived there for decades and wished that the image be protected. Sŏnmyŏng was his pupil, and she decided to gather the funds and materials, and so built a hall of several spans to the east of the monastery. Later, in 1881, Sŏnmyŏng and others reconstructed the Naewŏn Hermitage, which was a nunnery on Mount Sŏnggŏ that belonged to Wŏnt'ong Monastery. The nunnery had been rebuilt over a century earlier, but the tiles leaked, the pillars and beams were askew, and it was about to be abandoned. The elderly nuns encouraged Sŏnmyŏng to garner funds from the district capital and renew the nunnery. The inscription lists the donors and chief nuns.[76] In another case, in 1880, the monk Purun responded to the call of the nun Uwŏn and joined forces with her to rebuild Ssangam Monastery and rethatch the Dharma Hall. Uwŏn encouraged a lay believer, a woman of the Kong clan, to make donations.[77]

These sources only provide evidence from the late Chosŏn period. For example, in the 1880s and 1890s there was considerable activity in the Kŏnbong Monastery and Yujŏm Monastery systems. In 1893, the nuns Sŏngyun and Chŏngsim rebuilt Taewŏn-am on Mount Kŭmgang after it had burned down in 1888,[78] and nuns took part in the repair of buildings of Changan Monastery on the same mountains in 1881.[79] Laywomen and nuns also assisted with repairs to various hermitages or nunneries belonging to this monastery in 1819 and 1883.[80] The supervising monastery, P'yohun-sa, also had hermitages such as Ch'ŏngnyŏn-am in the Kŭmgang Mountains reconstructed by the nuns Chŏnggŭn and Chisim with the assistance of female lay donors in 1838 and 1878; Sillim-am was rebuilt by a nun in 1882.[81] Some of the buildings of the hermitages of Simwŏn Monastery in Kangwŏndo were rebuilt by nuns with the help of lay donors, including royal women, from 1860 to 1891,[82] and one of the donors of a triad for Ch'ŏngp'yŏng-sa in 1728 included the nun Ch'aehŏn.[83]

It is only in the *Chŏndŭng ponmal saji* that we find appended a genealogy of nuns, though none of more than seven generations. These lineages are divided into those of Ch'ŏngnyŏn-sa, Hwajang-sa, Wŏnt'ong-sa, and Chŏngsu-sa.[84] This suggests that lineages of nuns may not have been long-lasting due to poor economic circumstances and the government's anti-Buddhist policies. It also hints at a regional revival of Buddhism by nuns after the end of the royal nunneries.

There were thus at least three main regions where nuns and female donors played an important role in maintaining Buddhism: (1) the capital, (2) Kanghwa Island and the Kaep'ung-gun district, and (3) the Kŭmgang Mountains. To these Taesŭng-sa in Kyŏngsang Pukdo could possibly be added. There may have been other districts, but as far as the available sources indicate, these were the most important. While the region of the capital can be explained by the influence of royal women and the presence of wealthy donors, that of Kanghwa and environs may have been a result of the closure of the royal nunneries around 1661 and the expulsion of nuns from Seoul, since the activities there began around 1800. Yet there is evidence that some of the nunneries were extremely poor, while others had access to donations from wealthy patrons, many presumably from Seoul. In the Kangwŏndo region surrounding the Kŭmgang Mountains, for example, the evidence suggests that nuns' activities began earlier, at least as early as 1728, and that some of the women may have come from elite families and so had access to some funds for donations.

The gazetteers, however, have an inherent bias toward describing the construction of buildings and donations of land, paintings, and statues. They tell us very little more about the women, except that some had to beg and that most recited Amitabha Buddha's name (*yŏmbul;* C. *nianfo*), a practice performed by believers of the Pure Land school. Further research into unpublished gazetteers and materials scattered through Kwŏn Sangno's compilations in the *Han'guk sach'al chŏnsŏ* may reveal more centers and earlier activities. However, most gazetteers were compiled relatively recently and have information mostly on the latter half of the nineteenth century, as already noted. Other evidence may emerge from inscriptions on Buddhist artworks. Heejong Kang has shown that elite women financially supported the production of Buddhist images beginning in 1395, with the presumed assent of their husbands, and that commoner women donated more paintings than men did and were more concerned with the afterlife than elite women were.[85]

CHOSŎN BUDDHIST LITERATURE ON NUNS IN GENERAL

Unfortunately, the other works of Chosŏn Buddhism—the commentaries, records, and belles lettres found in the *Han'guk Pulgyo chŏnsŏ* (Complete Texts of Korean Buddhism, hereafter *HPC*)—reveal very little, for they are almost entirely male-oriented. The dedications for buildings and images invariably delete the lists of donors, and the monks did not write about nuns, for to do so might invite accusations of violating the rules of gender separation and hierarchy. Elite monks were also colonized by Confucianism, and so could filially write about their mothers while in mourning, or encourage and transfer merit to them, but did not write about nuns. Many literate monks wrote poetry, but again these poems could not refer to nuns, otherwise suggestions might have been made about amorous liaisons.[86]

Elite laywomen, and donors such as queens, were mentioned in a few dedications of the early Chosŏn,[87] but after that, there is almost total silence. The donors for an 1839 printing of the *Pulsŏl ch'ŏnji p'alyang sinju-gyŏngju* (Commentary on the Sūtra Spoken by the Buddha on the Divine Mantra of Heaven and Earth and the Eight *Yang*) by Kyŏnghwa (1786–1848) included a royal concubine and a number of nuns who made donations for the merit of their parents,[88] and a printing of the *Sammun chikji* (The Three Gates of Direct Pointing) of 1769 mentions female donors.[89] Only one stele for an eminent monk lists female donors, including nuns, on the reverse,[90] and a stele for Ansim Monastery on Mount Taedun of 1759 mentions a nun and some female donors.[91]

The only writing by a monk dealing specifically with the social role of nuns was composed by Ch'ŏnŭng (1617–1718) around 1661, when he appealed an order to abolish two nunneries in Seoul, the Ch'asu and Insu cloisters. He wrote that these nuns would have nowhere to go and, being the king's people, deserved pity. Moreover, the abolition would destroy the system established by previous kings and queens: "These pure nuns will display an image harboring sadness born of a shared misery, which will wound the hearts of the common women."[92] This implies that they would gain the sympathy of most women and upset them greatly.

Even in cases when monks discuss pious women and nuns, they are almost always women of China, not Korea.[93] The only Korean woman mentioned is Lady Pak in the *Kyŏngamjip* (Mirror Cliff's Collection) of about 1804, written by Kyŏngam Ŭngyun (1743–1804). Refusing to remarry after her husband died before the marriage was consummated, she mourned for three years and, when an official tried to marry her off, she slashed her breasts, took poison, and, chanting the name of Amitabha, expressed her wish to be reborn with her late husband in the Pure Land. Lady Pak died in 1793, and was praised as a virtuous woman. The nun Pongsŏng said that Buddhism contained the sense of the three bonds (*samgang*) of Confucian social relations. She claimed that loyal ministers, filial children, and virtuous women who knew the practice of *yŏmbul* would be reborn in the highest Pure Land, which is very rare. Pongsŏng maintained that virtuous persons who merely chanted the name of Amitabha at the moment of death, hoping to be reborn in his paradise, would do so. Therefore, the nun concluded that the widow Pak was an incarnated bodhisattva.[94] In this, too, we see an attempt by Buddhists to compromise with the dominant Confucian ideology.

Otherwise, the monks only wrote about the number of precepts for nuns, on the origins of those precepts, and on the eight forms of respect (*p'algyŏng*) a nun should pay to a monk.[95] Despite the fact that nuns had to confess to monks, and receive the precepts and other forms of guidance from them, some monks seem to have abandoned the ideals of nonduality when the topic of gender was raised. Thus, the famous Yu'il (1720–1799), who ironically had the style (*cha*) of Mui, tried to contradict a Confucian who lampooned the notion that the Pure Land was solely male. The Confucian said that all existence possessed *yin* and *yang*, and that there could be no pure *yang*. Yu'il countered with notion of the country of women (*yŏguk*) only, in which females were born by reflection from water, mentioned in the histories.[96]

FEMALE EDUCATION AND BUDDHIST NUNS

Given such attitudes, it would appear that monks encouraged women to aim to be reborn in the Pure Land, where they would become male and so be qualified for buddhahood.[97] Moreover, Pure Land *yŏmbul* was considered a simple practice for women and those with little education. The elite monks, like elite lay males, were educated in classical Chinese. Before the invention of *hunmin chŏng'ŭm*, or *han'gŭl*, in 1443, this was the only language for reading. Very few women had the opportunity or motivation to learn classical Chinese. Therefore, the invention of *han'gŭl* provided an opportunity to educate women and commoners. It was apparently inspired by the Buddhist ideology of King Sejong (r. 1418–1450), and Buddhist sūtras were "translated" before Confucian texts were because they supported royal power rather than the bureaucratic state. Under the following ruler, King Sejo (r. 1455–1468), the translation of Buddhist scriptures was made due to his personal piety. In the face of Confucian hostility, he was supported by the royal women and some Buddhist monks.[98]

King Sejong initially attempted to have the new alphabet used for official examinations and the promotion of Buddhism. The first works composed in *han'gŭl* were Buddhist; there were also practical works on pronunciation, farming, medicine, and government. However, *han'gŭl* was intended for spreading improving tracts about filial children, loyal ministers, and virtuous women among the people, and the *Samgang haengsilto* (Illustrated Conduct of the Three Bonds), an illustrated text on the three Confucian bonds written in 1432, was published in Korean translation in 1481. In particular, the section on virtuous women was distributed to improve the conduct of women high and low. In 1475, Queen Sohye wrote the *Naehun* (Instructions for the Inner Quarters) in mixed *han'gŭl* and Chinese characters to educate the women of scholar families.[99] Such works on Confucian morality in *han'gŭl*, often with illustrations, were printed throughout the rest of the Chosŏn period.[100]

In contrast, many Buddhist scriptures were translated or glossed with *han'gŭl* on the orders of King Sejo in the years 1462 to 1465, and some at the order of a royal consort in 1485.[101] But because most of these texts still used Chinese characters, albeit with explanations and pronunciation guides, and were Sŏn (C. Chan; J. Zen) in origin or tenor, they were not easy to read. Most of the "translators" were Sŏn monks of the Naong lineage.[102] However, some monks, such as Hakjo, friend of the nun Hyemyŏng (mentioned earlier), translated texts considered more suitable for women, such as the *Chijang-gyŏng* (Sūtra of Kṣitigarbha) and the *Ch'ŏnsu-gyŏng* (Sūtra of the Kwan'ŭm [C. Kuan-yin, J. Kannon, Skt. Avalokiteśvara] with a Thousand Hands), and several dharani (*tarani*) texts.[103] Hakjo was supported by the Royal Concubine Insu, who also wrote postfaces for these translations. Perhaps for this reason, Hakjo translated texts aimed more at women and commoners—namely, chanting texts such as dharanis and mantras (*chinŏn*)—rather than doctrinal works.[104] Most court ladies, including queens, were not versed in classical Chinese, so they tended to learn *han'gŭl*, while men avoided it.[105] After the peaks of Buddhist translation during the reign of Sejo and under the patronage of Concubine Insu, the majority of officially produced texts were on Confucian morality.[106] But it is clear that some monks promoted *han'gŭl* texts on Pure Land chants and dharanis, possibly because nuns and women might be able to use them. Thus, in 1637, an *ŏnhae* and *hyŏngt'o* punctuation version was made of Pou's *Kwŏnnyŏm yorok* (Essential Records Encouraging Recitation [of the Names of the Buddha]),[107] and Myŏngyŏn's 1704 *Yŏmbul po'gwŏnmun* (Texts Exhorting the Practice of Recitation) has Chinese followed by *han'gŭl*, and it advocates *yŏmbul* for women and contains chants and ritual texts in *han'gŭl*.[108] Again, Hoŭn Ugi (1707–1785), in his *Sinp'yŏn po'gwŏnmun* (New Compilation of Texts Exhorting Recitation) of about 1785, a text on Pure Land, has Chinese script followed by *han'gŭl*.[109] Most of these works were published in Haein-sa. Similarly, the section on *yŏmbul* in the *Sammun chikji* (The Three Gates of Direct Pointing) of 1769, by Chinhŏ Palgwan, has *han'gŭl* for the dharanis and chants.[110] Although some of this may have been to assist pronunciation by novice monks, it seems likely that they were made for the use of nuns and female devotees. Unfortunately, until the library holdings of Chosŏn nunneries are investigated, if that is possible, we will be unable to ascertain how successful these measures were.

CONCLUSION

Chosŏn Buddhist nuns were triply marginalized and effectively silenced by (1) the anti-Buddhist policies instituted by the Confucian bureaucracy and male elites, (2) the misogynist attitudes of the Confucian and Buddhist patriarchy, and (3) their lack of education in classical Chinese. Despite this, nuns existed right through the Chosŏn period, and survived all the obstacles placed in their way. They did have the sympathy of many women from the elites, and for considerable periods of time had the tacit support of the Yi royal clan. Moreover, some elite women gained the assent of their husbands to make donations to the Buddhist order and were able to support some of the nuns. Of course, being human, some of them strayed, and several notable criminal deeds by nuns gave the rabid anti-Buddhist Confucians the opportunity to further restrict Buddhism, and nuns in particular. Many nuns nevertheless struggled against poverty and other restrictions to build Buddhist facilities, such as nunneries and monasteries. The lives of the vast majority of nuns remain in obscurity, and we can only speculate that they spent their lives chanting the names of the buddhas, observing the precepts, and working around the nunneries.

GAZETTEERS CONSULTED

The following are compiled by Han'gukhak munhŏn yŏn'guso 韓国學文献研究所 and published by Asea munhwasa, Seoul, in a series called *Han'guk saji ch'ongsŏ* 韓國寺誌叢書 (Collected Gazetteers of Korean Monasteries), 14 vols.

Mandŏk saji 萬德寺誌 vol. 1, 1977
Chogyesan Songgwang-sa sa'go 曹渓山松廣寺史庫 vol. 2, 1977
Kŏnbong-sa ponmal sajŏk Yujŏm-sa ponmal saji
乾鳳寺本末事蹟 楡岾寺本末寺誌 vol. 3, 1977
Chŏndŭng ponmal saji Pongsŏn ponmal saji
傳燈本末寺誌 奉先本末寺誌 vol. 4, 1978
T'ongdo saji 通度寺誌 vol. 5, 1979
Taedun saji 大芚寺誌 vol. 6, 1980
Chikji saji 直指寺誌 vol. 7, 1980
Kŭmsan saji 金山寺誌 vol. 8, 1982
Taesŭng saji 大乗寺誌 vol. 9, 1982
Unmun saji 雲門寺誌 vol. 10, 1983
Pulguk saji (oe) 佛国寺誌〈外〉 vol. 11, 1983
T'aean saji 泰安寺誌 vol. 12, 1984
Pŏm'ŏ saji 梵魚寺誌 vol. 14, 1989

NOTES

1. I wish to thank Professor Eun-su Cho for giving me a number of articles by Professor Yi Ki-un and others that were not available in Australia, and for inviting me to the conference at which this work was first presented.

2. Han Ki-mun, *Koryŏ sawŏn ŭi kujo wa kinŭng* (The Organization and Functions of Monasteries during the Koryŏ Period) (Seoul: Minjoksa, 1998), 318, 332–333, 351 and passim.

3. Robert E. Buswell, Jr., "Buddhism under Confucian Domination: The Synthetic Vision of Sŏsan Hyujŏng," in JaHyun Kim Haboush and Martina Deuchler, eds., *Culture and the State in Late Chosŏn Korea* (Cambridge: Harvard University Asia Center, 1999), 137–138.

4. Martina Deuchler, *The Confucian Transformation of Korea: A Study of Society and Ideology* (Cambridge: Council on East Asian Studies, Harvard University, 1992), 283.

5. *Tongguk sŭngni rok*, in *Hsü-tsang ching* (Taipei: Hsin-wen feng, 1968–1970), 150 vols, 150: 695a.

6. Tongguk Taehakkyo Pulgyo munhwa yŏn'guso, *Hanguk Pulgyo ch'ansul munhŏn ch'ongnok* (Comprehensive Digest of Korean Buddhist Litera-

ture) (Seoul: Tongguk Taehakkyo ch'ulpanbu, 1976), 290–302. The exception is the nun discussed by Professor Heo in this volume.

7. Deuchler, *The Confucian Transformation*, 261.

8. Deuchler, *The Confucian Transformation*, 259.

9. *T'aejong sillok* 4, twelfth month; in Kwŏn Sangno, *Yijo sillok Pulgyo ch'ojon* (Abstracts on Buddhism from the Veritable Records of the Yi dynasty), 6 vols. (hereafter *YSP*) (Poryŏnkak: Seoul, 1924; 1976 reprint), 1:113.

10. Boudewijn Walraven, "Popular Religion in a Confucianized Society," in JaHyun Kim Haboush and Martina Deuchler, eds., *Culture and the State in Late Chosŏn Korea* (Cambridge: Harvard University Asia Center, 1999), 160, 171–172. Note that this measure was not very effective.

11. Deuchler, *Confucian Transformation*, 259–261, 52–53, 56, 68.

12. Deuchler, *Confucian Transformation*, 231–232.

13. Deuchler, *Confucian Transformation*, 283.

14. *T'aejong sillok* 13, sixth month, *YSP* 1:185.

15. Deuchler, *Confucian Transformation*, 221.

16. Buswell, "Buddhism under Confucian Domination," 138–139.

17. *T'aejong sillok* 7, twelfth month, *YSP* 1: 149. However, nunneries were often subordinate institutions attached to or administered by monasteries. It is unclear whether the surviving monasteries were permitted to maintain these branch hermitages and nunneries.

18. *Sejong sillok* 10, third and fourth month, *YSP* 1:369.

19. Deuchler, *Confucian Transformation*, 260.

20. *Sejong sillok* 16, fourth month, *YSP* 1:408–416.

21. *Sejong sillok* 26, sixth month, *YSP* 1:617.

22. Deuchler, *Confucian Transformation*, 260–261.

23. *Yŏnsan'gun sillok* 2, fifth month, *YSP* 4:336–337. Buswell, "Buddhism under Confucian Domination," 140.

24. John Jorgensen, "Conflicts between Buddhism and Confucianism in the Chosŏn Dynasty," *Pulgyo yŏn'gu* 15 (1989): 195. Buswell, "Buddhism under Confucian Domination," 140.

25. Buswell, "Buddhism under Confucian Domination," 145ff.

26. *Sejo sillok* 8, fifth month, *YSP* 2:392–393.

27. Deuchler, *The Confucian Transformation*, 259.

28. U Chŏng-sang and Kim Yŏng-t'ae, *Hanguk Pulgyosa* (History of Korean Buddhism) (Seoul: Sinheung, 1976 reprint of 1968 ed.), 138–139.

29. *Yejong sillok* 1, ninth month, *YSP* 2:545–546.

30. Pae Sang-hyŏn, *Koryŏ hugi sawŏnjŏn yŏn'gu* (Study of Monastic Lands of the Late Koryŏ) (Seoul: Kukhak ch'aryowŏn, 1998), 22.

31. Pae, *Koryŏ hugi*, 327.

32. Deuchler, *The Confucian Transformation*, 143–144.

33. Deuchler, *The Confucian Transformation*, 228–229.

34. William Shaw, *Legal Norms in a Confucian State* (Berkeley: Center for Korean Studies, University of California, 1981), 100.

35. Shaw, *Legal Norms*, 80.

36. *Sŏngjong sillok* 6, fourth month, twenty-third and twenty-seventh day, *YSP* 3:45–46.

37. According to laws dating back to the time of King Sejong, punishment of a pregnant woman was not permitted until one hundred days after the birth. Deuchler, *The Confucian Transformation,* 266.

38. This is the monastic name of Kim Si-sŭp (1453–1493). A Confucian student, he turned to Buddhism because King Sejo had deposed his nephew, Tanjong, who was just a boy. However, Sŏlcham still had thoughts of serving the state, and in 1463 he spent ten days at court working on a vernacular translation of the *Lotus Sūtra.* He again attended court in 1464 or 1465 to participate in a ceremony. See Gregory Evon, "Remembering the Past, Condemned to the Present: The Imaginative Retreat of Kim Sisŭp (1435–1493)," *International Review of Korean Studies* 1, no. 1 (2004): 49–81, esp. 53.

39. U Chŏng-sang and Kim Yŏng-t'ae, *Hanguk Pulgyosa,* chronology, years 1471, 1488, 1489.

40. *Sŏngjong sillok* 6, fourth month, twenty-third day to twenty-sixth day of seventh month, *YSP* 3:45–60.

41. Deuchler, *The Confucian Transformation,* 372 note 138.

42. U Chŏng-sang and Kim Yŏng-t'ae, *Hanguk Pulgyosa,* chronology, 1477.

43. *Sŏngjong sillok* 8, second month, twenty-ninth day, *YSP* 3:33–34.

44. *Yŏnsan'gun sillok* 1, third month, fifth day, *YSP* 4:224–225.

45. The Chŏngŏpwŏn was ordered cleared soon after this, *Yŏnsan'gun sillok* 10, eighth month, eleventh day, *YSP* 4:466. See also Yi Ki-un, "Chosŏn sidae wangsil ŭi piguniwŏn sŏlch'i wa sinhaeng" (The Beliefs and Foundation of the Palace Nunneries in the Chosŏn Period), *Yŏksa hakpo* 178 (2003):34.

46. *Yŏnsan'gun sillok* 10, fourth month, twenty-sixth day, *YSP* 4:457–458. Note that Confucians claimed burial was necessary for ancestor worship and that one should not harm the body one was born with, for it was a gift from one's parents. This pertained even after death. Therefore, they decried the practice of cremation, which destroyed the body, and rulers would desecrate graves and dismember corpses as a postmortem punishment.

47. *Yŏnsan'gun sillok* 10, eleventh month, thirteenth day, *YSP* 4: 466–467.

48. Yi Ki-un, "Chosŏn sidae," 32.

49. U Chŏng-sang and Kim Yŏng-t'ae, *Hanguk Pulgyosa,* 138.

50. *Chungjong sillok* 3, fifth month, tenth day, *YSP* 4:513.

51. *YSP* 4:514.

52. Jahyun Kim Haboush, "Constructing the Center: The Ritual Controversy and the Search for a New Identity in Seventeenth-Century Korea," in JaHyun Kim Haboush and Martina Deuchler, eds., *Culture and the State in Late Chosŏn Korea* (Cambridge: Harvard University Asia Center, 1999), 62–63.

53. Described in Shaw, *Legal Norms,* 97.

54. *Injo sillok* 24, sixth month, *YSP* 6:296–298.

55. Kim Haboush, "Constructing the Center," 68–69, 71, 75–76.

56. *Yŏngjong sillok* 38, fifth month intercalary, fourteenth day, *YSP* 6:437.

57. *Sukjong sillok* 30, tenth month, twenty-eighth day; *YSP* 6:375–376.

58. Yi Ki-un, "Chosŏn sidae," 30, 32.

59. Yi Ki-un, "Chosŏn sidae," 53–54.

60. *T'ongdo saji,* 358; *Pŏm'ŏ saji,* 97–98, for other mentions, 214, 243.

61. *Pulguk saji (oe),* 69–70, 75.

62. For their history, see Kwŏn Sang-no, *Han'guk sach'al chŏnsŏ* (Compendium on Korean Monasteries), 2 vols. (hereafter *HSC*) (Tongguk Taehakkyo: Seoul, 1979), 2:947c.

63. *Taesŭng saji,* 160, 184–185, 204–206, 209, 260–262, 273–275.

64. *Taesŭng saji,* 206.

65. *Taesŭng saji,* 160, 184.

66. *Nag'wŏn tang ni sujwa Sasin chi pudobi* (Stupa Stele for the Head Nun of Nag'wŏn Hall, Sasin).

67. *Yujŏm-sa ponmal saji,* 257–258.

68. *HSC* 2:740a–b.

69. *Chŏndŭng ponmal saji,* 61, 64; *HSC* 2:1086c gives 1816 for the reconstruction.

70. *Chŏndŭng ponmal saji,* 64; *HSC* 2:1013b.

71. *Chŏndŭng ponmal saji,* 108; *HSC* 2:1013b gives date of 1883.

72. *Chŏndŭng ponmal saji,* 108–109; *HSC* 2:1013c.

73. *Chŏndŭng ponmal saji,* 67; *HSC* 2:922a.

74. *Chŏndŭng ponmal saji,* 155; *HSC* 1:405c, who only mentions the monk.

75. *Chŏndŭng ponmal saji,* 205, 239; Taehŭng Monastery was on Mount Ch'ŏnma, Kaep'ung-gun. Note: Wŏnt'ong Monastery and Wŏnt'ong-am were different institutions in different areas.

76. *Chŏndŭng ponmal saji,* 198–199.

77. *Pongsŏn ponmal saji,* 142–143.

78. *Kŏnbong-sa ponmal sajŏk* (1928), 19; *HSC* 1:286d.

79. *Yujŏm-sa ponmal saji,* 336–338.

80. *Yujŏm-sa ponmal saji,* 383–384.

81. *Yujŏm-sa ponmal saji,* 417–418, 480.

82. *Yujŏm-sa ponmal saji,* 603, 622, 638, 640.

83. *Yujŏm-sa ponmal saji,* 719; for this monastery, see *HSC* 2:1099c ff.

84. *Chŏndŭng ponmal saji,* 295.

85. Heejong Kang (Hŭi-jŏng Kang), "Women as Patrons of Buddhist Art in the Early Chosŏn Dynasty." Paper presented at the Association for Asian Studies Annual Meeting, Washington DC, April 4–7, 2002.

86. Only one poem mentions a nun, in the abstract. This is by Kye'o (1773–1849), in the *Kasan'go,* preface 1852. The poem, "Kyŏn nisŭng odo si" (On Seeing a Nun and Being Enlightened), probably dates to around 1823, *HPC* 10:767b.

87. Kihwa (1376–1433), *Hamhŏ tang Tŭkt'ong Hwasang ŏrok* (Recorded Sayings of Reverend Tŭkt'ong of Hamhŏ), published in 1440, *HPC* 7:227b–228a, 229c–230a; Pŏpgyŏn, *Kiamjip,* published in 1648, *HPC* 8:173a.

88. *HPC* 10:818–819.

89. *HPC* 10:166a.

90. "Hŏbaek tang Taesa pi" (Stele for the Master of Hŏbaek Hall) of 1662, connected with P'yohun Monastery, Chōsen Sōtokufu, comp., *Chōsen kinseki sōran* (Survey of Chosŏn Period Epigraphy), 2 vols. (Seoul: Asea munhwasa, 1976 reprint), 2:915–916.

91. Chōsen Sōtokufu, *Chōsen kinseki sōran* 2:1193–1195.

92. "Kan p'ye sŏkkyo so" (Appeal Against the Abolition of Buddhism), *HPC* 8:341b–342a.

93. Cf. Pou (–1565), *Kwŏnyŏm yorok* (Essential Records Encouraging Recitation [of the Names of the Buddha]), published in 1637, *HPC* 7:612c, 613a–c; Paeg'am Sŏngch'ong (1631–1700), *Chŏngt'o posŏ* (Precious Texts on the Pure Land), published in 1686, *HPC* 8:505bff., on nuns and rebirth, beginning with the Sui and ending with the Ch'ing dynasty, but no Korean women, and 506a–509a, on laywomen and rebirth, but again no Koreans; Myŏngyŏn, in *Yŏmbul po'gwŏnmun* (Texts Exhorting the Practice of Recitation of the Buddha's Names), published in 1704, quotes only Chinese examples, *HPC* 9:51b–53c.

94. *HPC* 10:449a–449c.

95. Sŏngch'ong (1631–1700), *Ch'imun pohunju* (Glosses on the Precious Instructions to the Monkhood) of 1695, on instructions for clerics, *HPC* 8:584b–585b; Paekp'a Hwansŏn (1767–1852), *Chakbŏp kwigam* (Speculum of Ritual Procedure) of 1826, *HPC* 10:579b–580a.

96. *Yŏndam taesa imhanok* (Record from Beneath the Forest of Master Yŏndam), published in 1799, *HPC* 10:283a.

97. Cf. Myŏngyŏn, *Yŏmbul po'gwŏnmun*, *HPC* 9:45b.

98. Shim Jae-ryong, *Korean Buddhism: Tradition and Transformation* (Seoul: Jimoondang, 1999), 238–241.

99. Yi Kŭn-su, *Chosŏnjo ŭi ŏmun chŏngch'aek yŏn'gu* (Government Policy on Vernacular Writing of the Chosŏn Court) (Seoul: Kaemunsa, 1979), 119–128; Michael J. Pettid, "Devoted Wives and Chaste Maidens: Didactic Literature and Virtuous Women in Chosŏn Korea," in Gi-Hyun Shin, ed., *Korean Language, Knowledge and Society: Proceedings of the Third Biennial Conference Korean Studies Association of Australasia* (KSAA, 2003), 88–89.

100. Pettid, "Devoted Wives," 94.

101. Yi Kŭn-su, *Chosŏncho*, 131–134.

102. Yi Pong-ch'un, "Chosŏn chŏn'gi Puljŏn ŏnhae wa sasang e taehan yŏn'gu" (Research on the Vernacular Interpretation and Thought of the the Buddhist Scriptures in Early Chosŏn) (MA thesis, Tongguk University, 1978), 28–29, 33, 58–59.

103. Yi Chin-ho, "*Yukjo tan'gyŏng ŏnhae* ŭi t'ŭkching kwa kyoyuk ch'ŏlhakjŏk ŭiŭi" (Features of the Vernacular Interpretation of the *Platform Sūtra* of the Sixth Patriarch and the Significance of its Educational Philosophy), in Kim Chi-gyŏn, ed., *Yukjo tan'gyŏng ŭi se'gye* (The World of the *Platform Sūtra* of the Sixth Patriarch) (Seoul: Minjoksa, 1989), 412–413.

104. Yi Pong-ch'un, "Chosŏn chŏn'gi," 31, 52.

105. Yi Kŭn-su, *Chosŏncho*, 148, 152, 157.

106. Yi Kŭn-su, *Chosŏncho*, 131–132.
107. *HPC* 7:612.
108. *HPC* 9:45b, 55cff.
109. *HPC* 9:702.
110. *HPC* 10:144c ff.

7

Buddhist Nuns and Alternative Space in Confucian Chosŏn Society

Ji-Young Jung

In this chapter, I will use an alternative reading of the male Confucian elite's discourse on Buddhist nuns during the Chosŏn period to examine women who went beyond the boundaries of the dominant Confucian doctrine.[1] Buddhist monasteries provided upper-class (*yangban*) women an alternative cultural space from which their "female vitality" that the new Confucian norm tried to restrict could emanate. Buddhism in Chosŏn society formed an important part of popular culture that Confucian ideology was not able to completely subsume. Women in particular were key to maintaining its vitality.[2]

Scholars have previously focused on the status of women almost entirely in regards to their relation to the establishment of neo-Confucianism as the governing ideology of the Chosŏn dynasty. They see the transformation of the status of women as occurring in tandem with the spread of Confucian ideology. In particular, they have discussed the ways in which Confucianization affected such institutions as inheritance,[3] marriage,[4] adoption,[5] and ancestor worship.[6] As the past focus on the ideology of Confucian domination could not sufficiently account for the full scope of women's Buddhist activities in this era, the focus of this chapter shifts instead toward the subculture that developed therein, and the female agency that brought about its establishment.

To understand how Confucianism defined the proper role of women, we can look to the traditional female norm of "*samjong-ji-do*" (the Virtue of the Three Obediences). Here, women were defined solely as daughter, wife, or mother and their behaviors were proscribed through subordinated relationships inherent in each role. Ideologically, becoming someone's wife and then a mother to a son was an essential condition of leading a normal female life in Chosŏn dynasty. However, we may ask whether all women living under this Confucian ideology actually succumbed to these requirements and lived as wives and mothers of sons in contentment. Were there not any alternative lifestyles? It is true that numerous restrictions on the activities of women outside the home were legislated during the Chosŏn period? Yet I wonder if we should view these many legal restrictions not as proof that women led primarily domestic lives, but as evidence that so few women in fact submitted willingly to a life restricted to the domestic sphere.[7]

There is a need for scholarship to go beyond generalized descriptions of Chosŏn women and to focus specifically on the detailed context, process, and contents of Confucianization. It is especially necessary to view how Confucianism, even while steadily progressing during the seventeenth and eighteenth centuries, continued to arouse opposition and encounter resistance. We should be careful, moreover, not to view this resistance simplistically. Perhaps rather than simply defining the Chosŏn dynasty as the "Age of Confucianism," we should view it as a period during which, even while Confucian morality was changing society, numerous countermovements were also coming into being and forming a new balance with these new Confucian customs. The persistence of non-Confucian elements in Chosŏn society is one of the main issues demanding further discussion.[8]

If we look at documents from the Chosŏn dynasty, we find numerous references to women who do not fit within this Confucian ideology: from the bureaucrats' wives who came home dead drunk after carousing late into the night at banned religious ceremonies, to Buddhist nuns traveling in groups and staking out positions in the countryside.[9] One can approach the issue of women's responses to the Confucianized domestic sphere by investigating the Buddhist beliefs of *yangban* women, with special focus on their activities within Buddhist monasteries.[10] We might then try to understand the thoughts and lives of women within Chosŏn's Confucian society, focusing on how women's interests—material, intellectual, and emotional—caused them to make space for themselves outside of the domestic sphere.

In this chapter, I search for the traces left by nuns[11] who led alternative paths outside the boundaries prescribed by the Confucian patriarchal ideology. Few records tell of these women. They themselves left no historical records and the few written about them are distorted by male-dominant views. Most of the relevant discourses were produced during the development of the Chosŏn state into a Confucian society, with the objective of the narratives aimed at the containment of Buddhism and Buddhist nuns. Despite these biases, with these sources we can at least trace these nuns' existence. This chapter examines the women who did not conform to Confucian norms through a feminist reading of the discourses that expressed anxiety about women becoming Buddhist nuns or argued for the regulation and punishment of their activities.

STORIES OF THOSE WHO BECAME NUNS

In *Sijipsariyo* (Suffering under the In-laws), a Chosŏn song about the life of a married woman, the protagonist Kkoktukaksi is harassed by her in-laws for not working hard enough in the field. When her husband Pak *ch'ŏmji* (i.e., Mr. Pak) takes a concubine and refuses to give her any property, Kkoktukaksi tells him, "I want to go to Kŭmgang Mountain to become a nun. Give me some travel expenses." She leaves, becomes a nun against her husband's wishes, and lives as a wanderer.[12] How are we to understand such a woman, who decided to leave her unjust in-laws behind and become a nun? Can we not read the subjectivity of a certain segment of Chosŏn women from this song, those who actively refused the unjust and oppressive familial structure? The following record from 1478 (Sŏngjong reign year nine) relates some information about nuns in Chosŏn society.

> These days, unmarried women and widows continuously shave their heads and become nuns. Saying that they are either encouraging good virtue or picnicking in the mountains, they gather in groups and mingle with nuns; these kinds of wanton acts disrupt the good custom of proper families. They provide no benefits to the state and only harm to the people. We [the officials] are curious as to why your majesty does not shut down the monasteries, even when everyone in the court, including your advisors, is telling your majesty to do so.[13]

This claim, which clearly intends to describe nuns in a bad light, is certainly limited in the truth it can provide regarding the true reality of this situation. Yet, from the expressions "continuously shave their heads" and "gather in groups," we can surmise that nuns were not so rare in Chosŏn society. We can also surmise that becoming a nun was not so much a forced outcome born out of necessity but a deliberate choice.

To further our understanding of who these women were, let's examine a record from the twenty-second year of Sŏngjong's reign.

> These days, not only those from the middle class but also those from the literati class shave their heads and become nuns. They become nuns when their husbands have only just passed away. Even unmarried women compete with each other to go to the monasteries to become nuns. This is not appropriate. It is only natural that men have wives, and women have husbands. For women to become nuns when they are still young and never yet married harms the harmonious energy. I beg your majesty to order them back to the secular world.[14]

We can see from this record that there were many women, both unmarried and widowed, of various classes, who became nuns. And these nuns were criticized for "disturbing the harmonious energy" for not being in a marital relationship. The *sillok* (Annals) of King Sŏngjong record many cases of literati women becoming nuns. Thus, there was much debate whether to ban the practice.[15]

To further understand the development of this subculture, we need to examine the circumstances under which these women become nuns. According to *Sŏngjong sillok,* "Some of them became nuns after losing their virtue. Others became nuns after they were widowed, claiming that they would pray for their deceased husbands. However, the real reason behind this action was to wander around numerous monasteries and engage in wanton acts."[16] From these materials, we can see that the male Confucian intellectuals believed that there were three types of women who became nuns: unmarried women, widows, and housewives. The first were said to have become nuns due to adulterous acts,[17] the persuasion of others,[18] illness,[19] out of sadness for a parent's death,[20] or for being ousted from their home. We must consider, however, that all these reasons were given by men and did not necessarily represent reality.

The state banned unmarried women from becoming nuns, yet it considered those who did as objects of relief. Nuns were portrayed as destitute women, deprived of the married lives that they yearned for.[21] Some were viewed as having chosen the path, but most were considered to have become nuns because of the coercion of others. Government officials said, "Literati women are not allowed to become nuns, but of late, due to lax inspection, many are forced to shave their heads and not marry."[22]

During Sŏngjong's reign, an unmarried woman, Miss Kwŏn, became a nun, and a debate ensued between the king and Kyŏng Chun, an official in the Inspector-General's Office, about whether the woman became a nun through her own will or through coercion by a woman named Hong Sadang. King Sŏngjong thought that she became a nun through her own will because she had an illness. Kyŏng Chun argued that since she became a nun through Hong Sadang's coaxing and her parents' lack of interest, it was not due to her free will.[23] If so, his argument followed, the person who coerced her into shaving her head was to be punished. There were also incessant discussions aimed at forcing those who had already become nuns to return to the secular world and marry. In *T'aejong sillok,* we can find a petition: "Please order the young nuns, except those who had entered the monastery as widows, to keep their chastity, to return to their homes, and to marry."[24] The male officials thought that "although the nuns regret their decision [to become a nun] and want to return, they cannot say it aloud, and thus their hearts are always troubled."[25] As such, those who became nuns without ever having married were considered objects of relief.

The second type of woman to become nuns was widows. Many widows became nuns soon after they were widowed, claiming that it was necessary to preserve their chastity. This seems unlikely, since if keeping their chastity was the real purpose, they would have first completed the period of mourning for their deceased husband. Some women became nuns even before the funeral of their departed husbands. Mrs. Yun, the wife of Yu Chahwan, who became the abbess of Chŏngŏpwŏn, was such a case.[26] She ran away and became a nun on the day her husband was buried.

> The wife, Mrs. Yun, daughter of minister Yun Hyŏng, was easily led to jealousy and lechery. Even when her husband Yu Chahwan was alive, she would secretly socialize with nuns, and she had no expressions of sadness when her husband passed away. When the relatives prepared to go to [the husband's] hometown [to bury him], she pretended as if she was going to go with them. But on the evening before the burial she ran away and became a nun. Afterwards, she wandered the mountains and met many monks, received scriptures from them, and stayed with them. She would say that she was "praying for her deceased husband," but actually she was only looking to please her mind.[27]

We do not know exactly why Mrs. Yun ran away to become a nun without attending her husband's burial. Could she not endure life as someone's wife under the Confucian family order? Although male officials criticized her by saying that she was pursuing pleasure, she was likely just active in her religious activities as evidenced from the fact that she received scriptures from the monks she met. Moreover, she was capable enough at networking in her religious community to later become the chief priest of Chŏngŏpwŏn. For such a woman, living within the strict Confucian norms as someone's wife must have been so unbearable that she could not even wait until the burial rite was performed before retiring from the world. Or perhaps she had already transcended the norms that obligated her to attend her husband's funeral.

While the rationales offered in the denunciation of unmarried nuns were quite simple, since such women were considered to be the objects of relief, the ideological stance to take toward widowed women who became nuns was more complex. Since remarriage was practically banned in the Chosŏn dynasty,[28] the idea that widows became nuns to keep their chastity was warmly accepted. The widows of Chosŏn could open up the way of becoming Buddhist nuns by justifying it with "chastity," a female value imposed on them. They made a crack in the Confucian regulation by utilizing the very same regulation. During Sejong's reign, there was a move to ban sons and unmarried women from entering the monastery as monks and nuns, but an exception was made for widows.[29] There were, however, incessant suspicions about the behavior of these widowed nuns. Criticism of widowed nuns who engaged in lecherous acts with monks was constantly raised. These widows practiced the norms of chaste widows by becoming nuns, but, by doing so, they were able to transgress the traditional spatial boundaries between the chaste and the unchaste.

The last group included those who had "betrayed their husbands."[30] These women had been married but left their homes to become nuns. They may have resorted to becoming nuns because of oppressive in-laws or unfaithful husbands,[31] but, in the eyes of the abandoned husbands, these women were regarded as "wives who betrayed." There were also those like Sabangji,[32] whose sexual identity was unclear, as well as court ladies who became nuns.[33]

MONASTERY AND PLAY: STAYING OVERNIGHT, TALKING, AND MINGLING

Chosŏn Korea was a state built on Confucianism as its ruling ideology. From the beginning of the dynasty, the Chosŏn court, through numerous policies, attempted to remake itself into a Confucian society. Laws restricting the daily lives of women were put into effect from the beginning, including the *Naeoe pŏp* (laws defining which male relatives could meet freely with what women), *Punyŏ sangsa kŭmji pŏp* (laws restricting women's entrance into monasteries), and *P'yŏnggyoja kŭmji pŏp* (regulations outlawing the use of open sedan chairs by women), as well as *Chaeganyŏ chason kŭmgo pŏp* (laws preventing the descendants of twice-married women from taking civil service exams).[34]

These policies based on Confucianism stressed the regulation of women's bodies as a focus for moral cultivation. In this sense, activities such as "leaving the inner room" and general forms of play can be seen as a kind of resistance to the social and ideological norms of the time. Monasteries provided women with a liberated area from these regulations.[35]

Since the fourth year of T'aejong's reign, women were ordered not to enter Buddhist monasteries.[36] But this ban was never successfully carried out. Occasionally, there were Buddhist functions sponsored by the royal court itself, and many literati men and women attended them. Prince Hyoryŏng Yi Po opened a *Suryuk* festival[37] held for seven days near the Han River. Men and women gathered and literati women offered food at the altar.[38] Nuns were criticized for not being sequestered in the mountains but mingling with women and sponsoring monastery events.

Those who strongly argued that women who frequented monasteries should be punished pointed out the fact that these women were mingling with monks. During Sejong's reign, Mrs. Tong, the widow of an high official Yi Hwa-yŏng, convinced not only her mother and daughter, but also other female relatives, to stay at a small monastery with monks. She also had her jewelry melted down to write the *Lotus Sūtra* and made honey cookies to offer to the monks.[39] In the sixteenth year of Sejong's reign, Hoeam Monastery in Yangju hosted a Buddhist event attended by many women and nuns. When three monks started performing a dance called *muae-hŭi*, the women began to take off their clothes to offer as donations.[40] Another source described the scene: "musicians were hired, gold and silver decorated the Buddha, and men and women were mixed."[41]

Advisory officials demanded that the king punish the husbands of the violators. "Although it is well known that women are not allowed to enter the monasteries, of late, those like Mrs. Yun, Mrs. Yi, and Mrs. Hwang have traveled to numerous monasteries and stayed for two nights. Their manners were not in accordance with the *Book of Rituals*, and surprised those around them."[42] In response to these memorials, the king avoided punishing them by saying, "these women were merely unaware of the law." In the end, only one literati woman and one nun were flogged eighty times while others were just fined.[43]

Buddhist events organized by nuns and women continued. It was impossible to stop them from frequenting the monasteries with these bans. Another reason why these incidents were difficult to punish was because these events were sponsored by the royal court and the women participating were from the families of high officials. A *Sahŏnbu* record laments, "These women do not fear the ban and act as they wish!"[44]

The sillok of the Chosŏn dynasty recorded that women from the literati class would go up to the monasteries and pray, stay overnight, and chat with each other. What did the nuns and the women chat about all night? These dialogues never appeared in the pages of history, but were recorded as "lecherous mixings" through the eyes and mouths of male recorders.

The kings, however, knew very well that they could not break these women's wills. "If they consider it [going to the monasteries] a virtuous act and admire it with all their heart, then this means that these women have given up [Confucian cultivation], and we cannot do anything about it."[45] From this we can see that the women who frequented Buddhist monasteries were considered by the state as having abandoned the state-sanctioned ideology and instead chosen to live according to their own will.

In a society where civilized life was defined in Confucian terms, women continued to believe in Buddhism, pray at Buddhist monasteries, and participate in monastery events. State control and punishment could not change this cultural trend. In the monastery, nuns were able to build their own world. Mrs. Yun, who became a nun even before carrying out her husband's funeral, became an abbess at Chŏngŏpwŏn. The niece of Hong Kyŏng-son, who became an unmarried nun, is recorded to have gone to South Kyŏngsang Province to picnic in the mountains.[46] The significance of a nun picnicking in the mountains becomes clear once we remind ourselves that women during the Chosŏn dynasty were kept indoors by the Confucian rules of conduct. While other women were restricted from going outside, nuns were free to roam outdoors and picnic in the mountains.

The male intellectuals' descriptions of the activities of the nuns and women at Buddhist monasteries as lecherous and debauched were intended to disparage both the women and Buddhism. Thus, it is hard to say that the narratives are factual. It is more likely that they were recording the fact that Buddhist prayers were being held overnight with such descriptions as "men and women mingled." It is possible that the women at the Buddhist monasteries expressed not only their religious belief but also their sexual pleasure seeking and chitchatting desires—those things seen in the eyes of Confucian male intellectuals as "lecherous"—to their heart's content. What does it say about the male ruling class when they could not prevent women from frequenting the monasteries? It shows that by permitting the women's activities at the Buddhist monasteries, the male ruling class's discipline of women according to Confucian norms was not as seamless as it has often been characterized.

NUNS AND THE DISCOURSE ABOUT BUDDHISM ENDANGERING THE STATE

The nuns and women at the monastery did not just step outside the boundaries of Confucian norms through their partying, singing, and dancing. According to *Chungjong sillok*, "The evil acts of nuns are worse than that of monks; some frequent the homes of ministers, some frequent the court, and they do disrespectful acts. I beg your majesty to ban them from entering the capital."[47] These nuns seem to have used these visits to meddle with"outside matters." We can surmise that behind the discourse that criticized these nuns for being "lecherous," there may have been vigilance against their political power. Perhaps for this reason, the discourse on nuns during the Chosŏn dynasty was mostly negative: they were described as lecherous, willful, dirty, and harmful to the people. They were also "not afraid of the laws and conceited."[48] As soon as women became nuns, they began to exist outside the Confucian norms of conduct. It is not surprising that these women who possessed mental faculties, desire, passion, and collective power were considered lecherous and dirty from the perspective of those living within the prescribed boundaries.

The establishment of Confucianism was only enabled through the suppression of Buddhism.[49] "A king's reign is shortened when Buddhism is popular."[50] This statement represents the typical discourse espoused during the Chosŏn period in order to suppress Buddhism. The neo-Confucian elite argued for stronger suppression of Buddhism by strengthening the *toch'ŏp* system.[51] The state encouraged nuns to return to the secular world, and there were discussions to punish the heads of families when an unmarried daughter became a nun.[52] Monks and nuns were ostracized in Confucian society, and nuns were considered particularly dangerous. Unmarried women disrupted the family-centered order and because they were outside the bounds of marriage, nuns were thus considered dangerous to the state.

Nuns were regarded as a congregation of women who had disrupted the Confucian order. They did not benefit the state and only harmed the people. Especially when unmarried women became nuns, the basis of the state structure, which was the harmonious relation of *yin* and *yang*, wife and husband, was being disrupted. "If they had married and engaged in productive industry they would have become good people, but since they idle and consume clothes and food, they only disrupt the order of the state."[53] As such, monks and nuns were considered disruptive to the state. This is why the Chosŏn dynasty had a policy that made unmarried nuns return to society and marry.[54] Through marriage, the Chosŏn dynasty tried to bind men and women together into a 'normal' family unit. This policy was in a sense a relief policy for those women who could not marry, but also an encouragement for the women to be reborn into a 'normal' woman that society demanded.

In *Sejong sillok*, debates over never-married nuns continued. It was argued that never-married nuns should be rescued because they harmed the harmonious energy of the nation. One year there was a drought, and a memorial was submitted saying, "[it is natural that] the sky responds to the changes in the human world; the harmonious energy was harmed because there are women in their thirties and forties that have never married."[55] The censorial official Saganwŏn continued:

> The scripture said make sure that there are no resentful women. This is because the scriptures regarded the importance of the *yin–yang* harmony between husband and wife. Here, young nuns accumulate impure desires in their hearts but disguise them with a chaste appearance; although they want to get married, they cannot say it out loud, and spend their days sighing with regret. These surely are the hidden resentments! Would your majesty not order the officials around the state to have nuns under thirty years of age grow out their hair and marry?[56]

By saying that the young nuns resented their ill fate, the possibility that these women had made voluntary decisions was erased. Yet for those nuns who had no prospect of being relieved, they were subjected to measures that restricted them from entering the cities and prevented them from socializing with 'normal' women. The following passage from *Sukchong sillok*, which relates to Saganwŏn's argument to destroy Buddhist nunneries, aptly demonstrates how nuns were perceived at the time.

> The reason why monks and nuns were banned from entering the city walls was to protect the people against lechery

> and cunningness, so as to correct the ways of the people. This is why the previous king destroyed all the nunneries. Yet, these days Buddhism has once again became popular, and nuns in groups of tens or hundreds live together within the ten *li* from the eastern suburbs and build big houses. These houses sparkle in gold, and six out of ten are built so close to each other that one could look into one house from another. These houses have become the gathering places of wives who betrayed their husbands, maids who betrayed their masters, and unchaste widows. I cannot numerate the evil and lecherous deeds of these women. I ask your majesty to order these houses to be destroyed and the women to be sent to their proper places; please correct this wrong, and transform these women into proper people.[57]

From this record, we learn that from the Confucian state's point of view, the nuns were adulterous and cunning beings and what's more, that even during the late Chosŏn dynasty of the seventeenth through nineteenth centuries, women did not stop favoring Buddhism. Even though the majority of records about women frequenting monasteries came during the T'aejong and Chŏngjong reigns, this is only because the T'aejong and Chŏngjong reigns were when the Chosŏn state made regulations regarding the matter; it was not because women became less interested in Buddhism after the seventeenth century.

We also learn that nuns were not rare: according to the previous passage, they were as numerous as to build houses in groups of tens and hundreds. Fearing that the nuns would cause disorder in the ways of the people, the state ended up banning nuns from entering the city walls. In the first year of Yŏngjo's reign, the ban was expanded to include monks.

> A royal secretary (*sŭngji*) Yi Chŏng-ju pleaded, "Because there are so many Buddhist monasteries close to the cities, many good daughters from proper families are lured into shaving their heads and becoming nuns. Your majesty must ban this practice." The king said, "Currently, the Confucian way is prosperous in the state; how could a petty number of heretics harm it? Simply ban the nuns from entering the city walls."[58]

Nuns were considered dangerous women who could taint proper women if left to their devices. Although there were differences between the types of nuns (unmarried, widowed, those who had committed adultery), the commonality between them was that they were not contained by the Confucian family order.[59]

Even though the *Chosŏn wangjo sillok* records put the nuns in such a negative light, the subtext of these dictums evokes the prosperity of Buddhism at the time. Also, we learn that in spite of Saganwŏn's continual requests to have the nunneries destroyed, the king persistently declined. The king knew that Buddhism, as a women's religion and culture, could not be destroyed merely by destroying a number of monasteries.

CONCLUDING REMARKS

The Chosŏn dynasty tried to squelch the influence of Buddhism in everyday life and rebuild the society on the basis of Confucianism. The builders of the new state espoused Confucianism as an antidote to Buddhism, the state ideology of the previous Koryŏ dynasty. The major obstacles in achieving this goal were the women who were not willing to give up their Buddhist practices. Following the long cultural tradition, women believed in Buddhism, prayed at the monasteries, and socialized with monks and nuns.

Those women who became nuns did so not just because of their religious convictions but also to protest against the Confucian patriarchal order. The monastery in the Kŭmgang Mountain was an alternative space to the marital home that could be chosen or imagined. Thus, women living during the Chosŏn dynasty were able to create an alternative space outside of Confucian social norms through Buddhism.

What is the significance of this alternative Buddhist culture created by nuns and laywomen within the Confucian culture of the Chosŏn dynasty? Jahyun Kim Haboush and Martina Deuchler note that "whereas the public space was occupied by what was manifest, orthodox, and legitimate, marginalized groups, such as Buddhists and practitioners of popular religion, were tolerated as long as they remained 'invisible,' that is, as long as they did not claim part of the public space. By the late Chosŏn period, diminished and consigned to 'invisible' spaces in their spheres of activity, neither Buddhism nor popular religions were perceived as threatening the existing socio-religious order, and the state felt no need to persecute them."[60] Thus, though it can be said that Buddhism played an important part in the popular imagination, this role did not appear in the public sphere, and, as such, was not seen as a target for particular persecution.

This explanation takes off from the point of view that Confucian hegemony reigned supreme in the Chosŏn dynasty. However, is the distinction between what appears in the public sphere and what remains invisible really so explicit? Chosŏn women who became nuns did not exist in a domain separate from Confucianism. They were all ensconced within the moral strictures of Confucianism and, generally speaking, these women lived lives faithfully devoted to the roles delineated by Confucianism. Lay believers and nuns lived outside the confines of an oppressive social order, yet, at the same time, they remained within it, or emerged from it. Considering the ambiguity between these ideas of "inside" or "outside," we must question whether we can simply consider Confucian ideology as oppressive and Buddhism invisible.

From the perspective of the Chosŏn elite, though the Buddhist women had to be rendered invisible, this consisted of a process that embraced the visualization of these women only then to have it be eliminated. Visits to monasteries by Chosŏn women proved to be the source of endless headaches, bringing anguish to the elite males forced between the position of officially persecuting or approving such behaviors. Chosŏn dynasty records, produced by men, described nuns as lecherous and cunning beings. They were thought to be luring proper daughters to stay with them at the monasteries all night long and engage in lecherous activities with monks. In short, nuns were regarded as harmful to the Confucian state and its foundational ideology. As such, the reason these women came to be seen as such "harmful beings" was due to the fissure that emerged within the dominant Confucian social order.

The state tried to prevent the nuns from influencing other women. At the time, Confucian intellectuals and the royal court did not exercise extreme control over these activities, although they certainly limited them. This shows the complex ways in which intellectual and religious communities negotiated state control through the flexible adaptation of their ideologies and practices. This negotiation opened a niche in which women could maintain their Buddhist cultural life, handed down since Koryŏ, while at the same time appear to conform to Confucian norms. This niche was rendered possible by the constant resistance by some women, such as Buddhist nuns, who were not completely subsumed under Confucian regulations.

How can we find the erased voices and the diverse lifestyles of those women who transgressed the socially prescribed boundaries? How can we tell the stories of women who did not adjust easily to the new Confucian patriarchy or of those women who wanted to lead alternative lives? No written records of Chosŏn nuns survive, and their place within the modern history of that era has also been completely erased. Nevertheless, this does not mean that the women of the age simply led lives of unstinting oppression in the face of a dominant Confucian ideology. The thought system of Buddhism, along with the spatial presence of its monasteries, created a crack within the edifice of Confucian ruling discourse and control, and to women dreaming of a place "outside" this social order, it provided an alternative space for those who were unable to adapt to the strictures this order placed on their lives. Chosŏn dynasty women made space for themselves by utilizing all the means allowed them. We can read in the lives of Buddhist nuns and the space of Buddhist monasteries the traces of women who transgressed the Confucian boundaries in the Chosŏn dynasty.

NOTES

An earlier form of this chapter first appeared in *The Review of Korean Studies* 11, no. 4 (December 2008).

1. There are studies on female Buddhist monks during the Chosŏn period that examine the establishment of Buddhist monasteries for female monks by the royal household and the ways in which female monks are portrayed in novels and stories during the period. See Suk-chong Chŏng, and Pyŏn-sŏn Pak, "Chosŏn hugi pulgyo chŏngch'aek kwa wŏndang—nisŭng ŭi chonjae yangsang ŭl chungsim ŭro" (The Policy on Buddhism and Wŏndang in the Late Chosŏn Dynasty—Focusing on the Existence of Bhikṣuṇīs), *Minjok munhwa nonch'ong* (Collective Papers on National Culture) 18 (1998): 223–256; Ki-un Yi, "Chosŏn sidae wangsil ŭi piguniwŏn sŏlch'i wa sinhaeng" (Buddhist Practice and the Establishment of Palace Nunneries in the Chosŏn Period), *Yŏksa hakpo* (Research Essays on History) 178 (2003): 29–56; In-gyu Hwang, *Chosŏn chŏn'gi Chŏngŏpwŏn kwa pigunijuji* (The Chŏngŏpwŏn and Its Head Nuns in the Early Chosŏn Dynasty), *Han'guk pulgyohak* (Korean Buddhist Studies) 51 (2008): 103–129; Il-nam Kyŏng, "Kojŏn sosŏl e nat'anan yŏsŭng ŭi inmul yuhyŏng kwa munhakchŏk kinŭng yŏn'gu" (The Character Types and Literary Function of Buddhist Nuns as Represented in Classical Novels), *Ŏmun yŏn'gu* (Studies on Languages and Literature) 44 (2004): 207–230.

2. Min Sun-ŭi offers a feminist analysis of Buddhism by focusing on the Buddhist faith of the royal household, such as queens Sohye and Mungjŏng. Her feminist framework emphasizes women's experiences, understanding and looking after others on the basis of maternal thinking, women's solidarity and sisterhood, and gender politics. She analyzes the Chosŏn women's Buddhist activities as an embodiment of sisterhood. Min, Sun-ŭi, "Pulgyo rŭl t'onghan hŏstori pokku ŭi illye—Chosŏn wangsil ŭi pulgyo sinang ŭl chungsim ŭro" (A Case Study on the Restoration of 'Herstory' through Buddhism—Religious

Belief in the Royal Family), *Chonggyomunhwa yŏn'gu* (Studies on Religious Culture) 6 (2004): 45–64.

3. Edward Wagner, "Two Early Genealogies and Korean Women's Status in Korea's Early Yi Dynasty," in Laurel Kendall and Mark Peterson, eds., *Korean Women: View from the Inner Room* (New Haven: East Rock Press, 1983), 23–32.

4. Pyŏng-in Chang, *Chosŏn chŏn'gi honinje wa sŏngch'abyŏl* (The Marital System and Gender Discrimination in the Early Chosŏn Dynasty) (Seoul: Iljisa, 1997).

5. Mark A. Peterson, *Korean Adoption and Inheritance: Case Studies in the Creation of a Classic Confucian Society* (Ithaca: Cornell University Press, 1996).

6. Martina Deuchler, *The Confucian Transformation of Korea* (Cambridge: Harvard University Press, 1992).

7. Ji-Young Jung [Chi-yŏng Chŏng], "Chosŏn sidae punyŏ ŭi noch'ul kwa oech'ul" (Escaping the Inner Room: Women between Regulation and Resistance in the Chosŏn Dynasty), *Yŏsŏng kwa yŏksa* (Women and History) 2 (2005): 149–181.

8. Confucian reformers attempted a thorough transformation toward a very different social order, so contemporary Koreans have faced an arduous transition out of this Confucian embrace. See Martina Deuchler, "The Tradition: Women during the Yi Dynasty," *Virtues in Conflict: Tradition and the Korean Woman Today*, ed. Sandra Mattielli (Seoul: Royal Asiatic Society, 1977), p. 45.

9. Ji-Young Jung, op. cit.

10. Ŭn-sŏn Yi, "Chosŏn sidae sŏngnihak chŏngch'ak kwa yŏsŏng ŭi sinang hwaldong" (The Establishment of Neo-Confucianism and the Religious Life of Women in the Chosŏn Dynasty), *Sahak yŏn'gu* (Studies on History) 54 (1997): 109–140; Sun-gu Yi, Chosŏn ch'ogi yŏsŏng ŭi sinhaeng saenghwal (Women's Religious Life in the Early Chosŏn Dynasty), *Yŏksa hakpo* (Research Essays on History) 150 (1996): 41–82.

11. Nuns were called *sŭngni* (僧尼) or *nisŭng* (尼僧) during the Chosŏn period.

12. Chae-hae Yim, "Kkoktukaksi kŏri e nat'anan pubu kaldŭng kwa yŏsŏng ŭisik" (The Consciousness of Women and Spousal Conflict in the Kkoktukaksi Puppet Play), *Yŏsŏng munje yŏn'gu* (Studies on Feminist Issues) 12 (1984): 143–156. Previous studies state that the decision to become a nun was considered a passive response to marital conflict. See Chang, Sŏng-jin, "*Sijipsariyo* ŭi yuhyŏng kwa inmul" (Character Types and Personalities in the [Songs titled] *Suffering under the In-laws*), *Yŏsŏng munje yŏn'gu* (Studies on Feminist Issues) 12 (1984): 377–395. However, when we consider that by becoming a nun, a woman entirely abandoned the oppressive familial structure, such a decision could be seen as quite active.

13. *Sŏngjong sillok* 9, eleventh month, thirtieth day.

14. *Sŏngjong sillok* 22, fifty year, twenty-second day.

15. *Sŏngjong sillok* 9, third month, tenth day.

16. *Sŏngjong sillok* 4, eighth month, fourth day.

17. *Chosŏn wangjo sillok* calls these cases *silhaeng* (inappropriate acts), which usually refers to premarital sex (*Sŏngjong sillok* 4, eighth month, fourth day).

18. A record from the Sŏngjong reign states, "Hong Kyŏngson's sister became an unmarried nun, and his niece also became an unmarried nun." It seems likely that Hong Kyŏngson's sister became a nun first and then influenced her niece to do so as well (*Sŏngjong sillok* 2, eleventh month, twenty-second day).

19. *Sŏngjong sillok* 6, fifth month, twenty-sixth day.

20. *Sejong sillok* 7, sixth month, twenty-third day.

21. *Sejong sillok* 25, fifth month, sixteenth day.

22. *Sŏngjong sillok* 6, fifth month, twenty-sixth day.

23. *Sŏngjong sillok* 8, second month, twenty-ninth day.

24. *T'aejong sillok* 2, second month, eighteenth day.

25. *Sejong sillok* 8, sixth month, twenth-third day.

26. See In-gyu Hwang, op. cit., for more information about female chief priests at Buddhist monasteries.

27. *Sejo sillok* 13, second month, twenty-fifth day.

28. The *chaeganyŏ chason kŭmpo pŏp* (law preventing the descendants of twice-married women from taking the civil service exams) was promulgated in 1485 (the sixteenth year of sŏngjong's reign). It practically coerced the widows of Yangban class not to marry again even though it did not explicitly forbid widows' remarraige. See Lee Sangbaek, "Chaega Kŭmji sŭpsok ŭi yurae e taehan yŏn'gu," (Research on the History of the Ban on Remarriage), *Chosŏn Munhwasa Yŏn'gu Nongo* (Studies on Chosŏn Cultural History) (Seoul: Ŭryu Munhwasa, 1948); Ji-Young Jung, "Widows' Position and Agency in Late Chosŏn Dynasty," *The Journal of Korean Studies* 14-1 (2009), 12): 61–82.

29. *Sejong sillok* 2, eleventh month, seventh day.

30. *Sukchong sillok* 30, tenth month, twenty-eighth day.

31. The previously mentioned Kkoktugaksi in *Sijipsariyo* falls under this group.

32. *Sejo sillok* 8, fifth month, second day.

33. *Yŏnsan-gun ilgi* 10, twelfth month, twenty-third day.

34. Yong-ok Pak, *Yijo yŏsŏngsa* (Women's History in the Chosŏn Dynasty) (Seoul: Han'guk ilbosa, 1976).

35. Regarding monasteries and play as a general theme, we can refer to Hur's research about Asakusa Sensoji, a Buddhist monastery, in late Tokugawa Japan. He selected the topics of "prayer" (*kito*) to identify the religious dedications at Sensoji and "play" (*asobi*) to illustrate how socioeconomic and cultural matters eventually assumed greater significance in the monastery's affairs. By the end of the seventeenth century, the government's neo-Confucian advisors were anti-Buddhist, and the shogunate essentially terminated official financial support. Seeking new sources of income, Sensoji administrators used the monastery's adjacent land for a variety of profitable enterprises. Nam-lin

Hur, *Prayer and Play in Late Tokugawa Japan: Asakusa Sesoji and Edo Society* (Cambridge: Harvard University Press, 2000).

36. *T'aejong sillok* 4, twelfth month, eighth day.

37. A Buddhist ceremony performed for the lonely and hungry ghosts wandering on water and land.

38. *Sejong sillok* 14, second month, fourteenth day.

39. *Sejong sillok* 7, eleventh month, eighth day.

40. *Sejong sillok* 16, fourth month, tenth day.

41. *Sejong sillok* 25, fourth month, eleventh day; *Sejong sillok* 25, fourth month, twenty-eighth day.

42. *Sŏngjong sillok* 4, seventh month, eighteenth day.

43. *Sejong sillok* 16, seventh month, seventh day.

44. *Sejong sillok* 29, fourth month, twenty-seventh day.

45. *Munjong sillok* 1, fourth month, thirteenth day.

46. *Sŏngjong sillok* 6, fifth month, twenty-sixth day.

47. *Chungjong sillok* 1, tenth month, twenty-ninth day.

48. *Sejong sillok* 16, fifth month, fourth day.

49. John Jorgensen, "Chosŏn wangjo esŏŭi pulgyo wa yuhak kanŭi taerip" (The Conflict between Buddhism and Confucianism during the Chosŏn Dynasty), *Pulgyo yŏn'gu* (Buddhist Studies) 15 (1998): 145–187.

50. *Sejong sillok* 2, eleventh month, seventh day.

51. *Sejong sillok* 11, fourth month, sixteenth day. This was a system that required Buddhist monks to carry a *toch'ŏp*, an identification tag for monks. Anyone who wished to be a monk had to receive a *toch'ŏp* after fulfilling certain duties for the country. When a monk died or returned to secular life, the *toch'ŏp* had to be returned. Anyone who wished to be a monk had to pass a national exam and make a payment in bolts of cloth in order to receive a *toch'ŏp*.

52. *Sŏngjong sillok* 2, eleventh month, twenty-second day.

53. *Sŏngjong sillok* 9, eleventh month, thirtieth day.

54. Ji-Young Jung [Chi-yŏng Chŏng], "Chosŏn sidae honin changryŏch'aek kwa toksin yŏsŏng" (The Marital Encouragement Policy and Single Women in the Chosŏn Dynasty), *Han'guk yŏsŏnghak* (Korean Feminist Studies) 20, no. 3 (2004): 5–38.

55. *Sejong sillok* 25, fifth month, sixteenth day.

56. Ibid.

57. *Sukchong sillok* 30, tenth month, twenty-eighth day.

58. *Yŏngjo sillok* 1, fifth month, third day.

59. Catholic women were considered in the same light as Buddhist nuns by the Chosŏn state. During the Sinyu Year persecution in 1801, "not marrying" was one of the "evil deeds" charged against women who were executed for "being baptized and luring others into evil ways."

60. Jahyun Kim Haboush and Martina Deuchler, eds., *Culture and the State in Late Chosŏn Korea* (Cambridge: Harvard University Press, 1999), 7.

8

The Establishment of Buddhist Nunneries in Contemporary Korea

Pori Park

The anti-Buddhist policies and the neo-Confucian ideologies of the Chosŏn dynasty (1392–1910) had a long-term damaging effect on the Buddhist order and on Buddhist nuns in particular.[1] Korean Buddhist nuns had to endure gender discrimination, living in a society in which women had long been relegated to lesser status than men. It was not until 2003 that the Chogye (Jogye) order, the largest Buddhist order in Korea, appointed a nun to a head position in its central administration.[2] Further, the twenty-five head monasteries of the Chogye order still belong only to monks. In the Central Council, there are only ten nuns and sixty-one monks.[3] In other words, nuns are still underrepresented in the central politics of the Chogye order.

Despite the apparent inequalities between nuns and monks, Korean nuns are the first and only group of nuns in a Buddhist nation to receive full ordination from their own senior nuns, rather than from monks.[4] Korean nuns including novice nuns number about seven thousand, slightly less than monks. In 2008, approximately equal numbers of nuns and monks received full ordination in Korea.

The major Buddhist nunneries in Korea began to appear after the "Purification Movement" of the 1950s (discussed below). They included the Naewŏn-sa in 1955, Unmun-sa in 1955, Taewŏn-sa in 1955, and Sŏngnam-sa in 1957. These monasteries represent the emergence of the independent operation of nuns in Korea, who established their own lecture halls (*kangwŏn*) and meditation halls (*sŏnwŏn*).

This chapter examines the process by which Buddhist nuns have established their independent environment of practice during a relatively recent and short period of time. The investigation of major nunneries and leading nuns shows that Korean nuns gradually emerged as a confident group, operating their own monasteries and system of education and training. I argue that, in addition to the perseverance and determination of leading nuns, their underdog status in the Chogye order ironically helped them consolidate and build up the nun community.

NUNS PRIOR TO THE PURIFICATION MOVEMENT

During the colonial period, the hermitages Kyŏnsŏng-am, Yunp'il-am, and Chijang-am were the major places known for holding Sŏn (C. Chan; J. Zen) retreats for nuns. Kyŏnsŏng-am is under the umbrella of the Sudŏk-sa Monastery in South Ch'ungch'ŏng Province. It must have been built just prior to 1913, when the renowned Bhikṣuṇī Pŏphŭi (1887–1975) took residency there.[5] Pŏphŭi was one of the pioneer nuns, accomplished in Sŏn meditation, in the modern era. She received certification of her enlightenment from the Sŏn master Man'gong (1871–1946) in 1916. Kyŏnsŏng-am held its first official group retreat in 1928 and emerged as the first prominent place for nuns' Sŏn training.

Man'gong was the Sŏn master, together with Hanam (1876–1951), who wielded the most influence over nuns during colonial rule. Almost all the prominent nuns during the colonial period had met these two teachers and received life-changing instructions from them. Bhikṣuṇī Iryŏp (1896–1971) was one of the so-called New Women. She was one of the earliest recipients of modern education and had initiated the women's movement as a writer, entering monastery life in 1928, under the influence of Man'gong. She contributed to the fame of Kyŏnsŏng-am by making it her main residence from 1933 until her death in 1971.[6] She provided spiritual support to celibate clerics by writing several short articles in major newspapers justifying the Purification Movement initiated by celibate monks and nuns against married monks during the 1950s and 1960s. Other earlier eminent nuns, such as Mansŏng (1897–1975), Taeyŏng (1903–1985), Sŏn'gyŏng (1904–1996), and Pongong (1907–1965), all practiced under Man'gong while staying at Kyŏnsŏng-am.

Bhikṣuṇīs Mansŏng, Sŏngyŏng, Pongong, Sedŭng (1926–1993), and Inhong (1908–1997) practiced under the care of Hanam (1876–1951) at Sangwŏn-sa in Kangwŏn Province. In 1938, under Hanam's guidance, Pon'gong initiated the Sŏn retreat at Chijang-am on Mount Odae, which became a popular place for nuns who wanted to practice with Hanam.[7]

Yunp'il-am is located in Mun'gyŏng in North Kyŏngsang Province and is under the jurisdiction of the Taesŭng-sa Monastery. After receiving certification of her enlightenment from Man'gong in 1935, Bhikṣuṇī Pon'gong began the Sŏn retreat at Yunp'il-am the same year. Yunp'il-am was further developed into a Sŏn center by Wŏrhye (1895–1956) and Ŭnghap and Ŭngjun. It was also at this nunnery that a prominent contemporary doctrinal master, Myoŏm (1931–), began her religious life in 1945, with Wŏrhye as her teacher.

Kyonsŏng-am and Yunp'il-am continued to develop until the present as important retreat centers for nuns. Such meditation nuns as Pŏphŭi, Mansŏng, Sŏnkyŏng, Pon'gong, Inhong, Sedŭng, and Ch'angpŏp proved their ability to reach as high as monks in their spiritual pursuit of enlightenment. They engaged in dharma talks with monk Sŏn masters on equal terms and gradually established a self-reliant tradition of nun masters teaching nun disciples.

The nuns' doctrinal studies also were heavily dependent on monks at the beginning. During the colonial period, nuns who wanted to study usually audited classes in monks' doctrinal schools. An alternative was to follow monk masters with whom they wanted to study and ask the teacher to hold special sessions for a group of nuns. For example, even after liberation in 1945, the bhikṣuṇī doctrinal master Myoŏm followed doctrinal master Unhŏ (1892–1980) to several monasteries as he moved around.[8] From 1953 to 1956, she learned Buddhist scriptures from him at Tonghak-sa in Kongju, Kŭmsu-sa in Pusan, T'ongdo-sa in Yangsan, Yŏnhwa-sa in Chinju, and Haein-sa in Hapch'ŏn. She and her fellow nuns stayed at nun hermitages near these bhikṣu monasteries and commuted to them to study with the master.

The first bhikṣuṇī dharma master was Chŏng Kŭmryong (1892–1965). She was also the first nun who received formal doctrinal transmission from a monk master. After being recognized by Kuha in 1922, she gave lectures for thirty years as a dharma master. Kŭmryong was the one of the three eminent nun doctrinal masters, together with Pak Hyeok (1901–1969) and Chŏng Suok (1902–1966). Kŭmryong transmitted her teachings to Kwangwu in 1958, which became the first case of doctrinal transmission from nun to nun.[9]

Hyeok studied at Ch'ŏngam-sa in Kimch'ŏn, and at Haein-sa and Pŏpchu-sa. At the age of fifteen, her master entrusted her with giving a public dharma talk at Ch'ŏngam-sa. She was said to have radiated light (achieved samadhi) on three different occasions during dharma talks over the years. Suok appears to have been the first nun to hold a regular lecturer position; she taught for three years at Namjang-sa in Sangju, beginning in 1937, and for another three years at Pomun-sa nunnery in Seoul, beginning in 1947. Pomun-sa opened the first doctrinal school for nuns in 1936.[10] Suok studied Buddhist scriptures from doctrinal master Kogyŏng at Haein-sa, and at Taeŭn-sa in Seoul. She then went to Japan to study further at Minoni middle school for three years, returning to Korea in 1937. She seems to have been the only nun to study in Japan during the colonial period, whereas many monks went there to study. She transmitted her doctrinal lineage to Myŏngsŏng, a doctrinal master at the prestigious doctrinal school at Unmun-sa.[11]

Thus, these outstanding early nuns, who studied mostly with monk masters, became doctrinal masters in their own right and began to transmit their teachings to nun disciples. In other words, nuns had sufficient numbers of their own teachers to train young nuns without relying on monks. Indeed, several nunneries that emerged after the Purification Movement—including Tonghak-sa, Unmun-sa, Pongnyŏng-sa, and Ch'ŏngam-sa—were complexes known mainly for doctrinal studies.[12] With their own schools and nun masters in residence, nuns gradually established an independent system of doctrinal learning.

THE PURIFICATION MOVEMENT AND NUNS

After liberation, Korean Buddhists had to purge themselves of the remnants of colonialism, identifying and punishing so-called traitors and eliminating the Japanese institution of "temple ordinance." But the ideological confrontation and political chaos immediately following liberation frustrated the initial decolonization efforts of the Buddhist order. Korea was divided in two by the "liberating" forces of the Soviet Union and the United States, and the nation was soon engulfed in civil war from 1950 to 1953.

At the instigation of South Korea's first president, Yi Sŭngman (Syngman Rhee, 1948–1960), who abruptly ordered married monks' resignation in May 1954, celibate Buddhist clerics embarked on the Purification Movement, making the wholesale accusation that married monks were the product of colonized Buddhism. After a yearlong battle between the two factions, with the strong and repeated backup of the president, the celibates managed to gather at Chogye-sa in Seoul in August 1955 and pass a constitution for the saṅgha. They elected fifty-six saṅgha assembly members and filled the administrative positions with members of the celibate faction. The celibates then began to take over major monasteries. Due to the resistance of the married monks who operated the monasteries, the process of seizing them was difficult. With the help of police, the celibates forced the married clerics out.[13]

By October 1955, the celibates had taken about 450 out of 1,000 monasteries from the married faction. Of the remaining ones, they gave the right of operation only to those married monks who agreed with the Purification Movement. In reality, however, these monasteries remained under the ownership of the married monks because the minority celibates simply did not have sufficient manpower to run all of them.

The major contemporary nunneries were also assigned to nuns around this time. Thus, the three principal Sŏn nunneries (*sŏnwŏn*) appeared. Chŏng Suok (1902–1966) was appointed to Naewŏn-sa in South Kyŏnsang Province in 1955, Kim Pŏbil (1904–1991) was appointed the abbess of Taewŏn-sa on Mount Chiri in South Chŏlla Province in September 1955, and Inhong (1908–1997) was appointed to Sŏngnam-sa in South Kyŏngsang in 1957. These three nun leaders were close friends and decided to share the great task of building monastic compounds for nuns' practice.

The major nunneries for doctrinal studies (*kangwŏn*) also were established. An Kwangho (1915–1989) was appointed to Tonghak-sa on Kyeryong Mountain in South Ch'ungch'ŏng in 1956. Chŏng Kŭmryong (1892–1965) was appointed to Unmun-sa in North Kyŏngsang in 1955 as the first nun abbess, with Yu Suin (1899–1997) appointed the second abbess in August 1955. Pak Hyeok (1901–1969) was appointed to Ch'ŏngam-sa in Kimch'ŏn in North Kyŏngsang in 1956, which was later developed into a doctrinal school in 1987.

During the Korean War, most Buddhist temple structures were burned down. The monasteries that were assigned to nuns, in particular, were in the worst condition. These pioneer nuns had to start from scratch, building and repairing the compounds on their own.

At the beginning of the Purification Movement, celibate monks numbered from 200 to 300 and nuns around 400, while there were about 7,000 married monks.[14] Nuns were active participants in the movement, assisting the minority celibate monks. The monk leaders asked nuns to join the moment, and nuns came to Seoul whenever major events occurred, or even stayed in Seoul as constant assistants. Bhikṣuṇī Tŏksu (1922–) at Kyŏnsŏng-am later testified that she and other nuns stayed in Seoul at Taebiwŏn and helped monks run errands and take care of things behind the scenes.[15]

Whenever the celibates confronted the married faction, nuns were placed on the front line to reduce the physical fights with them. Nuns led the famous protest march of December 13, 1954 to Kyŏngmudae, the presidential residence, walking through downtown Seoul in the snow. Five or six nun leaders, including Chŏng Suok and Kang Chaho, were in front, followed by hundreds of other nuns—double the number of monks at this protest.[16] On September 28–29, 1954, a total of 30 nuns and 116 monks had participated in a nationwide conference for celibate clerics.[17] On November 3, 1954, the Central Council of the Saṅgha (*chonghoe*) had added 10 nuns to its 50 members. On December 25, 1954, the celibates submitted their plans for saṅgha reforms, with the signatures of 366 monks and 441 nuns. And the August 1955 conference of the celibate faction was attended by 423 nuns and 250 monks.[18]

Almost all nuns, except for the elderly and sick, participated in every meeting and confrontation with the married faction, and nuns provided spiritual guidance to the movement. As already mentioned, Kim Iryŏp (1896–1971), a Sŏn master at Kyŏnsŏng-am, wrote several articles in major newspapers supporting the cause of the celibate camp. She had become a nun in 1928 and focused exclusively on Buddhist practice, despite her fame as an intelligent, modern woman before her monastic career. In April 1955, she contributed an article on "The Buddhist Movement for Reformation" to the *Chosŏn Daily*.[19] This was her first publication since becoming a member of the saṅgha.

Iryŏp stated that celibacy was the most decisive precept of Buddhist clerics. To be free from the cycle of birth and death, Buddhist clerics needed to extinguish not only the physical desires but also the mental ones. She observed that monks who assumed direct responsibility for taking care of a family existed only in places where the Buddhist dharma was dormant, such as Korea. She declared that great awakening requires great restriction, and that one cannot enter the right path of life without giving up the self.

In 1959, Iryŏp wrote another piece, "The Urgent Matter of Buddhist Reformation: Waiting for the Decision of the Supreme Court," which was serialized over three days in the *Donga Daily*.[20] After the celibate faction had begun taking over the saṅgha administration in August 1955, the married faction had appealed to the court to recover their ownership of monasteries. A long court battle had ensued. This was the backdrop against which Iryŏp justified the Purification Movement. She asserted that being a Buddhist cleric meant first leaving home, then leaving the body, and finally transcending the world of birth and death. Buddhist clerics needed to risk their lives on the path of attaining great freedom. To her, it was beyond comprehension for monks to keep spouses and children.

Iryŏp also criticized those who thought that the saṅgha needed married monks for their social and financial abilities, as a means to maintain the current size and system of the Buddhist order.[21] She wrote that the Buddhism practiced by married monks was not legitimate because it pursued worldly benefits. To attain the final freedom, one had to be selfless. This was accomplished by abolishing the traits of consciousness, in addition to physical attachments to the world. She pointed out that returning to this Buddhist pursuit was the "right path" of life, and that the Buddhist reformation would enable people to find this right path. Arguing thus, Iryŏp affirmed the validity of the Purification Movement not only for clerics but for everyone.

Thus, whereas monks led the movement and were in the spotlight from the media and the general public, nuns contributed much at the grass-roots level. Nuns' participation continued through the second republic and Pak Chŏnghŭi (Park Chung Hee)'s regime, until 1969, when the married faction formed its own sect, called T'aego-jong.

In 1955, several head monasteries of the colonial period were assigned to nuns for the first time. The first was Tonghwa-sa in Taegu. Sŏngmun (1895–1974) was appointed its abbess, and the nun Inhong (1908–1997) its prioress (*ch'ongmu*). It was designated the ecumenical center (*ch'ongnim*) for nuns, but this status was transferred to Unmun-sa in 1958, around the time Tonghwa-sa was taken over by monks. Two more head monasteries were given to nuns: Chino (1904–1994) was appointed to Kimryong-sa in Munkyŏng in North Kyŏngsang in 1955, and An Kwangho (1915–1989) was appointed to Sŏnam-sa on Chogye Mountain in South Chŏlla in 1956. In addition, Hyeun was appointed to Ch'ŏnŭn-sa in South Chŏlla around this time. Nuns were put in charge of only a handful of monasteries, yet the monks complained about the nuns' occupation of important ones.[22] Eventually, these three head monasteries and Ch'ŏnŭn-sa were taken over by monks. Those nuns who had participated in the Purification Movement complained that, although their sacrifice for the cause was as great as that of their celibate monk counterparts, they had not received due treatment from the Chogye order.[23]

After the Purification Movement, the Chogye order was divided over who would represent the saṅgha. The celibate monks plunged into another whirlpool of conflict, this time among themselves. Instead of rebuilding the saṅgha from the ground up, the monks banded together along partisan lines. Major "families" had formed around celibate monks who had led the battle against the married monks, such as Ch'ŏngdam, Tongsan, Kŭmo, and Hyobong.[24] The two most powerful groups, the Pŏmŏsa and Tŏgsung families, came from Tongsan and Kŭmo, respectively. As a reward for their bloody engagement in the Purification Movement, these so-called dharma families took charge of the main monasteries and thus assumed great power. In the ferocious hegemonic fights among these dharma families, which have happened repeatedly, as recently as 1999, we can see patterns of violence and legal battles similar to those during the celibate–married conflict.

Because of their exclusion from power, nuns do not waste their energy on internal strife and, instead, they quietly build their own system of training, focusing on education and meditation practice. The following is a presentation of major nunneries that have emerged since the Purification Movement.

NUNNERIES ESTABLISHED AS MEDITATION TEMPLES (*SŎNWŎN*)

Naewŏn-sa

Naewŏn-sa belongs to the administrative district of the head temple T'ongda-sa, and is located in the foot of Mount Ch'ŏnsŏng in South Kyŏngsang Province. It was built around 1,300 years ago, during the Silla Kingdom. During the colonial period, its reputation was as high as that of Sangwŏn-sa, in the northern part of the peninsula, for producing great numbers of outstanding Sŏn masters, including Hyewŏl, Hyanggok, and Koam.

Naewŏn-sa emerged as a nunnery when Suok (1902–1966) was appointed abbess in 1955. It was in ruins after the Korean War (1950–1953). Already an established doctrinal master, Suok assumed the task of rebuilding the temple, which took five to six years.[25] She had entered the saṅgha at the age of fifteen, and completed her doctrinal studies in 1929, at the age of twenty-seven. As noted earlier, she went to Japan to further her studies and became one of the earliest nun doctrinal masters. Her dedication to and hard work in rebuilding Naewŏn-sa were recognized. She received several awards for rebuilding the temple and preserving its cultural properties. These were given by the governor of South Kyŏngsang Province in 1959, President Pak Chŏnghŭi in 1962, and the Supreme Patriarch of the Chogye order in 1964.

In 1958, Naewŏn-sa completed a meditation hall called Sŏnhae Ilryun and began to accept meditation practitioners.[26] Eminent nun Sŏn masters such as Pŏphŭi, Pon'gong, and Sŏn'gyŏng led the meditation group. Sŏn'gyŏng (1904–1996), in particular, served as succentor (*ipsŭng*) from 1963 to 1973, which thus contributed to Naewŏn-sa's becoming the leading nunnery for Sŏn practice. In 1972, Naewŏn-sa built the Sŏnnawŏn, a meditation hall for advanced practitioners. During Sŏn'gyŏng's residency, Sŏn masters Hyanggok and Kyŏngbong came regularly to give dharma talks.[27]

In 1979, fifty nuns began a three-year retreat, with Toyong as their succentor. By 1999, the nunnery had completed the three-year retreat six times, further establishing its reputation for Sŏn practice. About fifty Sŏn nuns usually gather there to conduct sitting meditation in each summer and winter retreat season.

Taewŏn-sa

Taewŏn-sa is a branch temple of Haein-sa and is located in Sanch'ŏng, South Kyŏngsang Province, under Ch'ŏnwang-bong, the main peak of Mount Chiri.[28] It was rebuilt from ashes after a fire in 1913, and during colonial times had two major meditation halls so large that practitioners in the different halls did not know one another. Leading Sŏn masters of this time all practiced in these halls. In 1948, however, Taewŏn-sa was burned down, except for a pagoda, during the Yŏsun Rebellion. In the conflict between the right and the left after liberation, the South Korean Army started the fire in the name of eliminating leftist guerillas hidden on Mount Chiri.

Taewŏn-sa emerged as a nunnery in 1955, when Kim Pŏbil (1904–1991) came there as abbess.[29] Pŏbil had graduated from a girls' high school in Seoul—a rarity for women of her generation—before entering the saṅgha in 1936, at the age of thirty-two. Graduating from the doctrinal school at Taewŏn-sa in 1940, she then practiced Sŏn meditation, completing thirty summer retreats.

The temple had been in ruins for eight years when Pŏbil arrived there in 1955. She and her disciples dedicated their lives to rebuilding it for the next forty years. Because Taewŏn-sa had no income or lay devotees in the beginning, the nuns had to go elsewhere to find donors. While raising funds, Pŏbil slept on the road, enduring winter storms and summer heat. Her hard work paid off with the completion, in 1957, of T'apchŏn, the meditation hall. The temple began to accept Sŏn practitioners and continued to grow. Meanwhile, the temple engaged in a legal battle with married monks over the ownership of the complex. The nuns finally won in 1959.

In 1986, the meditation hall was extended, and Taewŏn-sa became established as a major Sŏn center for nuns. During each season, about forty nuns gather at the Sŏn retreat.

Sŏngam-sa

Sŏngnam-sa is located on Mount Kaji in South Kyŏngsang Province. It was built about 1,200 years ago by national master Toŭi and was essentially destroyed during the Korean War.[30] It became a nunnery when Yi Inhong (1908–1997) was appointed abbess in 1957, and repair and construction began.[31] Inhong had left home for the monastery at the mature age of thirty-three. She practiced under the guidance of bhikṣu masters Hanam and Sŏngch'ŏl and became a leading Sŏn master for nuns. She earned her epithet, "the Tiger of Kaji-san," for her rigorous teaching style.

When Inhong arrived, the roof of the main hall needed major repair and the other buildings had rotten floors and leaking roofs. The temple was in great debt and did not own any land. Under these conditions, every nun in the compound engaged in the physical labor of repairing and rebuilding. In 1962, Inhong formed Sŏllimhoe, a lay organization that raised funds to buy land for the temple.

In 1957, Inhong built a meditation hall, called Chŏngsu Sŏnwŏn, and established the temple as a Sŏn center. This meditation hall hosted three-year retreats from 1963 to 1999, when one-year retreats replaced them. The Simgŏmdang Sŏnwŏn was built for advanced practitioners in 1963, and the Kŭmdan Sŏnwŏn was built to accommodate the increased numbers of Sŏn practitioners in 1995. In 1999, Sŏngnam-sa was designated a special temple for Sŏn meditation by the Chogye order.

In any season, about a hundred nuns practice there. Sŏngnam-sa is especially known for the strict observation of precepts, and its nuns begin their daily schedule by prostrating 108 times each morning. Everyone is also required to contribute physical labor to the upkeep of the complex.

NUNNERIES ESTABLISHED AS DOCTRINAL TEMPLES (*KANGWŎN*)

Tonghak-sa

Tonghak-sa is located on Mount Kyeryong in South Ch'ungch'ŏng Province. It opened its doctrinal school in 1864.[32] Its fame for doctrinal teaching sprang from the fact that the renowned Sŏn master Kyŏnghŏ, who revitalized Korean Buddhism at the end of the Chosŏn dynasty, stayed there and attracted many young clerics.

Tonghak-sa became a nunnery when Taehyŏn (1916–1963) was appointed abbess in 1956. She opened the first bhikṣuṇī doctrinal school in February 1956 by inviting the bhikṣu doctrinal master Kyŏngbong to teach there. When nuns took over the monastery, the complex was in ruins because it had been burned down during the Korean War.

As a result, the nuns suffered such extreme financial difficulties that in 1957 they appealed to the government to rescue them from dying of hunger.[33]

Bhiksu Kyŏngbong served as doctrinal master there until 1963, when he transmitted the certificate of teaching to his nun disciples Myoŏm and Hyesŏng. In 1969, Hyesŏng became the first nun doctrinal master (*kangju*) at Tonghak-sa. Bhiksu Hogyŏng (1904–1987), who taught at Tonghak-sa from 1967 to 1984, transmitted his teaching lineage to six nuns, contributing greatly to the independent operation of the doctrinal school,[34] since in 1985 nun masters began to teach the nuns at Tonghak-sa without the help of monk teachers.

Kyŏngwŏl (1943–) had received dharma teachings from Hogyŏng along with five other nuns, including Kyŏngch'ŏn, Kyŏnghae, and Kyŏnghwa. She taught at Tonghak-sa from 1977, when she received doctrinal transmission from Hogyŏng, until 1994. From 1994 to 2002, Sŏan (1947–) served as doctrinal master. In 2002, Kyŏngwŏl returned to Tonghak-sa and has been dean of the Saṅgha College ever since.

Kyŏngwŏl entered the monastery at the age of eighteen and graduated from the doctrinal school at Tonghak-sa in 1971. She also served as abbess there from 1986 to 1990. Sŏan studied at Tonghak-sa from 1966 to 1972 and graduated from the Buddhist seminary school at Tongguk University in 1980. She then taught at Pongnyŏng-sa and received doctrinal transmission from the doctrinal master Bhikṣuṇī Myoŏm in 1992. Myoŏm had received the transmission from the monk masters Kyŏnbong and Unhŏ but transmitted her teaching lineage to nuns, including Sŏan, Sŏnghak, Hyejŏng, Taeu, and Irun.

As of 2008, Tonghak-sa had produced 881 graduates, and 88 nuns were studying there. As in monks' doctrinal schools, nuns study for four years, concentrating on a different set of Buddhist texts each year.[35] In addition, they study Indian, Chinese, and Korean Buddhist history, the Japanese language, calligraphy, flower arranging, and computer skills.

Unmun-sa

Unmun-sa was built in 560, during the Silla Kingdom. It is located at Ch'ŏngdo in North Kyŏngsang and is a branch temple of Tonghwa-sa. It became a nunnery when the doctrinal master Kŭmryong was appointed abbess in 1955. Yu Suin (1899–1997) served as the second abbess from 1955 to 1966 and established Unmun-sa as a leading place for nuns' education.[36] She had entered the saṅgha in 1907, at the age of eight, and completed her doctrinal studies under Bhiksu Haedam at

T'ongdo-sa in 1922. She then practiced Sŏn meditation and completed more than twenty retreat years.

Due to the Korean War, Unmun-sa was in horrible condition, and every structure needed significant repair. Suin visited each of the owners of the land that had belonged to the temple before the land reforms enacted by the government in 1949. It was unusual for peasants to return land to the temple, but Suin persuaded many of them with her sincerity and dedication, and Unmun-sa came to repossess most of its lost property. Suin also had to fight, over an extended period, with the married monks who claimed ownership of the temple.[37]

Unmun-sa opened a doctrinal school for nuns in 1958,[38] and Bhiksu Cheŭng was invited to instruct there. Bhikṣuṇī Myoŏm served as doctrinal master from 1966 to 1970. When she began teaching, about forty students studied under her. The numbers continued to increase, reaching a hundred students.[39] Yet Myoŏm wanted to find a new place where she could focus on her practice, rather than spending all her energy on teaching, so she later rebuilt Pongnyŏng-sa in Suwŏn.

Chŏn Myŏngsŏng (1931–) came to Unmun-sa in 1970 as a doctrinal master, served as abbess from 1977 to 1998, and continues to teach there. Because of her long years of service at Unmun-sa, she is credited with Unmun-sa's reputation as a model nunnery. She entered the saṅgha at the age of twenty, after working as an elementary school teacher. She received her teaching lineage in 1958, from Bhiksu Sŏngnŭng at Sŏnam-sa and from Bhikṣuṇī Suok. She received her master's degree in 1970 and her doctorate in 1974 from the Buddhist seminary school at Tongguk University. She transmitted her doctrinal lineage to her nun disciples, Hŭngryŭn and Ilchin, in 1985.

Unmun-sa began the Saṅgha Graduate School for producing doctrinal instructors in 1997. As of 2008, 197 students study at Unmun-sa. For four years, nuns study Buddhist scriptures, Buddhist history, English or Japanese, calligraphy, piano, flower arranging, and computer skills. Learning flower arranging and piano is unique and different from the curriculum at monks' schools.

Other Nunneries for Doctrinal Studies

The first two nun schools at Tonghak-sa and Unmun-sa were opened in the 1950s, and other doctrinal schools started much later. Pongnyŏng-sa was able to open its doctrinal school in 1974 by taking thirty students. It is located in Suwŏn, Kyŏnggi Province, as a branch temple of Yongju-sa. As previously mentioned, Yi Myoŏm (1931–) came to Pongnyŏng-sa in 1971, after teaching at Unmun-sa. When Myoŏm moved in, Pongnyŏng-sa was a small, dilapidated hermitage. She and her thirty nun companions repaired and rebuilt the complex with their own hands. Impressed by their dedication, donors and helpers came to rescue them financially.

Myoŏm was born the second daughter of the renowned Sŏn master Ch'ŏngdam (1902–1971) and entered the saṅgha at the age of fourteen.[40] Sŏn master Sŏngch'ŏl (1912–1993), a very close dharma friend of Ch'ŏngdam, was instrumental in teaching her during the earlier years of her training. She studied with doctrinal masters Unhŏ and Kyŏngbong and received lineage transmissions from both. She graduated from the Buddhist Studies Department at Tongguk University in 1966. She became the founding teacher of the doctrinal school at Pongnyŏng-sa and transmitted her teachings to her nun disciples in 1992. She continued to teach there and currently serves as the dean. The school became a saṅgha college (*Sŭngga taehak*) in 1987 and, as of 2008, had 56 nuns studying there.[41]

Samsŏn Saṅgha College was opened in 1979 in Seoul, as a commuter school for nuns who combine their studies and service at their own temples.[42] It produced a total of 230 graduates from 1976 to 2007.

Lastly, Ch'ŏngam-sa opened a doctrinal school in 1987, which is located in Kimch'ŏn, North Kyŏngsang Province, and is a branch temple of Chikji-sa.[43] This monastery was famed as a doctrinal school during the Chosŏn dynasty, when the doctrinal master Hoeam Chŏnghye (1685–1741) taught there. It became a nunnery in 1956, when the doctrinal master Hyeok (1901–1969) was appointed abbess. The doctrinal school was begun in 1987 by doctrinal master Chihyŏng. Chihyŏng graduated from Tonghak-sa doctrinal school and studied with doctrinal master Bhiksu Chigwan. She graduated from Tongguk University in 1980, began teaching at Ch'ŏngam-sa in 1987, and continues to the present. As of 2000, 102 students studied there.

CONCLUSION

Major nunneries, such as Naewŏn-sa, Sŏngnam-sa, Taewŏn-sa, Tonghak-sa, and Unmun-sa, were established around the same time, after the first victory of the celibates in 1955. Nuns participated loyally in the Purification Movement, yet came to occupy only a handful of temples. The temples that were assigned to nuns were all in terrible condition due to the Korean War. Nuns began to rebuild them from almost nothing as the centers for their Sŏn practice and doctrinal learning.

As many nuns pointed out, celibate monks began to fight among themselves after ending their conflict with the married faction in 1970. The celibate Chogye order has been plagued by hegemonic strife among different dharma "families" as recently as 1999. While monks depleted their energies in this way, nuns concentrated on building their own system of training. They transformed the major temples into places where nuns could gather for doctrinal studies or hold Sŏn retreats. Their focus was on group training rather than on promoting personal gain. With meager means and resources, nuns sacrificed individual needs to build a community.

As the nunneries emerged as centers for nuns, nuns began to produce their own doctrinal teachers and Sŏn masters. They thus became less dependent on monks for their studies and training and finally became a self-sufficient group. In August 1984, instructors at the nuns' doctrinal schools convened and even proposed to the central administration that the curricula and length of education at the cleric doctrinal schools be standardized.[44] At the time, the Chogye order did not have a uniform system for clerics' education. This proposal was discussed at a nationwide conference of the doctrinal instructors, who then decided on the current system of four years of instruction and curricula.

In learning and practice, there was no discrimination against nuns. Nuns now have five major doctrinal nuns' schools. If they want to study further, they can go to the Central Saṅgha College or to Tongguk University, which are operated by the Chogye order.[45] Those who want to focus on Sŏn training can go to Sŏn centers for nuns, operated by nunneries.

Nevertheless, compared with the monks' situation, the nuns' is inferior. In 1997, there were 46 Sŏn centers for monks but only 31 for nuns, although 1,012 monks and 969 nuns practiced at these centers, respectively. Nuns practice in crowded and financially disadvantaged places, as compared to monks. In addition, monks have fifteen doctrinal schools, whereas nuns have only five, all quite crowded: in 2008, Unmun-sa had 197 students; Pongnyŏng-sa, 56; and Tonghak-sa, 88. In comparison, the Haein-sa school had the largest number of monks, at 86, and Paegyang-sa had 16. The other monks' schools had an average of 20 to 30 students.

As the saṅgha begins to recognize the importance of nuns representing the Chogye order, it needs to involve more nuns in the central administration and operation of the head monastery districts. Nuns still do not share the privilege of voting with monks, and thus are mostly excluded in every election of major posts and in the making of the saṅgha's policies.[46] The quality of nuns' education and Sŏn training would be enhanced if resources were shared fairly. Given the history of saṅgha conflict, however, a prudent approach is required. Nuns' demands could trigger another conflict within the saṅgha or work against them by stirring the minds of defensive monks. The situation may improve by creating a feeling of community among the members of the saṅgha, in which nuns need to play a salient role.

NOTES

1. I would like to express my thanks to Professor John Jorgensen, who gave me valuable comments at the HanMaum conference that I incorporated into the final version of this chapter.

2. Bhiksuni T'agyŏn was appointed to the head position in the Department of Cultural Affairs of the Chogye order in March 2003.

3. Silch'ŏn Pulgyo chŏnguk sŭnggahoe, ed., *Chogyejong chungang chonghoe hwaltong yon'gu* (Seoul: Haengwon, 1997), 121.

4. The Central Council revised the laws to permit nuns to be in charge of their own ordination in June 1982; Tonguk taehak Sŏngnim tongmun hoe, ed., *Han'guk Pulgyo hyŏndaesa* (Seoul: Sigongsa, 1997), 59.

5. *Sŏnwŏn ch'ongnam* (Seoul: Pulgyo sidaesa, 2000), 679–680. Today about one hundred nuns practice at Kyŏnsŏng-am during the retreat seasons of summer and winter, and about sixty nuns stay even during the free seasons of spring and fall.

6. For Bhiksuni Iryŏp's biography, see Ha Ch'unsaeng, *Kkaedarŭm ŭi kkot* (Seoul: Tosŏ Ch'ulp'an Yŏrae, 2001), 1:67–86.

7. Ha Ch'unsaeng, *Kkaedarŭm ŭi kkot* 1:96–97.

8. Refer to the biography of Myoŏm in Yun Ch'ŏngkwang, *Hoesaek komusin* (Seoul: Sigongsa, 2002).

9. Ha Ch'unsaeng, *Kkaedarŭm ŭi kkot*, 1:185–194.

10. Pomun-sa announced its separation from the Chogye-jong in 1972 and became the first bhikṣuṇi order, Pomun-jong. As of 1997, this order had only 212 nuns.

11. Ha Ch'unsaeng, *Kkaedarŭm ŭi kkot*, 1:207–220.

12. Tonguk taehak Sŏngnim tongmun hoe, *Han'guk Pulgyo hyŏndaesa*, 240.

13. For detailed information on the Purification Movement, read Pori Park, "The Buddhist Purification Movement in Post-Colonial South Korea: Restoring Clerical Celibacy and State Intervention," in J. Craig Jenkins and Esther E. Gottlieb, eds., *Identity Conflict: Can Violence be Regulated?* (Somerset: Transaction Publishers, 2007), 131–145.

14. Kim Kwangsik, *Kŭnhyŏndae Pulgyo ŭi chaejomyŏng* (Seoul: Minjoksa, 2000), 419.

15. Han'guk Pukgyo Kunhyŏndaesa Yŏn'guhoe, ed., *22in ŭi chŭng'ŏn ŭl t'onghae ponkŭnhyŏndae Pulgyosa* (Seoul: Sŏnudoryang Press, 2002), 263–282.

16. Han'guk Pukgyo Kunhyŏndaesa Yŏn'guhoe, *22in ŭi chŭng'ŏn*, 269.

17. Kim Kwangsik, *Kŭnhyŏndae Pulgyo*, 393–397.

18. Ibid., 401.

19. *Chosŏn Daily*, April 26, 1955; cited in *Sinmun ŭro pon Han'guk Pulgyo kŭnhyŏndaesa* (Seoul: Sŏnudoryang Press, 1995), 207–209.

20. *Donga Daily*, March 22, 23, 24, 1959; cited in *Sinmun ŭro pon Han'guk Pulgyo kŭnhyŏndaesa*, 273–277.

21. Iryŏp, *Chisŏng'in ŭi hoesang* (Yesan: Sudŏk-sa, 1960).

22. Han'guk Pukgyo Kunhyŏndaesa Yŏn'guhoe, *22in ŭi chŭng'ŏn*, 272.

23. Ibid., 278.

24. Yŏ Ikgu, "Han'guk Pulgyo ui inmaek/chimaek," *Sintong'a* (May 1985): 396.

25. For the biography of Suok, read Ha Ch'unsaeng, *Kkaedarŭm ŭi kkot* 1:207–220.

26. *Sŏnwŏn ch'ongnam*, 696–702.

27. Martine Batchelor, "The Life of a Korean Zen Nun: The Biography of Son'gyong Sunim as Told to Martine Batchelor," *Korean Culture* (Spring 1992): 26–37.

28. For Taewŏn-sa, refer to *Sŏnwŏn ch'ongnam*, 716–718.

29. For the biography of Pŏbil, see Ha Ch'unsaeng, *Kkaedarŭm ŭi kkot* 1:249–262.

30. *Sŏnwŏn ch'ongnam*, 772–777.

31. For the biography of Inhong, see Ha Ch'unsaeng, *Kkaedarŭm ŭi kkot* 2:41–57.

32. Pulhak Yŏn'guso, ed., *Kangwŏn ch'ongnam* (Seoul: Taehan Pulgyo Chogye-jong, 2000), 359–390. Tonghak-sa's *Kangwŏn* (doctrinal school) was changed into a *Sŭŭnga taehak* (saṇgha college) in 1987: Tonguk taehak Sŏngnim tongmun hoe, *Han'guk Pulgyo hyŏndaesa*, 240.

33. *Kyŏnghyang Daily*, January 16, 1957; cited in *Sinmun ŭro pon Han'guk Pulgyo kŭnhyŏndaesa* (Seoul: Sŏnudoryang Press, 1995), 264.

34. Tonguk taehak Sŏngnim tongmun hoe, *Han'guk Pulgyo hyŏndaesa*, 247.

35. Robert Buswell, *The Zen Monastic Experience* (Princeton: Princeton University Press, 1992), 96.

36. For the biography of Suin, see Ha Ch'unsaeng, *Kkaedarŭm ŭi kkot* 2:75–88.

37. Newspapers reported that the first battle ended in 1957, but the battle resumed in 1959. *Sinmun ŭro pon Han'guk Pulgyo kŭnhyŏndaesa*, 272.

38. Pulhak Yŏn'guso, *Kangwŏn ch'ongnam*, 446–474.

39. Yun Ch'ŏngkwang, *Hoesaek komusin*, 293.

40. For Myoŏm's biography, see Yun Ch'ŏngkwang's *Hoesaek komusin*.

41. Pulhak Yŏn'guso, *Kangwŏn ch'ongnam*, 391–415.

42. Ibid., 417–443.

43. Ibid., 475–505.

44. Taehan Pulgyo Chogyejong Kyoyukwŏn, *Chogyojong sa: Kŭnhyŏndae py'ŏn* (History of Chogye Order—Modern and Contemporary Periods) (Seoul: Chogyejong Press, 2001), 279–280.

45. The Central Sangha College was founded in 1979 and promoted to a certified college in 1996. In 1997, it moved to a new campus in Kimp'o, Kyŏnggi Province. Tongguk University began as Myŏngjin School in 1906, was promoted to a college in 1946, and then to a university in 1953.

46. Chŏn Haeju, "Han'guk Bhiksuni Sangha ŭi hyŏnhwang kwa panghyang," in *Chonggyo kyoyukhak yŏn'gu* 8 (1999): 325–342.

Glossary

Ado 阿道 (我道)
An Chŏng-bok 安鼎福
An Kwangho 安光豪
Anamdong 安巖洞
Ananda, King of Anxi 阿難達, 安西王
Andong 安東
Anfuli 安富里
Anhŭng-sa 安興寺
Anilwŏn 安逸院
Ansim-sa 安心寺
Asuka period 飛鳥時代

cha 字
Ch'ae Che-gong 蔡濟恭
Ch'ae Hong-gŭn 弘謹
Ch'ae Hong-sin 弘愼
Chaeganyŏ chason kŭmgo pŏp 再嫁女子孫禁錮法
Ch'aehŏn 彩憲
Ch'aehwa 采華
Chang Pogo 張保皐
Chang Tŏg-nyang 張德良
Changan-sa 長安寺
Changdan 長湍
Chasin 孜信
Chasuwŏn 慈壽院
Chegwan 諦觀
Chengqingli 澄清里
Chengzong 成宗
Chiang-Huai 江淮
Ch'ien-shou ching 千手經

Chigong 指空
Chi'gyŏn 智堅
Chiho 智浩
Chihye 智惠
Chihyŏng 志炯
Chijang-am 地藏庵
Chijang-gyŏng 地藏經
Chijang-sa 地藏寺
Chikchi simch'e yojŏl 直指心體要節
Chikchi-sa 直指寺
chilja 質子
Ch'ilsŏng 七星
Chin Ŭi-gŭm 珍衣金
Chin'gak Hyesim 眞覺 慧諶
Chin'gang 晋康
Ch'ing-liang 清凉
Chinhŏ Palgwan 振虛 捌関
Chinhŭng, King 眞興王
Chinhye 眞慧
Chinnyŏng 晋寧
chinŏn 真言
Chinpyŏng, King 眞平王
Chinul 知訥
Chisim 知心
Chisŏn 智善
Chiwŏn 智遠
Cho Bayan Böqe 趙伯顏不花
Cho Pun 趙芬
Ch'oe, Lady 崔氏
Ch'oe Cha 崔滋
Ch'oe Ch'ung 崔忠
Ch'oe Ch'ung-hŏn 崔忠獻
Ch'oe Hang 崔沆
Ch'oe Maeng-son 崔孟孫
Ch'oe Sŏ 崔瑞
Chogye 曹溪
Chogye-jong 曹溪宗
Ch'ŏlsan Sogyŏng 鐵山 紹瓊
Ch'ŏlwŏn 鐵原
Chŏn 倎
Chong 琮
Ch'ŏngam-sa 清岩寺

Ch'ŏngch'ŏn 清川
Ch'ŏngdam 青潭
Chŏnggŭn 淨根
Chŏnggyŏn 正見
Chŏnggyŏng 貞敬
ch'ŏnggyu 清規
Ch'ŏnghŏ Hyujŏng 清虛 休靜
Chŏnghwa T'aekchu 靜和宅主
Chŏnghye-sa 定慧寺
Chŏnghyŏn 淨賢
Chŏngil 淨一
Chŏngjong 定宗
Chongmin 宗敏
Chongnam-san 終南山
Chongnang nanxiang 崇壤南鄉
Ch'ŏngnyŏn saji 青蓮寺誌
Ch'ŏngnyŏn-am 青蓮庵
Ch'ŏngo Hyŏnbyŏn 清悟 玄抃
Chŏngŏpwŏn 淨業院
Ch'ŏngp'yŏng-sa 清平寺
Chongrensi 崇仁寺
Chŏngsim 正心
Chŏngsim 淨心
Chŏngsin 正信
Chŏngsu Sŏnwŏn 正受禪院
Chŏngsu-sa 淨水寺
Ch'ŏngwŏn 清遠
Chŏngyu 定有
Ch'ŏnhŭi 千熙
ch'ŏnin 賤人
Ch'ŏnsu-gyŏng 千手経
Ch'ŏnt'ae 天台
Ch'ŏnt'ae sagyo-ŭi 天台四教儀
Ch'ŏnt'ae-jong 天台宗
Ch'ŏnŭng 處能
Ch'ŏnŭn-sa 泉隱寺
Chosŏn 朝鮮
Chosŏn wangjo sillok 朝鮮王朝實錄
Chu-fo yao-chi ching 諸佛要集經
Ch'ukhŭp 竺洽
chuk-pi-ja 竹篦子
Chungbi 仲非

Ch'ungch'ŏng Province 忠清道
Ch'unggam 冲鑑
Chungjong 中宗
Ch'ungnyŏl, King 忠烈王
Ch'ungsŏn, King 忠宣王
Ch'ungsuk, King 忠肅王
Ch'unsŏng 春城
Ch'unsŏng-dang 春星堂

Dachongenfuyuansi 大崇恩福元寺
Dade 大德
Dadu 大都
Daehaeng [Taehaeng] 大行
Dahuazhu Shenggong 大化主 省空
Daqingshousi 大慶壽寺
Daxingxian 大興縣
Ding 定
Ducongguan 都摠管
Duoerji 朶兒赤

El Temür 燕鐵木兒

Fangshan shijing 房山石經
Fawangsi 法王寺
Faxiang 法相
Fayuansi 法源寺
Fo shuo Chien-ku-nu ching 佛說堅固女經
Fu Jian 苻堅

Gaolisi 高麗寺
Guangji Chansi 廣濟禪寺
Guangjiaosi 光教寺

Haein-sa 海印寺
Haeju 海州
Haengju 幸州
Haewŏn 海圓
Hagyun 學潤
Hakjo 學祖
Hakuhō period 白鳳時代
Han River 漢江

Han Son-su 韓孫秀
Hanam 漢巖
Han'guk Pulgyo chŏnsŏ 韓國佛教全書
Hangzhou 杭州
Hanlin Academy 翰林院
Hansŏng 漢城
Hanyang 漢陽
Hŏ Kang 許綱
Hŏ Kong 許珙
Hoeam-sa 檜巖寺
Hoeryong-sa 回龍寺
Hogyŏng 浩鏡
Hong Hyu 洪休
Hong Kyŏng-son 洪敬孫
Hong Sadang 洪舍堂
Hongsŏng 洪城
Hon'gu 混丘
Hoŭn Ugi 好隱 有璣
Hsiu-hsiu 休休
hua-tou 話頭
Hua-yen Sūtra 華嚴經
Hŭi-bi 禧妃
Hŭiwŏn 希遠
Hŭngch'ŏn-sa 興天寺
Hŭnggyo-wŏn 興教院
hwadu 話頭
Hwajang 華藏
Hwangnyong-sa 黃龍寺
hwasang 和尙
Hwaŭi *Ongju* 和義翁主
Hye (Lee), Queen 惠妃 李氏
Hyemyŏng 惠明
Hyesim 惠諶
Hyesin 惠信
Hyeyŏng 惠英
Hyobong 曉峰
Hyŏn 晐
hyŏngt'o 懸吐
Hyŏnjong 顯宗
Hyoryŏng, Prince 孝寧大君
Hyujŏng 休靜

Ilsŏn 一善
Im, Lady, Dame of Changsŏng 長城郡夫人 任氏
Im Yŏn 林衍
Inhong 仁弘
Inju 仁州
Insu, Royal Concubine 仁粹大妃
Inwang-dong 仁王洞
Inye, Queen 仁睿王后
ip'an 理判
Irin 一印
Iryŏn 一然

Jie Xisi 揭傒斯
Jin 金
Jinchengfang 金城坊
Jinsun Mitosi 金孫彌陀寺

Kaegyŏng 開京
Kaep'ung-gun 開豊郡
Kaesŏng 開城
Kaji-san 迦智山
Kakan 覺岸
Kamŭn 感恩
Kamŭng 感應
Kang, Lady 姜氏
Kang Ch'ŏn-yu 姜千裕
Kang Pak 姜樸
Kang Yung 姜融
Kangjong 康宗
Kangwŏn 江原
kangwŏn 講院
kanhwa Sŏn 看話禪
karam 伽藍
Kasŏn 假善
Ki, Empress 奇皇后
Ki, Lady 奇氏
Ki Ch'ŏl 奇轍
Kiangnan 江南
Kilju 吉州
Kim, Lady 金氏
Kim Baianchai 金伯顔察
Kim Chi-suk 金之淑

Kim Chŏn 金塡
Kim Hyŏn 金現
Kim Iryŏp 金一葉
Kim Kaemul 金開物
Kim Ku 金垢
Kim Kyŏng-dal 金景達
Kim Pyŏn 金賆
Kim Sŏk-kyŏn 金石堅
Kim Temür 金帖木兒
Kim Yu-sin 金庾信
ki'nyŏ 妓女
Ko Inbok 高仁福
Ko Yong-bo 高龍普
Kodoryŏng 高道寧
Koguryŏ 高句麗
kongan 公案
Kongmin, King 恭愍王
Koryŏ 高麗
Koryŏsa 高麗史
kosŏng yŏmbul 高聲 念佛
Kuanŭm 觀音
Kuanyinnu 觀音奴
Kugil-am 國一庵
kuksa 國師
Kŭmgang-san 金剛山
Kŭmo 金烏
Kŭmryong 金龍
kung-an 公案
Kungno 國老
Kŭnhun 根訓
Kunni-sa 君尼寺
K'waeho 快浩
Kwan 貫
Kwansŏ 關西
Kwengbyŏn 宏辨
Kwengyŏn 宏演
Kwŏn, Miss 權氏
kye 戒
Kyehong 戒洪
Kyehŭn 戒欣
Kyemyŏng 戒明
Kyerim 鷄林

Kyeryong-san 鷄龍山
Kyeyu 癸酉
kyŏl 結
kyŏmin 慊人
Kyŏng Chun 慶俊
Kyŏngam 鏡巖
Kyŏngamjip 鏡巖集
Kyŏngbok-kung 景福宮
Kyŏngbong 鏡峰
Kyŏngch'ŏn-sa 敬天寺
Kyŏnghŏ 鏡虛
Kyŏnghŭng 憬興
Kyŏnghwa 敬和
Kyŏngju 慶州
Kyŏn'gonyŏ-kyŏng 堅固女經
Kyŏngsang Province 慶尙道
Kyŏngwŏl 鏡月
Kyŏnsŏng-am 見性庵
Kyunyŏ 均如

li 里
liang 兩
Liao 遼
Liao-jan 了然
Linzhi 臨濟
Li-i-nu 離意女
Lohan 羅漢
Longquansi 龍泉寺
Lotus Sūtra 妙法蓮華經

Manbul Hyangdo 萬佛香徒
Manbul-hoe 萬佛會
Man'gong 滿空
Manhae Han Young-un 萬海 韓龍雲
Manhang 萬恒
Mansŏng 萬性
Map'o 麻浦
Mengshan Deyi 蒙山 德異
Meng-shan 蒙山
Milchik 密直
Mi-lo 彌勒
Minch'ŏn-sa 旻天寺

Mit'a-am 彌陀庵
Mitosi 彌陀寺
Morye 毛禮
Mo-shan-ni 末山尼
Mou 畝
mu 無
muae-hŭi 無礙戲
mudang 巫堂
Mugŭk 無極
Muhak 無學
Mui 無二
Muk'oja 墨胡子
Munhwagun 文化君
Munjŏng, Dowager Queen 文定王后
Munjong, King 文宗
munjung 門中
Muŭija 無衣子
Muyŏl, King 武烈王
Myo 妙
Myobong 妙峯
Myoch'ŏl 妙哲
Myodŏk 妙德
Myohyang 妙香
Myojŏk-am 妙寂庵
myŏng 銘
Myŏngdŏk 明德
Myŏngjong 明宗
Myŏngsŏng 明星
Myoŏm 妙嚴
Myori Pŏphŭi 妙理 法喜
Myoryŏng 妙玲

Naehun 內訓
Naejang-sa 內藏寺
Naeoe pŏp 內外法
Naewŏn-am 內院庵
Naewŏn-sa 內院寺
Namhan 南漢
Namsan 南山
Nancheng 南城
Nangp'al 囊八
nanyak 蘭若

Naong Hyegŭn 懶翁 惠勤
Nara period 奈良時代
National Bhikṣuṇī Association 全國比丘尼協會
nianfo 念佛
Nieh-p'an 涅槃
Nihon shoki 日本書紀
nisŭng 尼僧

O Hong-un 吳弘運
Ongnyŏn-am 玉蓮庵
Ŏnyang 彦陽
Ŏrok 語錄
Ŏsadae 御史臺

Paegun Kyŏnghan 白雲 景閑
Paekche 百濟
Paengnyŏn-sa 白蓮社
Pai-hsiu 白修
Pak Böqe 朴不花
Pak *ch'ŏmji* 朴 僉知
Pak Hu 朴侯
Pak Hyeok 慧玉
Pak P'il-su 朴弼秀
Pak Swe No'oldae 朴鎖魯兀大
p'algyŏng 八敬
Pang Sin-u 方臣祐
Pangham-nok 芳啣錄
Park Chung Hee [Pak Chŏng-hŭi] 朴正熙
pigu 比丘
piguni 比丘尼
Pŏbil 法一
Pŏbun 法雲
Pogae-san 寶盖山
Pogak Iryŏn 普覺 一然
Pogwang-sa 普光寺
P'ogyŏm 包謙
Pohyŏn-am 普賢庵
Pohyŏn-sa 普賢寺
Poje 普濟
Pojo Chinul 普照 知訥
Pŏmo families (*munjung*) 梵漁 門中
Pomun-sa 普門寺

Pŏnam 樊巖
Pŏnamjip 樊巖集
Pongnyŏng-sa 奉寧寺
Pongnyŏng-sa bhikṣuṇīs Seminary 奉寧寺 僧伽大學
Pon'gong 本空
Pongsŏng 奉性
Pŏpch'an 法贊
Pŏphŭi 法喜
Pŏphŭng, King 法興王
Pŏphwa yŏnghŏm-chŏn 法華靈驗傳
Pŏpjin 法眞
posal haeng 菩薩行
Pou (T'aego) 普愚
Pou (Hŏŭng) 普雨
Pudo-am 浮屠庵
Puin sŏnuhoe 婦人禪友會
Puin sŏnwŏn 婦人禪院
Puin-sa 符印寺
Pukhan 北漢
Pulchu-sa 佛住寺
Pulsŏl ch'ŏnji p'alyang sinju-gyŏngju 佛說天地八陽神呪經註
Punyŏ sangsa kŭmji pŏp 婦女上寺禁止法
Purification Movement 佛教淨化運動
Purun 佛雲
Puso-san 扶蘇山
P'yohun-sa 表訓寺
Pyŏn Han 卞韓
P'yŏngan 平安
P'yŏnggang 平康
P'yŏnggyoja kŭmji pŏp 平轎子禁止法
P'yŏngyang 平壤

Qin dynasty 秦朝

sa 寺
Sa, Lady 史氏
Sabangji 舍方知
Sabun-yul 四分律
Saganwŏn 司諫院
Sahŏnbu 司憲府
sajok 士族
sallim 山林

Samch'ŏk 三陟
samgang 三綱
Samgang haengsilto 三綱行實圖
Samguk sagi 三國史記
Samguk yusa 三國遺事
samjong-ji-do 三從之道
Samjung 三重
Sammun chikji 三門直指
Samno 三老
Samsŏn Sanga College 三仙僧伽大學
Samsŏn-am 三仙庵
Sangwŏn-sa 上院寺
sannyŏnggak 山靈閣
sansin'gak 山神閣
sap'an 事判
Sasin 思信
Sassi 史氏
se 歲
Sedŭng 世燈
Sejong, King 世宗大王
Shangdu 上都
Shen-chung ching 神衆經
Shin (Yŏm), Queen 愼妃廉氏
Shundao (K. Sundo) 順道
Shundi 順帝
Shuyuan Huang Taihou 壽元皇太后
sibwangjŏn 十王殿
Sik'wal 食活
Silla 新羅
Sillim-am 神琳庵
Sillok 實錄
Sillŭk-sa 神勒寺
Simwŏn-sa 深源寺
Sin, Queen 愼妃
Sin Tang-ju 申當住
Sindon 辛旽
Singwang-sa 神光寺
Sin'gye-sa 神溪寺
Sinhaeng 信行
Sinhye (Ryu), Queen 神惠王后柳氏
Sinhyo-sa 神孝寺
Sinp'yŏn pogwŏnmun 新編普勸文

Sirhak 實學
Sogyŏng 紹瓊
Sŏjŏn 西殿
Sŏlcham 雪岑
Sŏllimhoe 禪林會
Sŏn 禪
Son, Lady, Dame of P'ohae 浦海郡夫人 孫氏
Sŏnam-sa 仙巖寺
Sŏnan 善安
Song 宋
Sŏngch'ŏl 性徹
Sŏnghyo 性曉
Sŏngjong 成宗
Sŏngnam-sa 石南寺
Sŏngŭn 性恩
Sŏn'gyŏng 禪敬
Sŏn'gyŏng Ongju 善敬翁主
Sŏngyun 性允
Sŏnjo, King 宣祖
Sŏnmyŏng 善明
Sŏnsa 禪師
Sŏnwon 禪院
Sŏnyŏlhoe 禪悅會
Sŏsan 西山
Sosŏwŏn (Kim), Lady 小西院夫人 金氏
Sosŏwŏn, Queen 小西院夫人
Ssangam-sa 雙巖寺
Such'un 壽春
Sudŏk-sa 修德寺
Sujwa 首座
Sukjong, King 肅宗
Sumyŏng 秀明
Sun 順
Sundo 順道
Sung 嵩
Sungan 崇安
Sunggyŏng 崇慶
Sŭngji 承旨
sŭngni 僧尼
Sŭngnoksa 僧錄司
Sŭngnyŏ 僧侶
Sŭngt'ong 僧統

Suok 守玉
Suryuk festival 水陸齋
Susŏn-sa 修禪社

taebang 大防
Taech'ŏng-do 大淸島
Taedŏk 大德
T'aego Pou 太古 普愚
T'aego-jong 太古宗
T'aehŭi 太熙
Taehŭng-sa 大興寺
Taehyŏn 大賢
T'aejo 太祖
T'aejong 太宗
Taesŏn 大選
Taesŏnsa 大禪師
Taesŏwŏn, Queen 大西院(夫人)
Taesŭng-sa 大乘寺
Taewŏn-am 大願庵
Taewŏn-sa 大源寺
Taiding 泰定
Talchŏng 達正
Tamjŏng 湛淨
Tang 唐
tarani 陀羅尼
Tasan Chŏng Yag-yong 茶山 丁若鏞
Three Kingdoms period 三國時代
T'ien-t'ai 天台
Toch'ŏp system 度牒制
To'gang 道康
Tohak 道學
Tŏksu 德修
Tŏksung, Mountain 德崇山
Tong, Mrs. 童氏
T'ongdo-sa 通度寺
Tongguk Cheil Sŏnwonn 東國第一禪院
Tongguk sŭngni rok 東國僧尼錄
Tonghak-sa 東鶴寺
Tonghwa-sa 桐華寺
tongnohwa 禿魯花
Tongsa yŏljŏn 東師列傳
Tongsan 東山

Toyunarang 都維那娘
Tumandir 秃满迭兒

U 瑀
Udambala hoe 優曇婆羅會
Ŭich'ŏn 義天
Ungmyŏn 郁面
Ŭngyun 應允
Unhŏ 耘虛
United Silla 統一新羅
Unmun-sa 雲門寺

Wang 王
Wang *toin* 王道人
wangsa 王師
Wanpingxian 宛平縣
Wei Su 危素
Wenzong 文宗
Wi, Lady 韋氏
Wŏlchŏng-sa 月精寺
Wŏllam-sa 月南寺
wŏn 院
Wŏn Sŏn-ji 元善之
Wŏndam 元湛
Wŏndon 圓頓
Wŏnjong 元宗
Wŏnmyo 圓妙
Wŏnt'ong-am 圓通庵
Wŏnt'ong-sa 圓通寺
Wŏrhye 月慧
Wu-fen lü 五分律
wu 無
Wuzong 武宗

Xingfusi 興福寺

yaksajŏn 藥師殿
Yaksan O Kwang-un 藥山 吳光運
yangban 兩班
Yangga-sŭngnok 兩街僧錄
yangin 良人
Yangjin-am 養眞庵

Yangju 楊州
Yangze 揚子
Yangzhoulu 楊州路
Yebu 禮部
Yen-ching 燕京
Yen-tu 燕都
Yi 李
Yi Che-hyŏn 李齊賢
Yi Chip 李緝
Yi Chŏng-ju 李挺周
Yi Hwa-yŏng 李和英
Yi I 李珥
Yi Inhong 李仁弘
Yi Kok 李穀
Yi Kye-ham 李季諴
Yi Kyu-bo 李奎報
Yi Po 李補
Yi Qutuq Temür 李忽篤帖木兒
Yi Sam-jin 李三眞
Yi Su-san 李守山
Yi Sŭngman 李承晚
Yi Tae-sun 李大順
Yi Tŏk-son 李德孫
Yijo sillok 李朝實錄
yin-yang 陰陽
Yŏch'an 如璨
yŏdaesa 女大師
yŏguk 女國
yŏmbul 念佛
Yŏngjo 英祖
Yongningsi 永寧寺
Yŏnhwa 蓮華
Yŏnsan-gun ilgi 燕山君日記
Yŏnsan'gun 燕山君
Yose 了世
Yoyŏn 了然
Yu Chahwan 柳子煥
Yu Suin 兪守仁
Yüan 元
Yuanshi 元史
Yüan-chi 圓寂
Yug'i 六怡

Yuil 有一
Yulgok 栗谷
Yumu 惟茂
Yun 倫
Yun, Lady 尹氏
Yun Hyŏng 尹炯
Yun Kwan 尹瓘
Yunp'il-am 潤筆庵
Yuram Sik'wal 律菴 食活
Yuri 琉璃
Yuwŏn 有願

Zhaozhou Congshen 趙州 從諗
Zhigong 智空
Zhishuicun 池水村
Zhu Yuanze Temür 朱完澤帖木兒

Contributors

Eun-su Cho is Professor in the Department of Philosophy at Seoul National Universty. She previously taught in the Department of Asian Languages and Culture at the University of Michigan. Her research interests range from Indian Abhidharma Buddhism to Korean traditions of Buddhist thought. Her publications include "From Buddha's Speech to Buddha's Essence: Philosophical Discussions of *Buddha-vacana* in India and China," *Asian Philosophy* (2004); "The Uses and Abuses of Wŏnhyo and the '*T'ong* Pulgyo' Narrative," *Journal of Korean Studies* (2004); "Wŏnch'ŭk's Place in the East Asian Buddhist Tradition," in Robert E. Buswell, Jr., ed., *Currents and Countercurrents* (2005); co-translator of *Jikji Simgyeong*: *The Essential Passages Directly Pointing at the Essence of the Mind*, with John Jorgensen (2005) and many other articles in Korean.

Heung-sik Heo is Professor Emeritus in the Department of History in the Graduate School of Korean Studies at the Academy of Korean Studies. Specializing in the Koryŏ period, he has written eleven books, including *Koryŏ kwagŏ chedosa yŏn'gu* (A Study of the Civil Service Examination System of the Koryŏ Period, 1981), *Koryŏ sahoesa yŏn'gu* (A Study of Social Structure in the Koryŏ Period, 1981), and *Koryŏ Pulgyosa yŏn'gu* (A Study of Buddhism in the Koryŏ Period, 1986), and has published numerous articles.

John Jorgensen is Senior Lecturer in Japanese Studies at Griffith University, Australia. His recent publications include *Inventing Hui-neng: Hagiography and Biography in Early Ch'an* (2005); "Problems in the Comparison of Korean and Chinese Buddhism: From the 16th Century to the 19th Century," in Geumgang Center for Buddhist Studies, comp., *Korean Buddhism in East Asian Perspectives* (2007); and "Korea as a Source for the Regeneration of Chinese Buddhism: The

Evidence of Ch'an and Son Literature," in Robert E. Buswell, Jr., ed., *Currents and Countercurrents* (2005).

Ji-Young Jung is Assistant Professor of Women's Studies at Ewha Womans' University. She received her Ph.D. in history from Sogang University. Her research interests relate to marginalized women (widows, single women, concubines, and remarried women) and gender politics of the Chosŏn dynasty.

Young Mi Kim is Professor in the Department of History at Ewha Womans University. Her major works include *Silla Pulgyo Sasangsa-yŏn'gu* (The History of Silla Buddhism, 1994), and as a co-author with Ki-back Yi, T'ae-jin Yi, and T'ae-yŏng Kim, *Han'guk Sasang-sa Pangpŏp-non* (The Methodology in Study of the Intellectual History of Korea, 1997). She writes primarily on the influence of Buddhism on Koryŏ women and the practice of Buddhist nuns.

Pori Park is Assistant Professor of Religious Studies at Arizona State University. She has recently published "The Buddhist Purification Movement in Postcolonial South Korea: Restoring Clerical Celibacy and State Intervention," in J. Craig Jenkins and Esther E. Gottlieb, eds., *Identity Conflicts: Can Violence Be Regulated?* (2007); "A Korean Buddhist Response to Modernity: The Doctrinal Underpining of Han Yongun's (1879–1944) Reformist Thought," *Seoul Journal of Korean Studies* 20.1 (2007); and "Buddhism in Contemporary Korea," in Stephen Berkwtiz, ed., *Buddhism in World Cultures: Comparative Perspective* (2006).

Tonino Puggioni is an independent scholar who works with the Italian Ministry of Foreign Affairs and teaches Korean History and Culture at the University of Rome. He received his Ph.D. in History from Seoul National University with a thesis on the development of Koryŏ's Pŏpsang sect. His publications include articles on Koryŏ religious exchanges with the Yuan dynasty.

Index